SUCCESSION TO HIGH OFFICE

EDITED BY
JACK GOODY

CAMBRIDGE UNIVERSITY PRESS

CAMBRIDGE

LONDON · NEW YORK · MELBOURNE

Published by the Syndics of the Cambridge University Press
The Pitt Building, Trumpington Street, Cambridge CB2 1RP
Bentley House, 200 Euston Road, London NW1 2DB
32 East 57th Street, New York, NY 10022, USA
296 Beaconsfield Parade, Middle Park, Melbourne 3206, Australia

© Cambridge University Press 1966

Library of Congress catalogue card number 66–14190

ISBN 0 521 05117 7 hard covers
ISBN 0 521 29732 X paperback

First published 1966
First paperback edition 1979

Printed in Great Britain at the
University Press, Cambridge

DATE DUE

595

CAMBRIDGE PAPERS IN SOCIAL ANTHROPOLOGY

No. 4

SUCCESSION TO HIGH OFFICE

WITHDRAWN

CAMBRIDGE PAPERS IN
SOCIAL ANTHROPOLOGY

CONTENTS

FIGURES

CONTRIBUTORS TO THIS ISSUE

JACK GOODY, William Wyse Professor of Social Anthropology, University of Cambridge, author of *The Social Organisation of the LoWiili* (1956), *Death, Property and the Ancestors* (1962), *Technology, Tradition and the State* (1971), *The Myth of the Bagre* (1972), *Production and Reproduction* (1977), *The Domestication of the Savage Mind* (1977), editor of *The Development Cycle in Domestic Groups* (1958), *Literacy in Traditional Societies* (1968).

G. I. JONES, Ph.D. (Cantab.), former Lecturer in Social Anthropology, University of Cambridge, author of *Basutoland Medicine Murder* (1951), *Report on the Position of Chiefs in Eastern Nigeria* (1957), *The Trading States of the Oil Rivers* (1963).

MARTIN SOUTHWOLD, Lecturer in Social Anthropology, University of Manchester; took his B.A. (1953) and Ph.D. (1959) at Cambridge; author of several papers on the Baganda, including *Bureaucracy and Chiefship in Buganda* (1961).

R. G. ABRAHAMS, Lecturer in Social Anthropology, University of Cambridge; took his B.A. (1957) and Ph.D. (1962) at Cambridge; author of *Political Organization of Unyamwezi* (1967), *The Peoples of Greater Unyamwezi* (1967) and several papers.

PREFACE

We had hoped to include a paper on 'The Succession War in Ankole' by Derrick Stenning, Director of the East African Institute of Social and Economic Research, who contributed to the first volume of this series. But this was still unfinished when he died suddenly in March 1964. We are grateful to R. G. Abrahams for filling the gap at short notice and would like this volume to stand as a memorial to a former student and colleague of this department. We are grateful to the Smuts Fund of Cambridge University for a grant towards the printing costs of this series.

MEYER FORTES
JACK GOODY
E. R. LEACH

The following conventions are used in the genealogical king-lists:

Letsie	Paramount chief
KANGO	Chief
Roba	non-ruler
△	males
○	females

INTRODUCTION

By JACK GOODY

Discussing the characteristic features of the dyad, Georg Simmel claims that the two-person group is peculiar among social units, because it automatically dissolves at the death of one of its members. In this respect, he notes, it resembles a strange society in Northern France called 'the Association of the Broken Dish', which had its origin in a dinner attended by a group of industrialists. During the meal, a dish fell on the floor and broke. One diner noticed that the number of pieces was identical with the number of people present, and took this to be an omen. As a result, they founded a society of friends who owed one another help and service. Each member took a fragment of the dish, and when one of them died his piece was sent to the president, who glued the parts together. The last survivor was to fit the final piece into place and then bury the reconstituted dish. 'The Society of the Broken Dish will thus dissolve and disappear.' Simmel goes on to remark that the whole outlook of the association would doubtless be different 'if new members were admitted and the life of the group thereby perpetuated indefinitely...' (1950: 124–5).

The self-liquidating character of the Association of the Broken Dish makes it a most unusual kind of human group, and one which could only take the form it did because of the triviality of its social functions. With groups of any significance, some provision is made either for their continuity or for their replacement.

SUCCESSION, INHERITANCE AND RECRUITMENT

What is true for the membership of groups holds also for the inheritance of property and the replacement of individuals in roles and offices.[1] Unless they are simply to disappear from the social scene, all organizations, whether they be trade unions, student societies, university departments, or national governments, must have some arrangement for the transmission of corporate property and for the succession of key personnel.

But while the transfer of property and of office are often closely linked (English lawyers refer to both as succession), certain broad differences must be borne in mind.[2] First, there is the extent of involvement. The inheritance of property involves all members of a community, especially in peasant societies where the means of production are in the hands of the producers themselves. But the actual incumbency of high office is the direct concern only of a narrow segment of the community, although others may be involved

I

as eligibles, still more as supporters of rival candidates, and the whole population as consenting (in some sense or other) to the particular office and the particular incumbent. Secondly, offices are not simply a restricted category of roles; they are usually indivisible units within an 'establishment', a table of organization. For if the offices carry specific functions, like cabinet posts, and are not simply 'titular', like earldoms, there are not the same alternative sources of supply as for many kinds of property. The tools of production can be remade, houses can be rebuilt, farms can sometimes be carved out of virgin lands. Whereas offices are part of a hierarchy of restricted and interlinked roles.

Of course, offices do increase in number. In the long run, the development of more complex organizations means further differentiation of roles and offices, a greater division of social labour. And on a much shorter time scale, some posts (particularly those in the lower echelons) can always be duplicated, regardless of functional demands; indeed this tendency to proliferation has been proclaimed as one of the inevitable characteristics of bureaucratic systems (Parkinson 1958). But we are specifically dealing here with the men at the top, and high office tends to be unique and non-duplicating; the Paramount, Premier, President, and the Chairman of the Board are by definition highly restricted roles; if you want the position, there is only one way to get it—by ousting the present incumbent. So that the very uniqueness, the scarcity of the resource, magnifies the conflict situation that centres around the transfer of an office from one individual to another. And this conflict may loom so large that some societies, both monarchies and party systems, refuse to name a successor lest he should be tempted to succeed too soon.

Succession to office, like the inheritance of property, involves the allocation of scarce resources. So too may recruitment to social groups. But in many cases the membership of groups is open to all, either on an ascriptive (e.g. descent groups) or on a voluntary basis (e.g. political parties); and here the process of recruitment, unlike succession and inheritance, in no way diminishes the holding of existing members and hence does not give rise to the same recurrent situations of conflict.

GAINS AND COSTS

In this introduction I examine some of the variable elements in systems of succession, particularly hereditary systems, and try to assess the gains and costs of each of these modes of transferring scarce resources. Conflict there is bound to be, but it varies in its incidence (those persons between whom it typically falls) as well as in degree. As with elective and appointive (or 'bureaucratic') systems, each method of perpetuating an office and its associated organization has its own implications and concomitants: each system solves certain problems and produces its own particular dilemmas.

Levenson has recently examined some of the gains and costs of bureaucratic methods of succession in modern industrial enterprises (1961). A firm that pays little heed to ensuring continuity may find itself too unstable to achieve its principal objectives; one that trains too many 'anticipatory successors' may have a number of disappointed employees on its books and find itself acting as a management school for rival firms.

Likewise each particular type of electoral succession has its own intended and unintended consequences—for the individuals, for the political system and for the wider society. The reckoning of simple majorities is the crudest and most clear-cut procedure; but where minorities are evenly spread across the various constituencies, important subgroupings may be totally unrepresented. Proportional representation (by single transferable vote) does make provision for such minorities, but also tends to increase the number of parties and hence make for less continuity in government (Black 1958: 82). Clearly, different systems are appropriate to different social situations. So, too, with methods of hereditary succession. The way in which the Franks divided their kingdom among their sons gives full recognition to the rights of each of the king's progeny, but only at the cost of splitting the kingdom, a process which was reversed mainly by recourse to fraternal strife. *Pre mortem* succession may help settle, confirm or promote the successor in an indeterminate system or in fluid situations; but the costs, anyhow of the more radical application of the method, are obvious from Geoffrey of Monmouth's account of the fate of King Lear. Here the transfer of authority during the old king's lifetime, and the division of the realm between his daughters, directly mirrored the author's own times, not only in the practice itself but also in its grave consequences.[3] When Henry II (1154–89) made a partial transfer of the realm to his sons, the result was rebellion against himself and war between the successors. Handing over the reins of government to the younger generation may make for a more vigorous administration, relieve the old from the responsibility of office and diminish the tension between incumbent and successor. On the other hand, the partial transfer of authority may simply whet the successor's appetite for yet more power; while the complete transfer of office may result in the neglect and rejection of the old leader.

An examination of the factors involved in hereditary succession can throw some light not only upon the institutions of exotic lands but also upon the past of European society. And indeed upon the present too, for we have only to recall the names of Rockefeller, Ford and Krupp to see that hereditary succession, long characteristic of some of the more archaic features of present-day nations such as the monarchy and nobility of Britain,[4] is no stranger to the board rooms of modern industry.[5] And the names of Churchill, Roosevelt, Cecil and Kennedy emphasize that dynastic succession is by no means absent from the cabinets of contemporary states, although here it requires a stamp of approval from both party and people. The theoretical attention paid to appointive and elective succession, and the practical attention lavished upon the spectacular rise of men from cowherd to president, from factory-hand to industrial magnate, have tended to obscure the degree to which property and position are handed down between kin, even in the most technologically advanced societies.[6]

One of the reasons for this neglect lies in the conflicting attitudes which Western nations now take to transfer between kin. What we think of in one context as 'providing for one's children', in another we see as social injustice, as the perpetuation of inequality. In terms of office, care for kin becomes nepotism (a vice unheard of in most other societies).[7] These differing attitudes derive from the fact that while kinship is disfunctional in certain areas of the social system, everywhere it is in kin groups that mankind is initially raised. From one angle the tendency for dynasties to form, and to perpetuate themselves, in politics, business or the professions, arises from the process of socialization itself; to inhibit their growth, a society has to adopt very specific regulations, such as confiscatory death duties, appointment by examination and other mechanisms of a levelling kind.[8]

FACTORS IN SUCCESSION

The material presented in this symposium inevitably bears mainly on hereditary succession, since it comes from the pre-colonial societies of Africa. But this mode of transfer is not the only theoretical concern. Elements of election and appointment occur even in the most rigidly hereditary systems, and many non-Western states like Dahomey, Buganda, Ashanti, and Benin have seen a considerable development of appointive office. In any case, a consideration of the factors involved carries the analysis from one system to another: the conflicts that are found between the king and the heir apparent are also to be found between the members of board rooms and cabinets. So that an examination of the social consequences of different types of kinship transmission helps to spell out, by contrast at least, the main features of other modes of succession.

Hereditary succession is found among most simple societies, where it is consistent with the general stress given to kinship in the social system. Bureaucratic or appointive succession predominates in large-scale organizations where the demand is for technical competence, such as the ability to read and write in the traditional administration of China. Elective succession predominates in the political activities of many contemporary nations which require some measure of the volume of popular support a candidate can muster; this system often provides the elected representative with an independent position *vis à vis* not only the permanent bureaucracy needed to run a complex governmental system, but also the army and judiciary that back it.[9]

As Weber himself recognized, these 'pure types' are highly abstract. In the context of long-range historical processes, Weber's insights have borne fruit not only in the many studies of modern bureaucracies but also in the work of sociologists who have been concerned with the conditions under which appointive succession develops in traditional African states (Fallers 1956; Colson 1958; Southwold 1961). These matters I shall discuss later in this introductory essay. But my first concern is to try to lay out more precisely some of the factors involved in systems of succession and to specify some of the gains and costs of this mode rather than that. In this way some progress can be made towards understanding the concomitants of particular systems, for example, the relationship between 'uncertain' succession and 'corporate' dynasties. An examination of the concomitants of different modes of transferring high office raises the general question of the 'power' of the office and its relation to the structure of the dynasty, the character of the whole governmental system and the organization of the armed force upon which it finally depends. But these wider questions, which lead into the whole analysis of political systems, can only be briefly touched upon at this place and time.

I shall begin by discussing four main factors in succession to high office which I have already mentioned. These are:

(i)   the uniqueness or otherwise of the office,
(ii) the time of accession,
(iii) the selection of the successor,
(iv) the relationship between successive office-holders.

The duplicating paramountcy

While high office obviously tends to be unique, this is not always the case; and since the question of uniqueness so radically affects the nature of the organization, and of the organizational conflicts, it merits consideration right at the outset of this essay.

I want here to distinguish the duplicating paramountcy associated with the fissiparous state from a number of formally related institutions discussed in this essay, namely, (i) co-rulership, where, as the result of partial *pre mortem* succession, the incumbent and successor hold office simultaneously; (ii) the dual paramountcy, as in the Anglo-French condominium of the New Hebrides where the major roles are doubled up; (iii) the contrapuntal paramountcy, where, for example, the offices of political and religious heads are separate but (in some sense) equal.

The possibility of partitioning the territory and duplicating the supreme office obviously provides some solution to the problem of the plurality of heirs (particularly in 'corporate' dynasties) as well as to incipient rebellion, and in reconsidering 'rituals of rebellion' Gluckman has recently been led to contrast fissiparous states with those characterized by a cycle of internal rebellions (1963).

States may split as the result of an occasional war of succession, as in the struggle for high office among the South-East Bantu (Schapera 1956: 175–6); or they may divide by a regular process of fission such as occurs among the Nyakyusa, where office is handed over from one generation to the next at the 'coming out' ceremony (Wilson, M. 1951: 22 ff.). It is clear that both processes will lead to a diminution in size of the independent political units unless there is a parallel process of reintegration of the previous elements or of incorporation of new peoples or new territory.

Most systems of multi-kingdom peoples (the result of this fissiparous process) involve the inclusion of subject groups, usually by force. Among the Azande of the Sudan-Congo border, fission continually occurs either when a ruler divides a large kingdom among his sons, or as a result of a war of succession that takes place at his death, or when a member of the royal dynasty establishes his dominion over neighbouring peoples. But it is military superiority that allows the kingdoms to proliferate without any decrease in size (Baxter and Butt 1953: 48 ff.).

But the proliferation of chiefdoms may also arise from peaceful penetration. Among the Alur of Uganda, members of the dynasty are called in by neighbouring peoples to act as protectors, judges and ritual officiants (Southall 1956). Fission of the occasional kind also occurs as one result of the gradual devolution of power to local jurisdictions when the extent of the kingdom outstrips its capacity for domination and its system of communications. The build-up of local military forces, particularly characteristic of cavalry states, the establishment of locally based dynasties, the difficulties of communication between national capital and divisional headquarters, all these factors tend to produce fission over time. An example of this process occurs among the Nyamwezi of Tanzania, discussed by Abrahams later in this volume; in this multi-kingdom set-up, the unity of kingdoms was constantly under threat because of the poverty of administrative resources, which is especially noticeable where communications are limited by the absence of writing, the wheel and the horse.

But part of the problem in all these cases has to do with the nature of the system of succession; the existence of a plurality of heirs, the 'corporateness' of the group of royal brothers, prepares the ground for the possible division of the realm between them. Fission of this kind was a recurrent feature of early European history, especially in France under the Merovingian and the Carolingian rulers. At the death of Clotaire, son of the founder of the Merovingian dynasty, the kingdom was divided between his four sons 'like some piece of private property...according to the German method' (Wiriath 1910: 805); it was united again only after a series of fratricidal wars. A similar dismemberment took place shortly after the death of Charlemagne. And the Norman kings likewise dismantled their realms through inheritance and built them up through conquest and marriage. Since the total estate of a king was divided between the sons, so it could be reunited by dispossessing a brother. William I, for example, gave Normandy to Robert, his eldest son, and England to Rufus, his youngest; the long struggle between the two brothers was halted for a while when Robert pawned his heritage to his brother in order to take part in the Crusades, but the conflict continued again in the next generation with undiminished vigour.

The other method of building up one's realm was through marriage. As brotherless women were bearers of rank and property they brought increase to their husband's estates; it was in this way, for example, that Henry II acquired Aquitaine on his marriage to the heiress Eleanor.

The problem of the uniqueness of the kingship and division of the realm is associated with the question of the plurality of royals discussed in a later section. The more members of the dynasty are seen (and see themselves) as having an equal claim over the throne, the more they will be disposed to split the existing kingdom, or, if conditions allow, to establish others. But apart from the relatively institutionalized forms we have discussed above, any dispute between equal claimants for the throne may lead to threats against the territorial unity of the kingdom, even where this unity is considered sacrosanct. The Ottoman emperors always resisted attempts to divide the empire by inheritance. But after the death of Mehmed II in 1481, there opened the usual civil war which lasted until Bayezid II had driven his brother Cem into permanent exile. Cem had set himself up as a rival emperor and proposed that the empire should be divided. However, this suggestion involved a direct violation of one of the fundamental canons of Islam: that there shall be only one supreme Imam. Bayezid refused to accept Cem's offer, saying 'The empire is the bride of one lord' (Alderson 1956: 6–7). Bride of one lord the kingdom may be, but the unity of the realm often turns on the disunity of the sibling group; and the royal princes face the alternatives of accepting an inferior status to their brother, dividing the realm, fighting each other, or of carving out new kingdoms from neighbouring countries. The setting up of two kingdoms in place of one, either by division or by duplication, does not mean the cutting off of all close ties; indeed, in the case of division, the continuance of these may lead to efforts to reunite the separated domains. But the fissiparous state does modify the uniqueness of monarchy and permit more than one of the royal heirs to enjoy the fruits of high office, providing as it were a form of institutionalized rebellion for both the dynasty and the wider political system.

JACK GOODY

The time of accession

(a) Pre mortem succession

The accession of the new ruler may occur immediately upon the death or dethronement of the former monarch, after a reasonable interval has elapsed, or while he still sits upon the throne. The process of the division of the English and French kingdoms among the king's sons sometimes occurred during the lifetime of the king, and this often involved the establishment of a co-ruler-ship. It was Henry II himself who installed his eldest son, another Henry, as king of England, duke of Normandy, and count of Anjou, while his other sons were each 'shown' their own portion of the heritage; Richard was to have Aquitaine (through his mother), Geoffrey had Brittany (through his wife) and Ireland was awarded to John ('Lackland'). These provinces were the impartible units of dynastic operations;[10] at times they were brought together to form a larger polity, which, unlike the smaller units could be split up again, for each of the brothers had some claim upon the total patrimony and the existence of a plurality of sons led to a division of the territorial resources between them.

Henry's action created a situation of co-rulership since he installed his son as king while he remained on the throne. In the same way Charlemagne crowned his only son, Louis the Pious, during his own lifetime. The aim was clearly legitimacy. The institution of co-rulership tries to dispense with the uncertainties of interregna and to ensure that office passes to the man who has won the approval of the present king or king-makers. It is obviously likely to occur in situations where the succession rules allow for uncertainty, where they emphasize the equal claims of a number of heirs. So it was that the Anglo-Saxon Offa appointed his son Ecgfrith to be his successor in an attempt to preserve the Mercian succession within his own family, and it is possible that for this purpose he borrowed the new ceremony of anointing (plainly imitated from biblical usage) from the Franks, where it had first been used some thirty-five years earlier to sacralize the installation of Pippin, a man who had no claim to rulership by virtue of royal descent (Ratcliff 1953).

Under these conditions, transfer of the realm to the appointed individual has a greater chance of success if the early or *pre mortem* succession is complete rather than partial, if it results in a single ruler rather than two kings in uneasy harness. But the difficulties are clear. For the sharp contrast that exists between king and ex-king, chief and ex-chief, makes it well-nigh impossible for a man easily to cast off the authority he has held by right of birth. This indeed is the problem for Lear, as for many figures in con-temporary political life where retirement occurs neither at death nor yet at a pre-determined age.

The standardization of the time and of the occasion make the transfer of office between the living a smoother and more acceptable affair. Among the Nyakyusa of Central Africa, the headmen approach their chief when the eldest sons of his contemporaries have reached about thirty-five years. After a period of delay, 'for he is unwilling to relinquish his own honour and power', the old chief agrees to hold the 'coming out' ceremony, when, with certain reservations, the control of the kingdom is handed over to his two senior sons (Wilson, M. 1951: 22–3). By a somewhat similar process, authority in parts of East Africa is often transferred from one formal age-set to the next.

Early (i.e. *pre mortem*) succession is more frequently encountered in bureaucratic organizations, where the efficient working of the institution is held to demand compulsory retirement at a given age. But even in Western societies this rule tends to apply to employees rather than to employers; kings retain their offices until the end, and the professional death of politicians, bishops, and company directors occurs at a substantially later age than in most other occupations.

The dramatic increase in the span of human life over the last hundred years has meant that the elected representatives of the people, together with the high officers of industry and the Church, continue in their various posts for longer than ever before, since no limit of age is set upon their tenure. The only checks upon gerontocratic rulers are the opinions of the electors, of their colleagues and of themselves, about their fitness to carry on with the job, an opinion greatly influenced by reluctance to deal harshly with the old, particularly those who have done the state some service. Indeed, there is often a special reverence accorded to successful old age in high office which partly neutralizes the 'efficiency criterion' and bestows charisma upon those who endure its burdens to the end. And this is rendered more possible where the role is political rather than technical in scope. But even those who are relieved of the highest office, whether by abdication or by the electoral processes, never entirely revert to being private citizens, or ordinary members of a dynasty. This aura that attaches to the ex-king creates problems not only for the individual himself but for his successor and the entire political system, problems which can often be resolved only by the banishment or killing of the king.

Checks on ageing in office exist even in hereditary systems. Frazer's divine kings suffered the equivalent of compulsory retirement when, either at the end of a set period or with the impairment of their faculties, they were killed off by their followers. But this institution was much less common than Frazer thought, and some scholars have suggested that even the material on his type-case, the Shilluk of Southern Sudan, should be interpreted in a rather different light. The Shilluk *reth* generally met with a violent death, but this end may have been due to the rebellion of princes when the ruler's powers, political rather than magico-religious, showed signs of decline (Evans-Pritchard 1948: 33–5). Rebellion is, of course, another mode of achieving the early retirement of the office-holder; and so too are the less violent forms of dethronement practised by the Ashanti and others.

The more institutionalized forms of *pre mortem* transfer are comparatively rare; in the simpler societies succession to high office generally occurs at the death of the previous incumbent, so that the funeral and coronation of the king become part of the same sequence of events.[11]

(b) The interregnum

Where succession occurs after death, the gap between death and succession is of critical importance to the state. It is the time when changes in organization, such as the establishment of a new dynasty, are most likely to occur. Whatever the continuity gained by the co-rulership of two kings in joint harness (partial transmission), by the immediate proclamation of a new heir (*le roi est mort...*), by concealing the death of the king, or by a highly determinate system of succession, the changeover from one ruler to the next is always a period of danger to the state.[12]

For not only is the government vulnerable to internal pressures for the redistribution of power, but the nation is also more open to attack from without, whether from neighbouring kingdoms or, as the Mossi and Nyamwezi show, from the pressures of colonial administration (Skinner 1960; Abrahams, below).

Like many other peoples, the Gonja of Ghana are well aware of this fact. At the death of the divisional chief, the market of Salaga (a town of considerable importance in the history of West Africa) became a bedlam. Young men rushed in, overturned the traders' stands and stole their wares. For three days misrule continued, providing a dramatic demonstration of the supposed consequences to the society and its complex network of trade if it were to be permanently without kings and kingship; and providing too a public expression of the inevitable resentment to which authority gives rise among those excluded from office.[13]

(c) The stand-ins and stake-holders

The dangers of this transitional period are recognized not only in acts of limited licence but also in the existence of special persons or groups who act as stand-ins and stake-holders while the transfer of power (and possibly the selection of the successor) takes place. The stand-in serves as temporary deputy, often with negligible powers. It is as if the kingship cannot be allowed to lie vacant even while the process of consultation, essential to all but the most predetermined systems, is carried out. In Gonja, sons are explicitly excluded from directly succeeding to their father's office, and it is the eldest son (*wurikŭ*) who nominally stands in as paramount until the elaborate procedure of election and installation is carried out. Among the

Mossi of Yatenga to the north, where a son is permitted to follow his father in office, it is the eldest daughter (*napoko*) who performs the function of stand-in, for she too is a royal neutral, capable of looking after the interests of the dynasty but unable to succeed to the throne, or even to pass on dynastic membership to her children (Tauxier 1917: 352).

The Mossi have yet another stand-in for the dead monarch, the *kourita*. After the new king has been chosen, but before he is consecrated, one of his own or his brother's sons takes over the personal regalia, earlier worn by the female stand-in, as well as two of the dead king's young wives. He does this 'to perpetuate for some time the memory of the old Moro-naba' (352). During this period, the prince can seize what he will; after the consecration of the new monarch, he becomes a village chief and the senior of the 'king's sons'. Thus, when a king has been chosen to fill the empty office, the dead man is further embodied (this time as an individual ruler not just one of a line of kings) in a living descendant—and in Wagadougou in an ancestral shrine as well.

It is not only excluded members of the dynasty (either in the shape of the residual sibling or the ineligible male) but outside neutrals too who may step into the crucial roles during the transitional period between the death and rebirth of the kingship. Especially suited for this role of outsider are the offspring of the residual sibling (sons, where uterine succession obtains, and sisters' sons where the dynasty is recruited agnatically), as well as eunuchs, whose particular neutrality debars them from a personal interest in continuity.

The stake-holders are those who take charge of the office regalia during the interregnum. Sometimes this role is doubled with that of stand-in and in other societies with that of elector, so that those who decide upon the new incumbent take temporary possession of the emblems of office.

Among the Bemba, there is a class of priest-councillors (*bakabilo*) who take charge of the king's relics during the interregnum, pass down the historic legends of office, bury the dead chiefs and install the new, watch over the chiefship and give advice upon matters of succession. Many of the councillors are linked by paternal filiation to the royal dynasty, which is recruited by matrilineal descent.[14]

In Ashanti, the stake-holders are a group of court officials known as the *wirempefo*. On the death of the chief, they swoop down and seize the Golden Stool (or in the case of a lesser chief the ancestral stool or stools) and also a 'white stool' belonging to the late king or chief. The white stool is afterwards blackened and becomes an ancestral shrine; the other stool is the throne and has to do with succession in this world rather than the next. 'As the "stool" is of paramount importance in the kingdom or in a division, and as a new king cannot possibly be enstooled, i.e. enthroned, without the "stool" which the *wirempefo* seize on such occasions, the power and political significance of the body may well be imagined' (Rattray 1927: 178).

In the north-west of Ashanti, where Rattray saw them perform their funeral roles, he noted that the *wirempefo* consisted of the chief official of the household, the *Gyase'hene*, together with the heads of some major court offices, namely the heralds, the stool-carriers, gunmen, sword-bearers, horn-blowers, drummers, umbrella-carriers, the bearers of the elephant-tail. None of the ruling lineage might act as a *wirempe*, and the name itself could only be spoken during a time of mourning. At such a period their 'power' is manifest. Messengers approach them with gifts and, referring to the dead chief, say 'If any fowl which you gave us to rear has been lost, it must have been a wild beast that caught it'. The messengers are driven off, but on the third occasion their gifts are accepted and used for the subsequent rites, when offerings are made to the shades. The *wirempefo* march round the town abusing all members of the ruling lineage and later rush wildly through the streets slashing at the leaves of growing trees.

The behaviour of the *wirempefo* illustrates a number of recurrent themes that run through these situations—the reversal of roles from servant to stakeholder that is also shown in the 'ritual of rebellion' against the ruling lineage; the display of limited violence during the transitional period; the exclusion of the eligibles; the seizure of the regalia whose possession alone gives legitimacy to the ruler.

The declaration of electors serves to resolve the indeterminacy of the system and of the disputes that cluster around succession to high office. The transfer of the regalia may perform a similar function. For possession is a unique act and one that demonstrates *de facto* strength, whether of arms, followers or of craftiness. And like the declarations of the electors, possession is also a public act which serves to announce the resolution of a disputed succession. The theme that possession means right is particularly clear where the seizure of regalia by the royals, rather than the electors, in itself appears to legitimize the new ruler. This theme is widely stressed in indeterminate systems, most spectacularly perhaps in the circulating kingship of the Anuak (Evans-Pritchard 1940).

It was also a feature of the history of European monarchies. When William Rufus was killed in the New Forest in 1100, his brother Henry left him unburied, rode post-haste to Winchester, and seized the royal treasures. Physical possession of this property was one of the main arguments in securing his election to the English throne in the face of the stronger claim of his elder brother, Robert.

Choosing the successor

In hereditary systems of the kind found in the surviving monarchies of modern Europe there exists a line or chain of succession specifying the precise order in which royalty should succeed to the throne. Most contemporary organizations, whatever their character, make similar arrangements of an automatic lineal kind, so that a deputy can take over should a position of importance suddenly fall vacant, and this chain of deputation usually follows the chain of command. But unless the selection of the deputy has doubled for the selection of the heir apparent, the automatic arrangement to cope with an emergency may be quite distinct from the line of succession itself.

No system of succession is completely automatic, even setting on one side the recurrent possibility of dethronement, abdication or usurpation. In the first place, high office generally demands some particular qualities of its incumbents, even if only *mens sana in corpore sano*. The health of the king often has a direct link with the health of the kingdom; and in a next-in-line system not all the automatic successors can meet the minimum demands of royal fitness. Hence some flexibility must exist or the dynasty will find itself out of power through inadequacy or incompetence. Secondly, where a large dynasty is involved in the military and civil government of a country, an element of ambiguity, of uncertainty, in the selection of a successor not only provides a spur to effort, but gives expression to the 'corporate' character of the royal kin group.

The problems of the 'corporate' dynasty are discussed in a later section. Here I want to stress that while, even in those systems we speak of as hereditary, some element of choice is always present, the extent of option varies greatly from next-in-line succession to 'dynastic election'. And despite the western idea that the automatic next-of-kin procedure is the normal type, dynastic election is in fact far more widespread.

(a) Time

The selection of one among a group of possible heirs raises problems as to the mode of choice and its timing. Somewhat similar considerations apply to the timing of the succession itself, as I noted in the earlier treatment of the installation. Indeed, where the selection takes place after the death or retirement of the previous ruler, then the two operations are virtually combined. But as we have seen in discussing co-rulership, the succession may be pre-empted by earlier installation; in this case it is the selection that is pre-empted, as happened at times in Baganda history when the king nominated his heir.

It was by means of the appointed successor that the transfer of high office acquired some measure of stability in the later Roman Empire. In theory, the abolition of the monarchy meant that only the Senate could determine the successor and confer on him the powers of Augustus. 'This difficulty was usually overcome by the emperor's associating with himself, in his lifetime, a son or adopted son or other younger colleague, and causing the Senate, most of whose members were only anxious not to be thought slow in expressing their loyalty, to confer on him a sufficient selection of the imperial powers to leave him in an unrivalled position when the reigning Augustus died' (Burn

1952: 6–7). It is but a short step from pre-emptive succession to co-rulership. In Rome, the sons or adoptees of the emperor were first designated Caesar (a family name taken over by all emperors) and later Augustus. The practice clearly represented an attempt on the part of the office-holders to effect a safe and predetermined handover in a fluid situation. So that when the Augustus-father died, then the Augustus-son would automatically take over (Ensslin 1939: 371). Often enough, however, the throne became vacant through assassination, and the choice then lay with the Senate; in practice the commanders of two or more frontier armies fought for possession of Rome, and for a position of power from which the senatorial acclamation could be duly secured.

A similar form of 'pre-emptive positional succession' was found in ancient Egypt, where the heir apparent, usually the eldest son, was promoted co-regent with his father. The king himself was identified with the god Horus, but at death he became Osiris, killed by his brother, Seth; meanwhile, the new Pharoah became Horus and automatically filled the temporal and divine roles of the late ruler (Frankfort 1948: 101, 110). The process of succession thus formed part of a great chain of being that linked both this world and the next, both the below and the above.

The selection of an heir during the lifetime of the king was one aspect of the Celtic institution known as *tanistry*, the 'preliminary election of a successor before the kingship became vacant'.[15] Here the specificity of pre-emptive selection is linked with the indeterminateness of dynastic election, that is, with the absence of a next-of-kin rule and hence the existence of a plurality of heirs, two features often associated with wide-ranging 'corporate' dynasties.

In Rome, pre-emptive selection meant that a ruler had a say in the appointment of his successor. However, in Ireland and in the Dalriadic kingdom of Scotland, tanistry was associated with a system by which the kingship rotated between two or more branches of the royal clan, whose members took it in turn to supply the monarch. The tanist was thus the head or representative of the next dynasty in line for the kingship. Here an early decision reduced the likelihood of interregnal strife among the many heirs; but it also had a rather different function, as a pledge to the segment out of office that it would have the next bite of the cherry.

Tanistry of this kind was practised in certain divisions of Gonja in Northern Ghana (e.g. Daboya and Tuluwe) where a special title was assigned to the head of a segment next in line for the chiefship. One advantage of this prince-of-Wales system is the unambiguous designation of the successor. Conflicts over the succession tend to be settled at an earlier stage in the replacement cycle, that is, at the election of the heir apparent rather than at the enrobement of the chief himself. By the time the heir-apparent succeeds, the legitimacy of the claim has become an accepted fact for the generality of his subjects. The cost of such a system, of course, is that of any determinate mode of succession, namely, a hardening of the incumbent-successor situation. Such considerations are quite explicit in the Swazi preference for a late rather than an early selection of the successor (Kuper 1947: 88). But in my account of Gonja later in this volume, I try to show that the precise designation of the heir has different implications in next-of-kin organizations (i.e. close succession) than it has for circulating systems (i.e. distant succession) of the kind that prevailed in Gonja and in many other kingdoms in West Africa, as well as among the Scots and Irish.

(b) Means

(i) Appointment

The selection of a successor to the kingship while the incumbent is yet in office is a feature of a number of indeterminate systems; by separating the selection from the transfer of office, it mitigates some of the inevitable uncertainties of the transition. Under such circumstances, the strongest factor in the selection is likely to be the voice of the present office-holder; in non-automatic systems, the appointive element will tend to dominate the elective as the ruler's power increases.

The link between the centralization of royal office and the emphasis on appointive succession also occurs at lower levels in the hierarchy. Indeed, Weber sees the use of appointment as one of the major ways in which bureaucratic systems, needing to fill the battery of specialized roles required by a complex organization based upon a division of administrative labour, gradually developed out of traditional polities of the patrimonial kind. To this question I return later. For the highest office, appointment clearly has but a restricted part to play, except where pre-emptive selection occurs. However, a form of appointment does occur where a military clique like the palace guard effectively arrogates power to itself and 'appoints' or 'elects' a representative of the dynasty as a figure-head to fill what is formally the highest office in the land. I discuss this situation, typified by the *kafes* period of the Ottoman Turks, in a subsequent section which deals with force as a means of selection. Here I would note that the acceptance by the dominant power group of the legitimacy of the blood royal provides a spring-board from which the dynasty can at some time in the future regain effective control. The ruling houses of Turkey and Ethiopia had a long and chequered history of just such a kind; whatever the power position, they were recognized throughout as the rightful rulers.

A somewhat similar situation arises in weak kingships with largely ritual functions, where the selectors may again be politically more powerful than the selected. But this clearly constitutes the limiting case.

(ii) *Election*

Just as no system of succession can be completely automatic, so none depends entirely upon appointment from above. All types of succession require a measure of acceptance by the body of the nation, except in the limiting case where a régime depends solely upon the control of physical force. And even the minimal compliance encountered in the initial phases of conquest states usually leads on to more active demonstrations of consent, the kind displayed in the acclamations of loyalty that enthronement so often demands. The bestowal of public approval, initially perhaps enforced, later voluntarily given, is one aspect of the role of those ineligible members of the community who act as enthroners, stand-ins, stake-holders (or guardians of the regalia). In crowning the English king, the archbishop of Canterbury not only conferred the active blessing of supernatural forces, but also gave the consent of the Church as a temporal organization.

In Gonja, as in other conquest states in the area, the enrobement of a new chief is carried out by representatives of the main social estates that are excluded from the high political office. These representatives of the commoners and the Moslems do mediate in cases of dispute, but they act as electors only to the extent that they could refuse to perform the installation ceremony for a prince of whom they disapproved. But their lack of political power makes refusal well-nigh impossible; in any case, there would doubtless be some blackleg priest, anxious to curry favour with the present dispensation, who would step forward to see the deed was done. The Moslem Limam and the commoner Earth Priest simply perform the laying on of hands and so bestow the final legitimacy upon a candidate already determined by the ruling dynasty itself. This role of the enthroners is often confused with that of electors proper. Apart from seeing to the mechanics of the installation, the enthroners publicly commit their groups and their gods to support the new ruler in whose selection they have played no major part.

Just as the early establishment of the pre-emptive successor introduces the appointive element in monarchical systems, so a later decision stresses the elective. Weber distinguished between the two in the following way. In the 'pure type of bureaucratic system', he writes, 'the official is *appointed* by a superior authority'; the elected official, on the other hand, 'does not derive his position "from above" but from below' (1947*b*: 200–1). In general, succession to the highest office can clearly be appointive only while the previous ruler is still alive, and is consequently limited to *pre mortem* transmission. But, in fact, the distinction between appointment and election is not as radical as might at first appear. It depends upon the relative power position of those who choose and those who are chosen; when the selectors are 'above' (in terms of the organizational hierarchy), they appoint; when they are 'below', the system is elective; in both cases there is choice among a number of alternative candidates, and the choosing may be carried out by one or more electors. But in appointive systems the tendency is to operate with a smaller number of selectors and a larger number of candidates, if only because of the nature of the organizational pyramid. For the higher the office the more persons there are 'below'; it follows that, given open eligibility, the greater the number of possible candidates, and given an elective system, the greater the number of possible electors. But as the body of electors to high office approximates to a universal suffrage, the fewer the actual candidates, since there are limits to the number a mass electorate can handle. The extension and secrecy of suffrage have been among the main features of the political history of Western states over the last century, and have become a distinguishing feature of multi-party democracies. But the secret ballot is preceded by a more open process by which the parties select their candidates and thus produce a manageable list of contenders. In one-party states the selective process within the ruling party is, in effect, the decisive one, with the ballot itself having an acclamatory rather than an electoral role.

In monarchical, as distinct from party states, the actual choice-making body is generally small and often stands partly outside the hierarchy, as we have seen in the parallel case of the Ashanti and Bemba stake-holders (although elector, stake-holder, and enthroner are three quite separable interregnal roles). While in a political sense electors are 'below' their rulers, at election times they are 'above'. Hence the reversal of roles during the installation ceremonies is no mere charade; it indicates the concrete but temporary change in relative social position.

The process of dynastic election varies in several ways, depending upon the extent of the electoral body and the range of choice they are normally allowed. Germany provided one of the best examples of a small compact group of electors, at the time when the monarchy was linked to the headship of the Holy Roman Empire. From the thirteenth to the nineteenth centuries, the German king was chosen by a body of princes (*Kurfürsten*), originally seven in number. Already, before this period, an element of election had obtained; as in the Kentish and West Saxon offshoots in England, the king had to be a member of one of the houses that traced their descent from the god Woden: *reges ex nobilitate sumunt*. The king seems to have been chosen by representatives of the dynasty itself, the choice swinging backwards and forwards from Franconian to Saxon, from Saxon to Bavarian, from Bavarian to Franconian, from Franconian to Swabian. In this way the growth of the central authority tended to be limited by the circulation of office through the semi-independent duchies.

The association with the Holy Roman emperorship that began in 962 made for the greater emphasis on election by a small group of men, which distinguished the German from other western European monarchies. In the place of descent from Woden, which had legitimized the claims of earlier pagan kings, the Church substituted the idea of the monarch acquiring his crown by God's choice, after the manner of Saul; and the will of God was made manifest in the choice of the Church, or, at any rate, of the general body of Churchmen (Barker 1910: 173). The system crystallized in the thirteenth century, after two long interregna had resulted in great chaos; seven electors were formed into a definite body, consisting of the three Rhenish archbishops (who held the arch-chancellorships) and four lay magnates (who were vested with the four offices of the royal household). Their power derived, in some measure, from the part they played during the coronation itself and led them at times to interpret their role more actively and to become watchdogs of the kingdom, even to the extent of trying to set up an alternative government in the emperor's stead.

In medieval Germany, the body of electors (who were non-eligible) was small, but in earlier times the whole dynasty had played a direct part in the process. In the Ashanti divisions, the ruling dynasty put forward the name of a candidate which had then to be approved by the State Council, on which sat representatives of the major lineages resident in the area. In theory, the Council could reject a candidate (indeed, even after installation the chief can be dethroned); in theory, the ruling lineage can select any member of the dynasty (Busia 1951: 9; Wilks 1959: 396). In practice, a near kinsman of the deceased usually succeeds, anyhow in the case of the paramountcy itself.[16] For in Kumasi, the development of the regimental system, appointive office and a more centralized and specialized administration placed greater power in the hands of the king, although even so the paramount was liable to be dethroned (Busia 1951: 91 ff.; Wilks 1966).

(iii) Force

In comparison with the medieval German kingship, the system which operated on the level of the Ashanti division widens the body of electors but retains dynastic eligibility (which the Germans recognized in practice). Among the Ankole of East Africa, eligibility was restricted to the sons of the late chief, but the electing body was extended by forcing the princes to seek what support they could from the people themselves. And instead of the choice among the sons being made by a formal show of hands indicating numerical predominance, or by those more elaborate methods of consultation which allow greater weight to be given to the voices of particular individuals, it was done through success in the civil war that followed the death of the king.

Whatever the system of succession, force is the final arbiter. But in some indeterminate systems, civil war and rebellion become, in effect, the regular means of selection and elimination. As Southwold points out below, this was so at various times in Baganda history. In the Ankole case, the successful brother had to gain considerable popular support in order to seize the kingship. But where military force is more specialized, either in weapons or in organization, then such procedures become less democratic and the choice of monarch may fall into the hands of a military elite. This is what happened to the marcher lords of the Mongol Empire who established the Ottoman dynasty. The Turkish sultans strengthened their position by getting rid of their brothers, but the lack of a large dynasty meant that they had no permanent backing to help ward off threats from other power groups in the society, such as the palace guard.

In most of the Islamic world, leadership passed not in the vertical father–son line ('Amûd-i-Nesebî) but 'in a zig-zag through brothers and nephews' ('Ekber-i-Nesebî) (Alderson 1956: 4). But at the time when the dynasty emerged, Turkish tradition describes an event which provided the charter for father–son succession from the thirteenth to the sixteenth centuries. This event was the slaying of his father's brother by the son of the founder. But

far from there being any theory of primogeniture at this stage, the law of succession may well be described as a 'free-for-all', in which the strongest of the sons inherited the throne, while the others—according to the Law of Fratricide—suffered death. The stakes were indeed very high and the resulting struggles correspondingly fierce, each prince being supported by those leaders and officials who thought that he would best serve their purpose. It clearly rested with the officials in power to decide which of a dead sultan's sons was to be sent the message which would bring him to the throne.

For sons were sent out of the capital to become provincial governors. 'This was also one of the reasons why it was necessary to conceal the death of a sultan until such time as his successor was in a position to be proclaimed; otherwise there would have been many more civil wars' (Alderson 1956: 5–6).

According to Islamic law, all sons are legitimate and equal; there is, therefore, no automatic means of establishing a line of succession. The selection was made partly by the early nomination of the heir presumptive by the present emperor; this man was also allocated the provincial governate nearest to the capital, which gave him a good chance of seizing the throne at his father's death, before any other claimant could get there (a strategem that by no means always worked). And the selection was completed by the systematic elimination of all the rivals, either in the civil war itself or under the Law of Fratricide.

The ruler was not simply the favourite of his father, the nominee of the dynasty (which was continually being thinned out), nor yet the most skilled in battle; his victory depended upon popular support, and the sultans were constantly up against the sentiment that 'the people were at liberty to choose whom they would and also to depose him freely', which provided some safeguard against the election of a weak, incompetent ruler. It is true that force was the measure of popular support, and that the 'people' were, in fact, the Janissaries or a small palace clique; but an elective element remained.[17]

Hence there was never any question of a distinction between the sultan *de facto* and the sultan *de jure*; whoever occupied the throne was its rightful possessor and the attempt to restore a deposed monarch usually ended in tragedy.

At the beginning of the seventeenth century a radical change came over the monarchy, and it reverted to fraternal succession. When Mehmed III came to the throne at the beginning of 1595, he executed his nineteen remaining brothers 'according to custom'. He then decided to keep all his own sons at court, rather than appoint even one of them to a provincial governate, probably because he feared their intrigues. In spite of this he was forced to execute the princes Selim and Mahmud, while two other sons died from natural causes before their father. As a result, when the sultan died, his elder surviving son, Ahmed I, was only thirteen and a half years old, while Mustafa I was about twelve. Neither had ever held a governate before, so that their qualities were unknown; it would have been dangerous to remove one of them by fratricide—particularly before an heir was born to the dynasty. Moreover, Ahmed and Mustafa were full brothers, and it is more than likely that their mother insisted Ahmed should spare Mustafa's life. Many of the quarrels between the sultan's sons were helped on by the ambitions of their mothers, who wanted to see their own offspring successful against the children of other wives. This situation is one of the costs of polygamous marriage, and particularly of royal polygyny in dynasties where the succession is not automatic.[18]

For whatever reason, Mustafa's life was spared, and he was transferred to the *Kafes*—a miniature court with sterilized harem situated in the palace. So that when Ahmed I died in 1617, there was a brother alive to take over the throne for the first time since 1298.

The earlier system had led to a dynasty that consisted simply of a thin red line; all collaterals were liquidated. Under the Kafes system, the brothers were kept alive. But although they were allowed female companions, measures were taken to see they had no children, or that such as were born did not survive; the mid-wife killed them by leaving untied the umbilical cord, since no-one could shed royal blood with impunity. Only very occasionally was a child smuggled out and reared by a foster-mother. As a result, the dynasty remained almost as narrow as before.

The Kafes (or cage) system worked in the following way. The sons of the sultan were transferred from the harem to the men's quarters at about the age of eight; before 1600 they had been sent out to act as provincial governors some four to eight years later, but they now stayed in the men's quarters until their father died. After his death, they were taken to the Kafes and kept there either until they died or until they inherited the throne and returned to the full life of the court. Their situation resembled that of Rasselas in Dr Johnson's novel (founded upon Ethiopian reality), with the Kafes as the Happy Valley;[19] the dynasty formed a pool of princes out of which the effective kingmakers drew out a new monarch, sometimes even before the death of the old. From the time of Bayezid I (1389), there were 17 depositions, that is, half the number of sovereigns. And this position, like other themes that remain half-expressed in other dynastic systems, was recognized quite openly by the Ottoman Turks. The military, who had earlier provided support in the civil war, or else exercised an approbatory role, now became the main instrument whereby a monarch was enthroned and deposed. In 1632 the Janissaries forced Murad IV to show them his brothers, with the words: 'The princes are our lord's sons; we have lost confidence in you, and just as you killed Hüsrev Paşa, so you will destroy the princes; bring out the princes and show them to us now.' When he refused, they threatened to depose him, saying: 'If you don't do as we say, you are no further use to us as Sultan.' And at this he gave in (p. 33).

The dynasty had been so thinned by violent methods that it could offer no effective resistance to the force ostensibly at its command, a force recruited from a religious minority with a view to increasing its dependence upon the monarch. But the result was the dependence of the monarch on his household troops. Nor is this by any means a unique case. In 1888, the Baganda king was expelled by his fusiliers. In the middle of the eighteenth century, the slave-recruited military (*ton-dyon*') of the Bambara state of Ségou seized power from the Kouloubali dynasty and themselves served as kings for two decades (Monteil 1924: 57). Similar slave dynasties arose in India, also as a result of their military role. The danger from such household troops increases with the concentration of fire power, and it is typically when such units acquire guns that they have power to assist or control their masters. And in many cases it is marginal units of this kind that first get equipped with the new weapons, partly because the equipment and traditions of the nobility commit them to the established means of warfare, and partly too because the monarch may see in such innovations a means of controlling his too-powerful subordinates, be they barons or fellow-members of his dynasty.

(iv) *Divination*

Whatever procedure is used for selecting among the possible successors, whether it be by bullet or ballot, the human choice often requires the confirmation of divine authority. Either the electors themselves are seen as guided by God (or by his clergy), or else they resort to some material device in order to divine the wishes of the unseen powers.

The Dagomba of Northern Ghana used divinatory procedures as an adjunct to human calculation. But other societies place yet more weight on the wishes of spiritual beings, and in effect lay the entire burden of choice upon them. As one might expect, such an emphasis is characteristic of theocratic states and ecclesiastical institutions.

In Tibet, divination by horoscope was used to choose the Dalai Lama. A similar method, the drawing of lots, was employed by the disciples to find a successor for Judas Iscariot (Acts i, 23–6). And, following Biblical precedent, the Moravian brethren used the same system to select their wives from among the women members of their own community.

Such randomizing procedures have positive advantages when all candidates are equally fitted for the job or where the final outcome is of little consequence. For in putting the onus upon luck or the Gods, men remove an element of friction from their own affairs.

But a divinatory system of the Tibetan kind does more than place the problem of succession in the hands of the Gods, for it accompanies a completely open system of selection. As we have seen in discussing elective systems, an important variable is the size of the body of potential heirs. But for the office of Dalai Lama, the potential heirs are the total population, from among whom the actual office-holder is selected by procedures largely beyond human control, and certainly beyond human questioning. Consequently, the system virtually eliminates the conflicts between potential heirs, to which indeterminate succession so often gives rise. Moreover, since the selection is made after the death of the incumbent, there can clearly be little conflict between an office-holder and his unknown heir. In other words, there is no dynasty and the minimum of succession conflicts. On the other hand, since the ruler is chosen in infancy, the royal powers are limited by the long minority, during which effective authority rests with his advisers.

Completely open succession is adopted only in rare circumstances; in Tibet it was associated with theocratic rule, where ecclesiastical office (the abbotship of certain Buddhist monasteries) had won control from earlier monarchical dynasties, at times with outside help. Since its practitioners were celibate, the monastic system did not recruit by birth, and some alternative to hereditary succession had to be found; and as a specialized religious body, it was, of course, committed to the principle of divine choice.

The open method they used made for difficulties at interregna and created the problem of a lengthy minority for the nation's rulers, although these disadvantages could be partly surmounted with the aid of supporting offices and supernatural sanctions; but it was clearly a method which encouraged commitment to the religious and political system. Any citizen might be the parent of the new king; all had a stake in the succession. So, too, commitment to some religious sects of the Messianic type, both in Judaism and Islam, is strengthened by the idea that any member of the congregation in proper standing can be the parent of the Saviour.[20]

In considering the problem of the choice of a successor, I have been concerned with a number of interrelated variables. First, there is the degree to which the succession was determined in advance. Indeterminate systems involve additional means of selection, and the timing of the choice becomes of major significance for political stability. So, too, do the means of selection themselves, how the body of selectors is constituted (the degree to which the whole population is involved, by direct participation, by representatives or by delegates), and the procedures it adopts. Indeterminate systems also vary in the body from which candidates are drawn, whether this be a sibling group, a descent group, a noble estate, or the country at large.

There are two aspects of indeterminacy I want to mention here. The first is that the larger the pool of candidates, the greater the potential distance between incumbent and successor. Close succession, as for example a next-of-kin rule, means that the tensions of the struggle for office fall on the nuclear domestic relationships. Distant succession, as when a new manager is always imported from outside the firm, limits the extent of these tensions within the organization itself.

The second point concerns conflict. Indeterminacy increases the tension between potential heirs; the very openness of the succession encourages the struggle for power. But it also does something to assuage the conflict between incumbent and successor, as Southwold notes for Baganda. Indeed, this function is explicitly recognized by the Swazi who nominate no successor while the king remains alive.

Swazi consider that when the heir is not known, the kinship group has greater solidarity: co-wives and their sons are more likely to remain on terms of equality and friendship, and the position of the father is more secure, since there is less likelihood of divided loyalties and a possible attempt to hasten his death.

(Kuper 1947: 89)

After the king has died, a successor is chosen from amongst the children by a council of kinsmen. On the rare occasions when the heir is known beforehand, he is 'usually sent away from home for safety and grows up "hidden" by trusted relatives' (89). The 'banished heir' is found in a number of African societies, for example among the Mossi of Wagadougou, who practise a modified primogeniture, and the institution does something towards lessening the tensions of incumbent and successor (as well as protecting the heir) where the system of succession tends to a more precise statement of that relationship. In agnatic systems, such conflict particularly centres around a man and his eldest son; and some societies, including the Baganda and the Yoruba, specifically ban this son from succeeding to his father's office. Here he is not so much the banished as the prohibited heir.

JACK GOODY

Corporateness and indeterminacy in dynastic succession

In dealing with the general ways in which selection operates, I have concentrated on the system often referred to by writers on the Middle Ages as 'dynastic election'. The true hereditary model is taken to be a next-in-line system, such as that presented by Burke's *Peerage* for the British monarchy. The 'mixture of heredity and election' in the Middle Ages is often seen as marking a transition between the Saxon method of election by the Witan and a later primogeniture. The Saxon system, in its turn, was held to be a 'development of the more ancient practice of choice by the armed manhood of the tribe' (Keith 1936: 1), which led to restriction within a dynasty and finally to the domination of 'the hereditary element'.

But there is no real incompatibility here between exclusive principles. Marc Bloch writes of feudal kingdoms: 'Men believed in the hereditary vocation not of an individual but of a dynasty' (1961: 384). Within such dynasties, conflicts inevitably arise owing to the plurality of potential heirs and the paucity of actual offices. As Bloch again remarks, 'The logical conclusion would doubtless have been the exercise of authority in common by all the sons of the dead king, or the division of the realm among them' (384). But the outcome of division is obvious and as far as high office is concerned the joint exercise of authority hardly works with father and son, let alone with kinsmen of equal rank. Dynastic corporations of this kind require leadership, a fact which necessarily means that some members are more equal than others.

In his perceptive analysis of the political system of the Soga of East Africa, Fallers pointed to the difficulties that arise from the fact that paramount authority could not be shared with lineage-mates, since 'complex, continuously-functioning administrative organizations tend to have a single head' (1956: 230). Noting the difficulties which exist in these systems, various sociologists have tried to answer the question of why indeterminate succession occurs at all.

In his paper *Rituals of Rebellion* (1954*a*) Gluckman observes that institutions which allow for a limited expression of hostility against the existing order may serve to strengthen the social system. And he goes on to suggest that civil rebellion itself may serve a similar function. He finds support for this suggestion in the fact that

rarely in Africa do we find clear and simple rules indicating a single prince as the true heir. Frequently the rules of succession are in themselves contradictory in that they support different heirs (e.g. Bemba), and more often still they operate uncertainly in practice (e.g. Swazi and Zulu). Almost every succession may raise rival claimants. Or the heir is selected from the royal family (Lozi). Or else kingship rotates between different houses of the royal dynasty which represent different territorial segments (e.g. Shilluk and Nupe). (1963: 131.)

While the struggle over the kingship may certainly confirm the value of that office in the eyes of both contenders and spectators, it would be a mistake not to recognize (as Gluckman now does) that such struggles may lead to organizational changes of the kind mentioned by Schapera (1956) and Richards (1961), as well as to structural changes relating to the distribution of power. In any case, the data on the uncertainty of succession do not appear to give support to the analysis in any direct way. It is not a matter of giving preference to arrangements that, intentionally or not, stir up dynastic conflicts which, in turn, keep the system going. Indeterminate succession may sometimes have such unintended consequences; but at others it has the opposite results. The explanation for indeterminacy lies elsewhere.

First we should remember, as Gluckman has observed, that 'clear and simple rules indicating a single prince as the true heir' are in fact rare throughout the world. That they are an exception rather than the rule is relevant to Fallers' analysis of the Soga. He sees the problem of conflict in dynastic descent groups as arising from the opposition between two types of political organization; 'the hierarchical, centralized Soga state and the corporate lineage organisation were structurally antagonistic'[16]. The appointive recruitment of political office is seen as opposed to the ascribed membership of lineages. 'In the lineage, authority was the property of a solidary company of near equals; in the state, it was the property of individuals arranged in a hierarchy of superiors and subordinates' (230). Hence these two structures, lineage and state, produce interpersonal conflict and institutional instability that are reflected most clearly of all in the position of the ruler. 'The ruler himself was both head of the state hierarchy and a member of the royal clan and lineage. His unique position at the head of the state was, however, in conflict with his membership in the royal company of equals...' (231).

Fallers goes on to contrast the conflict and instability that arise when lineage and state are found in the same political system with the 'greater stability in Baganda' (236), a stability which he attributes to the abandonment of the lineage principle at the state level, i.e. the absence of any royal clan. But reference to the Baganda situation suggests two further points. The problem does not lie primarily in the conflict of lineage and state. As many writers have observed, the opposition between the two needs some modification. In many states, we find lineages operating within a central administration and, while they clearly have fewer functions than in acephalous systems, we cannot simply regard them as survivals. Lineages disappear as societies get more complex, but then so do monarchs themselves. Looked at from a distance, kings too are 'transitional' between political systems of the acephalous kind and the nation state that derives popular support from an elective party system, through a single political party, or directly from the fountainhead of power, the armed forces.

It is not the existence of a lineage system in itself that gives rise to strain; the conflict derives from the presence of a plurality of 'royals' who regard the crown as in some sense a common property, even though it has to be held by one member at a time. The problem is similar to one which arises in connexion with the inheritance of property between members of the same unilineal descent group (Goody 1962: 346). Here, too, membership of a kin group implies a measure of joint ownership—this land belongs to us Mac-Donalds—but in peasant agriculture the productive system itself is based upon the joint activities of small groups of close kin. The same contradiction between 'ownership' and 'possession' is yet more apparent in the sphere of chiefship, where resources are scarcer, more restricted; and the conflict between the idea of joint or common ownership of the resources and control by one or more individual members is of much greater intensity.

From one standpoint, then, 'uncertain' systems of succession are linked to the 'corporate' nature of royal dynasties, which Richards (1961) has recently discussed.[21] For they serve to relieve the tension which accumulates between a king and an heir apparent, as well as promoting a sense of sharing in the scarce resource of chiefship.

But these functions are fulfilled not only in systems of corporate descent groups of the kind found among the South-East Bantu, the Soga or the Bemba. In these societies, the royal dynasty is one of a number of morphologically similar (but not identical) unilineal groups, associated in a social system that leans heavily on the notion of descent. However, we find similar problems concerning the equivalence of royal siblings arising in monarchies with differing dynastic structure.

I need here to distinguish four types of dynastic institution. The first is the 'royal descent group' of the Basuto, the southern Bantu generally, and of many other societies to which I referred earlier. The second is the dynasty which constitutes the only significant descent unit in the society, as is the case among the Gonja, Lozi, Hausa, Nupe, and in some of the Mossi states; I speak of these as 'dynastic descent groups' to indicate their limited role and distribution in the society. The third is the narrow, lineal dynasty of the Baganda in the nineteenth century, and more especially of the Ottoman Turks; this 'stem dynasty' results from constant and radical elimination. Finally, there is the 'bilateral' or 'familial' dynasty of the kind found in modern Europe.

I make this breakdown of dynastic structures in order to establish the point that the uncertainty of succession is not simply an aspect of the incompatibility of lineage and state, nor yet does it depend upon the existence of a descent group acting as a royal dynasty. The same uncertainty may prevail where the royal dynasty is a unique descent group, as well as in familial monarchies like the Norman kingdom of England. In all these cases there is

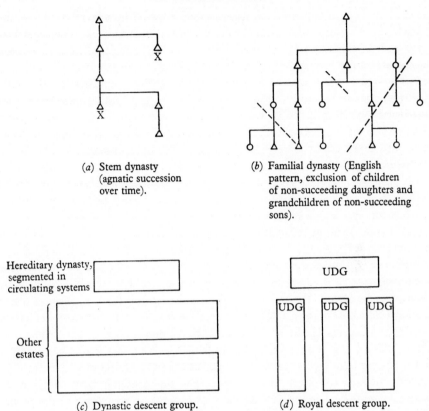

(a) Stem dynasty (agnatic succession over time).

(b) Familial dynasty (English pattern, exclusion of children of non-succeeding daughters and grandchildren of non-succeeding sons).

(c) Dynastic descent group.

(d) Royal descent group.

Fig. 1. Four types of dynastic structure; X, no children; - - -, line of exclusion; UDG, unilineal descent group.

a 'dangerous proliferation' of the royal personality. Where the dynasty provides neither a military force nor major office-holders (other than the king himself), brothers lack the obvious utilities they elsewhere possess. Yet 'uncertainty' is still present. The explanations are several. Fundamentally, it derives from the exigencies of family structure, that is, from the 'equivalence of siblings' (or in this case of brothers), which arises out of the fact that 'siblings share a common socialisation situation including a common sub-ordination to parents' (Fallers 1956: 237–8, n. 3; Radcliffe-Brown 1952: 64). Secondly, no dynastic system can operate on a completely 'lineal' basis; the most ruthless unigeniture must allow for occasional reversion to a collateral line should the king be without issue or should such issue die; high rates of infantile mortality make the provision of a plurality of heirs a measure of common prudence. Thirdly, uncertainty within the sibling group means that some allowance can be made for achievement as well as ascription; within the restrictions of the dynastic system, you can select the 'best man for the job'. Fourthly, the element of uncertainty may well increase the attachment between father and son; where there is no definite successor, the son who acquires the blessing of his father (given only after long and faithful service) has a head start on the rest of the field. And as a corollary, vagueness in the incumbent-successor relationship is likely to lead to a decrease in the tension between parent and child, although not between the brothers themselves.

Finally, indeterminacy may act as a constitutional check; in so far as it involves an elective procedure, it implies a set of rights on the part of those who select, and these sometimes include the 'right' to rebel or the 'right' to dethrone. In Ashanti, chiefship was subject to just such a possibility, even during the most centralized phases of the régime's history. For the electorate is not only active at the time of installation, but may make its power felt throughout the whole reign, in regular council, at annual ceremonies of the *incwala* type, or at critical junctures, as in Ashanti.

The points I have made about indeterminate succession are brought out in the history of the English monarchy, where there has been much discussion about changes in the hereditary element in the kingship, which is sometimes seen as assimilating 'the descent of the Crown to the descent of an estate in fee simple' (Anson 1935: 261). During the twelfth and thirteenth centuries, legal thought certainly found it difficult to distinguish between the rights and duties of the king, who held land as a private person on the one hand and as ruler of the realm on the other. And as Pollock and Maitland make clear, the relative poverty of legal ideas meant that the growing body of lawyers' writings tended to assimilate the rules of succession to rules of inheritance. 'The kingly power is a mode of *dominium*; the ownership of a chattel, the lordship, the tenancy of lands, these also are modes of *dominium*' (1898: I, 513); the transmission of the two tended to be brought into line.

But this problem is not simply a matter of the lawyers' difficulty in formulating distinctions. The process of socialization inevitably puts pressure on the modes of inheritance and succession to coincide, despite the essential differences between the transfer of property and office on which I have earlier remarked. For the group of brothers who have common interests in their father's property (and they are 'provided for' even under systems of unigeniture) also tend to have common interests in his office. And the uncertainty of succession is related to the difficulties of eliminating all except one member of the sibling group from accession to high office. Unigeniture, like other modes of automatic succession by a close kinsman specified in advance, is uncommon because it contradicts not only the idea of a corporate dynasty but also the 'corporateness' of the group of brothers, the 'equivalence of siblings' that results from the family situation.

But automatic systems too have definite gains as well as costs. At the very least, they minimize the danger of the interregnum, which is then uncomplicated by the problem of selection. The cry of the French herald *Le roi est mort, vive le roi* could be heard only where the succession was predetermined, either by an automatic rule or by early choice of the successor. For then, not simply the kingship but the king himself never dies. Keith has noted that 'it is now an accepted doctrine that the king never dies in the sense that there is no interregnum' (1936: 16); but formerly, under the indeterminate system of the Norman monarchy, the interregnum was a recognized fact, and a special officer, the Justiciar, took administrative charge of the kingdom until the process of selection was complete, since the king's peace was in abeyance.

Selection: the persons

In the previous section I have discussed the various ways in which the successor may be chosen as well as the general problem of indeterminate as against automatic selection. One major topic that remains to be examined concerns the who rather than the how of the selection process. Or to look at the other side of the coin, we need to see who is eliminated as well as who succeeds, and what happens to these dynastic discards. Those members of the sibling group who are not selected for the kingship may retain their position as potential kings or as fathers of kings; they may be excluded from the succession but still belong to the royal kin group; they may be demoted from the dynasty to some lower rank of the nobility; or they may be quietly liquidated.

Exclusion

(a) From the dynasty

In unilineal systems of succession membership of the dynasty is defined automatically; one sex transmits membership, the other is excluded. Major political office is basically a male prerogative, even where queens (ruling queens as distinct from kings' consorts) are permitted (as in England) or prescribed (as among the Lovedu). But the sex through which office is transmitted, that is, whether it is transferred by an agnatic or a uterine rule, has profound significance for the dynastic structure.

In systems of agnatic succession, a ruler has it in his power to expand his dynasty through polygamous marriages, by which means he accumulates sons who, as possible heirs, often make equivocal supporters. And the further problems that attach to such proliferation after the king's death are often explicitly recognized, as in the prophecy made by Sheik Abderahmân Es-Soyoûti to Askya Mohammed, ruler of Songhai (1493–1528) when he was travelling on the pilgrimage to Mecca: 'Tu auras de nombreux fils, cent environs, qui tous suivront tes préceptes pendant ton règne, mais qui après toi, changeront de conduite du tout au tout... en sorte que ton royaume soit bouleversé' (Rouch 1953: 213).

In uterine systems, plural marriages do nothing to enhance the numbers of

JACK GOODY

the dynasty, which reproduces itself through sisters. A man's sons, however, can be increased through marriage; and they give him less ambivalent support since they have nothing to gain from the king their father's death. Indeed they have much to lose, for their personal link with royalty is greatly weakened.

While the role of the offspring of the residual sibling has some structural similarities in kingdoms with agnatic and uterine succession (in both they often have important roles at critical junctures, as well as filling specific chiefships), sons usually have a role of greater political importance under uterine succession than sister's sons in agnatic ones (e.g. in the Trobriands, Bemba and Ashanti). This imbalance derives from a general aspect of the contrast between agnatic and uterine transmission. I have noted elsewhere that the transfer of property *inter vivos* to sons in systems of uterine inheritance is usually of greater importance than the corresponding transfers to sister's sons in agnatic systems (Goody 1959). This situation arises from the dominance of males in political and economic activity, which gives them a stronger position even when they constitute the excluded sex for the major transfers of relatively exclusive rights. Two significant aspects of this imbalance are that even in matrilineal systems the basic unit of socialization usually includes a man and his sons; and furthermore, even where marriage for commoners does not entail virilocal residence, wives are bound to move into the polygynous households of chiefs, which will thus tend to attract sons as well as their mothers.

In agnatic systems, then, the effects of polygynous marriage can mean a rapid growth of the dynasty over a very few generations; and even with uterine succession or monogamous marriage, better food and child care lead to a lower infant mortality. Such growth complicates the process of selection, because the larger the number of eligibles, the more difficult they are to handle. Where the support of such a large dynasty is not required, one solution is to lop off the unwanted branches, either by liquidation as in Ottoman Turkey or by relegation of distant royals to a category of ineligibles.

Dynastic shedding is even more necessary in 'bilateral' systems, since in the absence of a unilineal rule, the royals would proliferate through both males and females at every generation. In England, the line of succession (the numbered sequence of eligibles) is, in theory, all inclusive, but the dynasty (if one can speak of the 'royal family' as such) sheds members at each generation. This inner group of eligibles consists of the royal princes and princesses (that is, those having the title of H.R.H., although this category can be extended by Letters Patent); eliminated from this group are the children of non-succeeding daughters and the grandchildren of non-succeeding sons, an arrangement that reflects the preference which this 'bilateral' system gives to males within the group of siblings.

Despite the preferential treatment given to males, English royalty are recruited 'bilaterally'; there is no concept of a group of people passing on to the next generation the membership of a unit that retains its boundaries over time. The contrast can be made when we look at the Zulu or the Bemba, where the dynasty constitutes a named descent group (e.g. the Crocodile clan), eligibility to which is through one parent rather than the other. Such descent groups stand at the apex of a system of unilineal descent groups which automatically exclude certain categories of kin from membership of the group. But a unilineal rule defines the make-up of the dynasty; it does not prevent its growth. Homicide apart, the dynasty itself can only be cut down in size by shedding whole segments (i.e. lineages) whose claim to the throne has now become distant. And it is more difficult to ease a whole segment out of the dynasty than to shift certain categories of kin to a lower rung of the status hierarchy. Rebellion or secession could easily result, since the group to be eliminated has its own pre-existing organization.

(b) From the eligibles

The usual solution to the problem of what Richards has called 'the proliferation of royal lines' is the split dynasty. Instead of the elimination of persons from the royal kin group, the limits are placed upon those who may succeed to the kingship. Hence the ruling group retains an overall unity, despite a division between eligibles and ineligibles. Among the Baganda, princes are no longer liquidated in Ottoman fashion; but instead the dynasty is divided into the princes of the drum (that is, the sons and grandsons of the king, close members of the direct dynastic line) and peasant princes, the 'princes thrown away' (Richards 1961: 148). This very abrupt division is virtually the equivalent of dynastic shedding, and is linked to the minor part played by the wider group in the political system. Where members of the royal kin group are needed to support the régime (in an administrative, military, or more general capacity), then such a division tends to be at once less radical and less acceptable. Less radical because the prevailing ideology is likely to place more emphasis upon the corporate character of the dynasty, so that even where it is divided into eligibles and ineligibles, phrases such as 'the crown is ours' indicate that the king is seen as filling a representative role. Indeed high office always has some such facet, since a king cannot rule without support; and this aspect of royalty is particularly prominent in conquest régimes dependent upon a limited military technology.

But this ideology itself creates difficulties. For when ineligible royals are employed to administer the constituent units of the state, fission often results; unable to rise farther in the hierarchy, fearing replacement by more recent discards, these second-class royals can only acquire the full status of kingship by setting up on their own. And this situation creates the potentiality for fission that exists among some kingdoms of the Southern Bantu. However, among the Basuto this tendency appears to have been somewhat inhibited by the strict ranking by order of birth and the creation of new chiefships for a ruler's younger sons, at any rate during the period of expansion.

(c) Women

Before considering the position of male members of the dynasty, I want to add a few words about the position of its women. Since political and military leadership usually falls to males, women are often excluded from succession to the throne. Even in 'bilateral' systems like that of the English monarchy, they ascend to the throne only in the absence of male siblings, irrespective of age. In some sense, therefore, they are seen as substituting for males.

The point at which female substitution is allowed, i.e. the point where a closer female is preferred to a more distant male, varies in different social systems. As far as inheritance is concerned, there is a most important difference here between Eurasian and African societies (Goody 1962: 320). In England the preference for transmission to direct female descendants rather than indirect males is also found in the succession to royal office. In ancient Egypt, females had a similar eligibility for high office and the practice of brother–sister marriage in the royal family appears to be linked to the fact that women were not eliminated from inheritance and succession. Where women are excluded from office, one alternative is to employ them to promote affinal alliances with other dynasties, or with powerful noble houses inside the state. But the exclusion of women from the kingship does not, of course, imply their exclusion from other important offices in the political system. Among the matrilineal Ashanti, the queen mother is both 'sister' and 'mother' of the king, whereas in out-marrying dynasties based upon the agnatic succession of men to the kingship, only royal 'sisters' have the blood royal; the mothers of kings are outsiders. But in all such systems, female members of the dynasty may be used for its support both in sororal and affinal contexts. As a sister, a woman may hold an office which has to do with the regulation of women's affairs (as the Gonja *Wuriche*) or help increase royal numbers by contracting special unions (as in Dahomey). As a wife, a woman may create or continue an affinal alliance, externally with a neighbouring ruler or internally with the scion of a powerful house.

(d) Men

In those automatic systems which designate a specific heir on the basis of kinship criteria, the simplest method of selection is by vertical succession (Fig. 2(a)). One member of the sibling group (the sons or sister's sons) is designated as heir and the rest are eliminated, unless there is a failure in the main line. For obvious reasons, the selected heir is usually the eldest son; those factors which militate in favour of ultimogeniture in the inheritance of

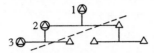

(*a*) Lineal or vertical (filial)
       Unigeniture (here primogeniture)

(*b*) Lateral or horizontal (fraternal)

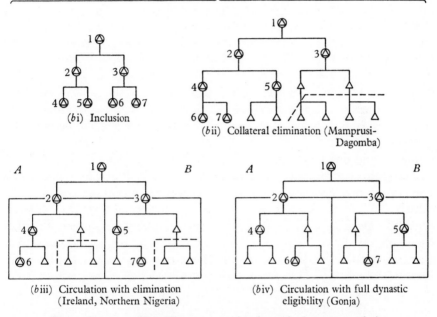

(*b*i) Inclusion

(*b*ii) Collateral elimination (Mamprusi-
         Dagomba)

(*b*iii) Circulation with elimination
          (Ireland, Northern Nigeria)

(*b*iv) Circulation with full dynastic
         eligibility (Gonja)

Fig. 2. Systems of hereditary succession (agnatic, between males).
(△), Ruler; - - -, line of exclusion.

property are relatively unimportant for succession to high office. On the
other hand, some systems deliberately exclude the eldest son.

I should add here that elimination within the sibling group may be carried
out by pointing not to a particular heir (either by prescriptive rule, election,
battle, etc.) but rather to the mother (or potential mother) of the heir, and
then selecting among her offspring. For in polygynous households the
definition of seniority by order of birth may present great problems.[22]
Examples of these anticipatory devices are widespread. Porphyrogeniture,
the exclusion of sons not born in the purple, i.e. before the father becomes
king, is practised among the Nupe of Northern Nigeria, as in the other
Byzantium (Nadel 1942: 87). In the Polynesian island of Tonga, only one
wife bred heirs to the holder of the title of Tui' Tonga; the king had many
wives, but only one queen (or heir-producing consort). Among some of the

Southern Bantu, one wife was selected (by the king or by a council) as the mother of the heir.[23]

All vertical systems pose two central problems, that of Prince Hal and that of the wicked uncle.

Where office passes between close agnates of adjacent generations, there is a potential heightening of tension within a relationship that usually carries the burden of the whole process of socialization. To the ordinary conflicts between father and son are added those arising out of the transmission of office; this is one of the problems Shakespeare sees in the uneasy relationship between Henry IV and Prince Hal, who almost fits the role of 'banished heir'. And the tensions between the two are epitomized in the prince's taking up the crown while his father still lived. Had such anticipatory or *pre-mortem* succession been legitimate, the early transfer of the kingship would have somewhat lessened the tension. A similar relaxation is also one of the gains of indefinite systems of succession which relieve the relationship of a man and his heirs, although at the expense of increasing the potential conflict between the claimants themselves.

The second problem is one of regency. With vertical succession, the sons may be mere children when the throne falls vacant, and their minority usually leads to the establishment of a regency. Where the regent is a member of a collateral branch of the dynasty, the temptation to try and make his temporary rule into something more permanent is considerable; for a brother of the late king, only the life of his young nephew stands between him and the throne. Once acquired, it continues to descend indefinitely to the heirs of his body. By one stroke, he becomes father of a line of kings. This is the problem which runs through the *Tragedy of Richard III*.[24] Where the regent is not a kinsman, the position of the dynasty is weakened as against other elements in the social system and great power often resides in the kingmakers.

Both these major problems that typify vertical systems of succession are brought out in Shapera's analysis of the Tswana. Chiefship was hereditary in the male line, the heir being the eldest son of the chief wife. In this determinate system, considerable conflict arose between father and son, incumbent and successor, which could lead to the latter's disinheritance. The regency problem gave rise to yet more open violence. When Pheto II died in 1810, his children were still minors. Pheto's brothers, Senwelo and Motlotle, tried to kill off his heirs and, in fact, the young king Letsebe eventually met his death at the hands of his uncle, Senwelo, who was later killed by the dead king's brothers, one of whom subsequently succeeded (Shapera 1955: 62, 308).

Another kind of vertical succession is found among the Basuto, discussed by Jones later in this volume. Although such vertical systems limit the numbers directly interested in succession to the highest office, junior siblings play an important part in the administrative set-up; the dynasty is wide, but

34

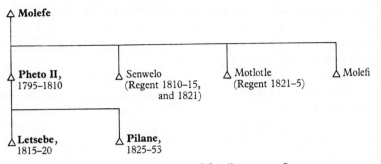

Fig. 3. The Tswana royal family, 1795–1853.

the members are precisely ranked according to their genealogical proximity to the king. Newly formed cadet branches were dispatched to administer outlying areas or to displace relatives of earlier monarchs in central districts.

A similar situation prevailed among the Mossi of Upper Volta, who practised a modified primogeniture; the eldest son was appointed to the office of Djiba Naba and lived as a 'banished heir' quite apart from the king his father (Tauxier 1912: 550; Delobson 1933: 8 ff.), first with his mother's brother and then at Djiba. The younger sons were regarded as possible rivals for the kingship; they too lived with their mother's kin until they were given a district chiefship (or other assignment), which, as with the Basuto, involved displacing an existing line. 'Almost all of the dynastic changes that occurred in the Mossi districts seem to have stemmed from a ruler's attempt to find districts for his brothers or his younger sons' (Skinner 1964: 49).

The basic alternative to a vertical system is a horizontal or fraternal one (Fig. 2(b)). Instead of excluding brothers, you include them. As a result, there is less strain on the father–son relationship; a wider range of kin acquires a direct interest in the throne; and you have older office-holders and shorter reigns.[25] But mortality still demands you make the jump to the junior generation, and this again raises the problem of who then gets the crown.

The logic of fraternal succession would imply that if you go down the line of brothers in generation 2 in order of seniority, then in generation 3 you ought to go down their sons in the same order (Fig. 2(b i)).

Here the dynasty remains truly 'corporate' as far as the crown is concerned. But the difficulties are obvious. In the genealogy shown in the diagram, the number of eligibles doubles at each generation.[26] You can only satisfy all of these by continually decreasing the lengths of reign to such an extent that you end with a dynastic merry-go-round. With each succeeding generation the problem of determining seniority becomes more complex, and the numbers of possible candidates become too great even for elective or appointive succession. The system cannot continue indefinitely. By the third and fourth

35

generations, you get strong pressures towards a reduction in the number of potential successors, towards some system of elimination.

One possibility would be simply to concentrate at generation 3 on the off-spring of a single brother, excluding all others even when their fathers had occupied the throne (Fig. 2(*b*ii)). The result is a modified unigeniture. But it would be a most explosive system, since it means that a man may be king and his children not. Indeed I know of no actual example of this possibility. It seems that attempts in this direction would lead either to a vertical system or else to a wider extension of eligibility at the third generation. Otherwise you would get a trial of strength between the brothers and the system as such would prove unworkable. Or rather, if you get elimination of the offspring of reigning brothers, then it must be by force rather than by design.

The history of succession among the Mossi of Yatenga (Upper Volta) bears out this contention. Tauxier (1917: 348) writes:

En principe toutes les branches collatérales de la famille royal doivent être représentées tour à tour dans le commandement du pays. En fait l'histoire dynastique du Yatenga a consisté à éliminer les unes après les autres par la force et par la violence les branches trop éloignées. En effet, dès qu'un naba puissant monte sur le trône, son idée est tout de suite d'assurer son héritage à son fils aîné ou tout de moins à son frère.

In the nineteenth century interminable civil wars were fought between the sons of Tougouri and the sons of those of his various brothers who had also been king. The former were more numerous and tried to eliminate their cousins from the succession. In the end they succeeded, but only with the support of the French invaders who thus established their overlordship at the end of the century (Appendix 11(*c*)).

The great kingdom of Bornu, ruled over by the Beni-Sef, had similar problems which Urvoy relates to their origin as a conquering pastoral tribe. The king was merely 'the president of the family council'; all the members of the royal family, at least those nearest to the direct line, continued to consider themselves as having a right to the throne equal to that of the reigning prince, and as a result exacted substantial compensation (Urvoy 1949: 37). Certainly from the thirteenth to the beginning of the sixteenth century, the kingship passed in an irregular fashion between the descendants of the two sons of Ibrahim Nikalé, with the occasional appearance of another royal line (Urvoy 1949: 77). Both before and after, succession was characterized by 'une filiation rectiligne et simple, signe de la paix politique'; but this period was marked by the violent elimination of collateral lines, 'le juste schéma d'un noeud de vipères' (Urvoy 1949: 51).

In matrilineal systems the struggle takes a somewhat different form, since the politically dominant sex has a less immediate interest in the continuity of claims. But the history of succession in the matrilineal Bemba monarchy of

Central Africa displays many similarities to the Mossi. Gluckman (1954b: 22) has summarized the situation in this eighteenth-century offshoot of the Baluba kingdom of the Congo in the following words:

In the history of this particular royal lineage at first the big territorial chieftainships were all held by a limited number of close relatives; within the first three generations there was no dispute about who was the rightful heir to the kingship, though there were irregularities in the succession to, and struggles for, the big chieftainships. When it became time for an heir to be taken from the fourth generation, there was a dispute between the senior men in two branches....

The dispute led to a fight which gave the winners control of the major offices, male and female, that had become scattered through the dynasty over recent generations. But here, as perhaps in most of these systems, elimination occurs not at generation 2, but at some later point when numbers have swelled and a greater social distance exists between potential heirs and the throne they seek.

A less violent method of selection is effected by the automatic elimination of the descendants of children or grandchildren who do not reign. Among both the Fulani and Habe of Zaria, Northern Nigeria, only those members of the dynasty whose fathers had themselves been paramounts have any claim to this office (Smith 1960: 234); the same rule applies to their southern neighbours, the Nupe, with the added restriction that the heir has to be born 'in the purple'. The Dagomba of Northern Ghana confine eligibility to the sons of previous paramounts, for it is a principle of chiefship that no man should rise higher than his father (Duncan-Johnstone 1932: 29; Tait 1961: 6; Rattray 1932); among the nearby Mamprusi, another of the Mossi group of states, grandsons may be considered for the kingship.[27] Among the Irish, eligibility to office, like Biblical sin, extended to the third or fourth generation, a situation which gave rise to the saw, 'five generations from king to spade' (Hogan 1932: 250).

Elimination from the eligibles does not necessarily involve elimination from the dynasty itself. Indeed complete exclusion is unlikely to take place where the society is divided into a number of unilineal descent groups, one of which provides the royals, since membership of these groups has many other implications apart from rights to kingship. The same is true of dynastic descent groups, where elimination from the eligibles is again likely to lead to an internal division between those who can and those who cannot succeed. It is in familial dynasties of the 'bilateral' kind that one finds the gradual but radical shedding that results in the descendants of royals merging, if not into the bulk of the population, at least into the non-royal nobility.

In his analysis of government in Zaria, Smith writes of the differential rank distribution in Fulani lineages, where the splintering process involves progressive isolation of those potentially successful descent-lines within each lineage or dynasty, and thus reduces lineage solidarities, the content of lineage membership, and the significance of lineage status. But while the dynasty is no longer fully 'corporate' with regard to the crown, the king can rely upon the support of a larger number of the 'princes' than are directly interested in the succession. And since the dynastic segments are not exogamous, ineligible members may be linked affinally to potential rulers. Such a dynasty may rebel against a particular ruler, but it is unlikely to revolt against the kingship with which it is so closely identified. And this identity will tend to increase when the discarded princes, instead of forming a compact body of potential rebels, are linked to particular segments of the dynasty between which the kingship circulates with varying degrees of regularity (Fig. 2(biii)).

Polysegmental dynasties of this kind exist in most of the states mentioned above and follow from the fact that when fraternal succession is combined with continuing vertical eligibility, office is bound to pass down several lines. These lines are limited by consolidation into a restricted number of dynastic segments, each eligible to provide a representative to govern the nation.

In a later essay in this volume, I consider the different ways of organizing such systems of circulating succession, and the costs and gains of each. I there discuss the degree of regularity with which office passes between the political units, the number of the units involved and the relationship between them.

These factors bear upon the functions of circulating succession. In centralized polities, these relate to the maintenance of a balance of power; rotational succession, either at death (as is usual in monarchical governments) or after a fixed period (as in most non-dynastic systems), maintains a degree of unity where other modes of transfer would only lead to fission. While it is characteristic of certain weakly centralized organizations, such as ancient Ireland and certain organs of the United Nations, it is also associated with more complex governmental institutions; the Zaria Hausa of Northern Nigeria had one of the most developed organizations in the whole of Africa, yet they were marked by a circulation of high office among segments of the ruling Fulani dynasties. One must distinguish between concentration of power in the governmental and in the dynastic fields. And the wide distribution of power that rotation entails is related to the nature of the support the dynasty provides. Similar support, which may be of an administrative or military nature (or simply one of 'compliance', non-rebellion), can also be secured by offering other inducements to members of the dynasty—titles, position, wealth—even when they are not considered eligible for the kingship itself. But such inducements are less effective than circulating succession, since a discarded royal can only become king by rebellion, murder, witchcraft, or secession.

The Gonja situation, which I outline later, draws attention to two further features of circulating succession. For it has a more specific 'distributive' function in societies where the position of the ruling group is dependent upon cavalry, since it offers the warrior estate, who themselves own the means of destruction, the prospect and opportunity of succession to high office. Hence it is found in some of the more centralized polities in Africa, such as those of Northern Nigeria that Nadel deliberately compared with Byzantium. But aside from political functions, circulating systems have one striking characteristic on the domestic level; since a man is never followed by his son, nor by any near kinsman, the tensions to which the transfer of office invariably gives rise are shifted on to distant rather than close relationships. In this, as in the political domain, there is major contrast between systems of close and distant, vertical and horizontal, filial and fraternal succession, at least when the latter are of the circulating kind.

SYSTEMS OF SUCCESSION IN TIME PERSPECTIVE

The main types of succession, heredity, election and appointment, are found in all societies, but they occur in different combinations depending upon the kind of polity. In the simpler societies, the emphasis on hereditary succession is part and parcel of the extensive role that kinship plays. The rudimentary offices of acephalous societies and weakly centralized federations are sometimes passed on by rotation, to maintain the balance between the constituent units. Or, alternatively, the main offices may be divided between the major segments of the society as in the Creek Confederacy (Murdock 1956: 137 ff.). Even in more centralized systems, circulating succession does something to solve the conflict between the uniqueness of office and the 'corporateness' of dynasty, particularly where administrative and military considerations make the support of such a group indispensable in maintaining the government in power. But in any case, simple states tend to rely upon a broad-based dynasty, and this inevitably raises the problem of which member to select to fill the kingship. By and large, indeterminate systems of succession are a characteristic of 'corporate' dynasties.

The concentration of royal power is accompanied by systems of succession that are at once more lineal and more determinate. Vertical transmission of office means a smaller group of eligibles, and the partial removal of the threat that strong collateral branches may offer. The seventeenth-century traveller, Ludolphus, remarked upon the absolute power of the Abyssinian king in civil as in ecclesiastical affairs, observing that only a few provincial governors were able to claim their positions by right of inheritance. The emperors, like most 'Eastern Kings', did not 'deem it a decent thing to command Illustrious Families' as they did not believe that 'servitude can be expected from those that are accustom'd to command themselves. Moreover, they presume that Hereditary Dignity is an obstruction to Virtue; that Men are more certainly made, than born great; and that they will prove more faithful, whom they have rais'd from the Dust, than such as claim their Fortunes from their Ancestors' (Ludolphus 1684: 234–5, quoted Pankhurst 1961: 125).

Raising men from the dust means an increase in appointive as against hereditary succession as well as an increased use of clients, retainers and of other similar roles where ties of subordination are personal rather than hereditary in kind. And many writers have linked appointive office and the institution of clientship to the development of more centralized systems of government.[28]

Max Weber saw appointive office as critical in the rise of modern institutions. For bureaucracy, he claims, first developed in patrimonial states of the 'traditional' kind where a body of officials was recruited from extrapatrimonial sources (1947b: 315), i.e. from persons linked to the chief by purely personal loyalty rather than from a household staff recruited by traditional ties. But under these conditions, he claims, five features of the truly bureaucratic administrative staff are absent:

(a) a clearly defined sphere of competence subject to impersonal rules,

(b) a rational ordering of relations of superiority and inferiority,

(c) a regular system of appointment and promotion on the basis of free contract,

(d) technical training as a regular requirement,

(e) fixed salaries, in the type case paid in money.

But, in fact, it is difficult to visualize any central government that did not meet the first two of these criteria, and indeed Smith has claimed that the government of the Hausa state of Zaria met all except the requirement of free contract (1960: 69). However, only in a limited sense was training technical and were salaries fixed, and consequently there are substantial differences between appointive office in states of the African kind ('patrimonial') and in industrial societies where 'true bureaucracy' is found. So great are these differences that, as Colson has remarked, it seems misleading to refer to both personal and impersonal forms of appointment under the same head (1958: 42). For, in industrial societies, appointive office is not simply optional but is forced upon them by the high degree of specialization, that is, by the division of labour itself.

Technical competence is a central criterion of bureaucratic office, a fact that makes kinship succession largely dysfunctional in industrial societies. On the other hand, in less specialized societies (e.g. in Buganda, Ashanti, and feudal Europe) there is a constant tendency for appointed offices to become subject to hereditary rules. Referring to the Ngoni, Colson writes: 'Appointment to office was a common phenomenon, for the state was expanding rapidly with the constant influx of captives, but the principle was established that each appointment meant the creation of a new hereditary right' (1958: 45). Here the control exercised by the monarch soon lapsed; the new chiefs were anyhow members of the conquering dynasty whose interests were broadly the same as the king's. Leadership of Ashanti regiments, a new one recruited by each monarch from slaves and captives, was passed on from father to son. In these cases, appointment was a means of establishing new institutions. But it is generally true that in societies with simple technologies, where the requirements of office are not of a highly specialized kind, there is little resistance to the pressures which the family, as the unit of upbringing, exercises over the transfer of scarce resources. Office inevitably tends to become hereditary as the personal link between office and office-holder is broken. So that despite the benefits that accrue to a ruler under appointive office, it is difficult to establish a system for the transfer of high office which is not susceptible to pressures that favour kinship succession. Slaves become freed men, clients infiltrate the nobility, the sons of appointees acquire the offices of their fathers. Ultimately, the only complete solution lies in the use of eunuchs, whose particular neutrality leaves them with scant interest in descent.[29] Otherwise it is largely in the military sphere that considerations of age and competence continue to override such tendencies, even over the long term. This was especially true of the regiments of some of the Southern Bantu monarchies; since they were based upon age-groups, the authority system was self-liquidating and the king retained control of appointments to military offices (Colson 1958: 44). It was also the case that, in the kingdom of Benin, the existence of political associations provided support for the development of non-hereditary succession.

In simple states, it was not only appointed officers who acquired an entrenched power that threatened the monarchy. When kings brought other institutions to the fore in order to curb the power of dynastic colleagues or a hereditary nobility, in time these too sought to assert their own independence. In European history, the problem sometimes arose in an acute form when monarchs built up the power of the Church to counter that of princes. In the tenth century, Otto I of Germany endowed his prelates with great gifts of land, as well as jurisdiction in civil and criminal cases. 'The emperor's idea was that, as Church lands and offices could not be hereditary, their holders would necessarily favour the crown.' However, the inevitable tendencies to consolidation set in and the alternative loyalties limited the king's dividends. '...he forgot that the church had a head outside Germany, and that the passion for the rights of an order may not be less intense than that for the rights of a family' (Holland 1911: 836).

In a yet more aggravated form, the problem arises in the attempt to establish military forces under the king's control. This is best done with the arrival or invention of new weapons, especially the gun which is typically the weapon of permanent forces under central control. Such weapons are often kept out of the hands of existing elites; their values will in any case predispose them to the obsolescent weaponry already under their control, a fact most noticeable in aristocracies with a horse culture. The new weapons are therefore handed to mercenaries, slaves, religious minorities, or other marginal groups, partly because of their more ready acceptance and partly because of the increased power accruing to the centre, which enables the king to neutralize, even eliminate, the dynasty upon which he was formerly dependent for support. Thus the location of armed force in specialized bodies, rather than a wide dynasty or a body of nobles, places the monarch in a powerful but dangerous position. While he has at his command the force to kill off his rivals, the choice of king may fall into the hands of the palace guards on whom he relies (as happened with the Turkish Janissaries), just as, in contemporary states, the government may fall under the control or influence of the armed forces on whose power it eventually depends.

The development of governmental systems of greater complexity and greater centralization depends then upon an increase in the potential 'power' available to the administration. Such power depends upon the government's ability to control human, economic and military resources. In the widest time perspective, succession systems can be linked to changes in the economic and military potential (human resources remaining for most purposes a constant), which in a considerable measure, although by no means exclusively, depend upon changes in technology.

Colson has argued persuasively that the economic conditions that prevailed among the Southern Bantu were such as to inhibit the development of appointive office; under conditions of extensive agriculture, land had little value and hence could not be the subject of 'estates in land'. In the states where appointive office was developed, in Buganda, Dahomey and in the Lozi kingdom, cultivation was on a semi-permanent basis and estates in land (suitably scattered throughout the kingdom) could be attached to national offices which the king filled by appointment (1958: 45–6).

Colson is referring to the development of a staff rather than a line organization, which is an attribute of all kingdoms, and, where it occurs, is usually supported by income or tribute from land. But while the productivity of land is often low, it is not the only means of supporting a further development of offices, whether appointive or hereditary, staff or line. War booty, slave production, and, most importantly perhaps, taxes on trade, were available in other parts of Africa, especially in the states of the West African savannahs, for the support of offices and their holders.

The states of Northern Nigeria have at once what is perhaps the most complex governmental system of Negro Africa (and one that had a restricted literacy), and at the same time a highly diffused system of succession, which over time distributes a strongly centralized royal power through the various segments of the ruling estate. This situation arises partly from the way in which the states were established by conquest in the last century. But it is also related to the means available for that conquest, in other words to the nature of the military technology. For the means of conducting war, and more especially raids, was by the use of cavalry armed with light lances.

The long-term trend towards more centralized political systems, towards more complex organizations, is a fact of history, and one that has involved an overall increase in appointive as against hereditary succession. But whereas hereditary systems, like personal appointment, provide their own built-in support, a governmental system cannot long maintain itself on the basis of bureaucratic office and impersonal appointment alone. It requires the support either of the army or of the populace, preferably of both. In the modern world, non-military support has been obtained through a wide extension of elective succession in the political arena, together with the use of other consultative techniques, such as the referendum, or the public acclamation often demanded by personal leaders. But acclamation only affirms a *fait accompli*, and the succession to personal leadership, which has rejected both hereditary and electoral transfer, remains a major problem in the modern world.[30] And under conditions of such uncertainty, the interregnum becomes a yet more critical period than in monarchical régimes. Succession lies with the party (the dynasty), but, without the restraining influence of an agreed system, the military readily becomes involved.

While long-term changes in systems of succession move in a definite direction, with appointment coming to dominate but not eliminate other forms, as ascription gives way to achievement, 'status' to contract, history also has many an ebb to set against the general flow. The units of a conquest régime like the Gonja kingdom or the British Empire, whether they be divisions or dominions, tend to become increasingly independent with the passage of time (particularly of 'peace time'), and the result of the new distribution of power may be either fission or a change in the system of succession.

There are other changes in the internal balance of power that affect not only the mode of succession, but also what is succeeded to. The interregnum is especially sensitive to any such influences. It is during this period that the major power groups, particularly those holding military power, may show their hand.[31] But it is also at this time that 'neutral' groups, electors, stake-holders, enthroners, extend their influence in the state. For such roles fluctuate in importance over time, as the balance shifts between king and kingmaker, between royalty, nobility, and commoner. And the most sensitive place at this most sensitive of times is the royal residence itself, where the household officials, who like the palace guard, are now required to transfer their loyalty from one lord to the next, are in a unique position to influence the course of events to their own advantage.

CONCLUSION

In the last section I discussed the development of appointive office, which, although it radically affects (or is affected by) the nature of the dynasty and its control over human, economic and military resources, is rarely the mode of succession that is used to fill the highest office in the land. In this sphere, hereditary succession prevails, although it is often modified by elective and other procedures. In the overwhelming majority of simple states, the highest office is a kingship, entitlement to which is passed down within a dynasty of varying structure. Whatever the use made of extra-dynastic personnel, whatever the development of institutions not manned by members of the dynasty, the kingship itself is a dynastic possession, however small and weak that dynasty may at times become.

I stress this point because discussions of simple states often appear to treat them as an extension of the relatively homogeneous polities of 'tribes without rulers'. In a truly segmentary state (which would of necessity imply only minimal government) it is conceivable that the interests of chiefs and people might be identical. But the more complicated states of pre-industrial times are found in social systems that are stratified in relation to access to office; they are, in other words, dynastic systems. In such states, particularly when they have been constituted by conquest (as is the case in most areas of the world), it would be naïve to identify too closely the interests of royals and other members of the society; it is equally a mistake to identify too closely the interests of the dynasty, the government and the military, even though at the apex of all three stands the king himself.

The nature of this domination exercised by the ruling dynasty varies with the nature of the resources controlled, and hence with the productive (economic) and destructive (military) systems. Therefore the 'power' of the kingship varies too; there is no given quantity of authority attached to all kingships. And there are clearly limitations to the central control of force when the military technology is based upon the bow and arrow, or agriculture upon shifting as distinct from hydraulic cultivation. So that it is not simply the uniqueness of high office that matters; there is also the functional aspect, the powers it wields, ritual, mediatory, judicial. And these factors necessarily influence the nature of the struggle for office, although even ritual offices produce their complement of succession conflicts.

It is important to stress not only the nature of the 'class' (or rather 'estate') interests involved, but also the nature of the resources under dynastic control. Some writers appear to give more weight to the dynasty's access to royal ancestors than to their control of more mundane resources, to be more interested in their marital transactions than in their military arrangements. Analytically, some further rethinking is required.

In this essay, I have given but little attention to these major aspects of dynastic systems. I have tried to point to some of the changes that have taken place in systems of succession, suggesting rather than demonstrating the way in which these are affected by differences in economic and military resources. I have tried at greater length to sketch some of the variables involved in systems of dynastic succession and consider the positive and negative aspects of their functioning. I have set out this analysis with a measure of formality in order to try and elucidate, in a more general way than is usually done, the complex and confused series of events that mark the history of royal dynasties.

I pointed out that the next-in-line methods of modern European monarchies were very rare. These highly determinate systems laid out a line of successors, and any intending usurper, like Richard III, had to eliminate those with greater precedence. Because of the determinate nature of the systems, they give rise to little unrest at interregna, with which they may indeed dispense. But the greater the precision, the greater the potential conflict between incumbent and successor.

In indeterminate systems, some mode of selection has to be adopted to sort out the blood royal, either by election, combat, appointment or divination. Interregna are likely to be lengthier and more troubled, unless an early selection is made, either by *pre-mortem* transfer of office, by co-rulership, or by the pre-emptive selection of the heir. Tension between incumbent and successor is relieved at the expense of increased conflict between the potential successors themselves.

The incidence of incumbent–successor tension is vitally affected by the emphasis given to fraternal as against vertical movement, and in the former, by the distance between the 'brothers'. Vertical systems of the agnatic kind aggravate inter-generational tensions (the Prince Hal complex) and, at the same time, since minorities breed regencies, bring into prominence the wicked uncle and the kingmaker. Fraternal systems mean older rulers, shorter reigns, a greater emphasis on the 'corporate' dynasty, and some relaxation of inter-generational tensions; while distant fraternal succession (i.e. circulation) means that political conflicts are largely removed from the domestic domain and the 'corporate' character of the dynasty is given yet stronger recognition, a recognition that may be demanded by its military or administrative roles.

I distinguished four types of dynastic structure (Fig. 1):

(a) The stem dynasty, with the possibility of only a limited degree of lateral succession, combined with a radical elimination that places the monarch in lone control but bereft of a support and therefore liable to fall under the sway of his troops or his officers of state (e.g. Turkey, late nineteenth-century Buganda).

(*b*) The familial dynasty (e.g. post-Norman England) with dynastic shedding (royalty to nobility), with male office holders but a bilateral emphasis that opens up the possibility of female kings. Only a limited degree of lateral succession is possible.

(*c*) Dynastic descent groups (e.g. Gonja, Hausa, Lozi). These are largely political in character and are often made up of the descendants of an invading army who maintain their claim to office by ties of descent; these ties are of minor importance for the population at large, which in the above cases is 'bilateral'. Such dynasties are often non-exogamous in character.

(*d*) Royal descent groups (e.g. Ashanti, Yoruba, Southern Bantu), where the dynasty is but one of a number of similar groups. This implies greater cultural homogeneity than in the case of dynastic descent groups, since the UDG's have a wider range of function that may include property rights, exogamy, and ancestor worship, with the royal ancestors being propitiated on behalf of the kingdom as a whole.

In both the last two systems, indeterminate succession is likely to be found because of the existence of large dynastic groups. But unless circulating succession is practised, there must be some elimination within the dynasty, a stratification into eligibles and ineligibles, the severity of which will depend upon the functions allocated to non-eligible members.

Monarchical systems, now few in number and marginal in scope, have played a dominant part in human history, where the polities of Greek and Rome stand out as rare exceptions. Otherwise virtually all the known states of pre-Renaissance times were dynastic in character, although the position of the dynasty varied greatly in different systems. By sorting out these variables we can make some progress towards understanding the total political situation with which different dynastic structures were associated.

Most contemporary states select administrative positions by appointment. But for obvious reasons, this system cannot work with the highest political office, nor yet with representative assemblies of the parliamentary kind. Some modern states kill or confirm their leaders every four or five years by the system of competitive elections which has had such a vigorous development over the last hundred years. But in the large areas of this world that have abandoned monarchical rule and set aside the transfer of power by true election, the problem of the transfer of power is both critical and unsolved. And succession to high office swerves uncertainly between appointment by the leader, an inter-party struggle, and the intervention of the military. But, except in the Society of the Broken Dish, the problem of succession to high office remains just as essential, as full of conflict, and as critical for social continuity and change, as in the monarchies of earlier times.

APPENDIX I: VISUAL AND NUMERICAL MEASURES OF
HEREDITARY SUCCESSION

The comparative study of systems of succession cannot of course be divorced from the study of the political situations in which they operate. But since it is notoriously difficult to compare the entire organization of different states, there is much to be said for starting at a more limited level. For hereditary succession to high office, two methods suggest themselves. First, a visual one. Depending primarily upon the mode of succession, the king-lists of different monarchies (and for different periods) will vary in their profiles. A remarkable example is the Ottoman king-list which dramatically illustrates the change from lineal (father–son) to collateral (fraternal) succession (see Appendix II(a)). The profiles of the Mossi states of Yatenga (Appendix II(c)) and Wagadougou (Appendix II(b)) embody the different histories of fraternal as against lineal (or vertical) succession. While the Leinster king-list (Appendix II(d)), although suspiciously perfect in form (and differing somewhat from the written account given in the same source), shows the operation of a system of rotational succession.[32]

Related to the differences in dynastic profiles are the numerical variations in length of reign. The first fourteen rulers of the Ottoman dynasty, under a system of vertical transmission, averaged 23 years a reign; with fraternal succession, the next twenty (up to 1909) averaged 15 years. The comparative figures for other states are: Roman emperors, 7; Byzantine emperors, 12; Abassid caliphs, 12; Russian czars, 18; French kings, 21; English kings, 23 (Alderson 1956: 4). In promotional systems one would expect shorter reigns than under either vertical or fraternal succession, since a man is already elderly when he qualifies for higher office.

Not all transfers of office take place according to the book, and systems can be compared in terms of the extent of 'wrong' successions. Of course, it would only be possible to calculate a usurpation rate when the I-S relationship is defined in advance. And even here it may be customary to push forward a 'false heir' as a decoy for both men and gods, while the true prince remains in the background until the last moment.

In his detailed analysis of succession in Cenél Eoghain, one of the eligible segments of the northern O'Neils who alternated with the southern branch in providing the kings of all Ireland, Hogan calculates two rates of 'wrong' succession for the period 879–1260. The first measure is of out-of-line succession, where eligible princes have succeeded in the wrong order. Out of a total of 48 rulers, there are 4 instances of father-son succession, two of which are doubtful. The second measure is of usurpation. From the same sample there were 6 cases of intrusion, 4 by 'complete outsiders' and 2 by men beyond the legal eligibility (1932: 219).

Hogan also attempts to calculate a third rate, one of dynastic homicide, and concludes that 'approximately 46% of the total recorded manhood of the Cenél Eoghain dynasty met with violent death, and of these approximately 50 per cent died at the hands of kinsmen'. Hogan concludes from this, as had MacNeil before him, that from the tenth century Ireland 'reeks with bloodshed, disorder, and internecine wars, resulting directly or indirectly from the succession system' (249). But two points should be borne in mind. First, that the percentage of kinship killings is a function of the extent of kinship ties and in Ireland the dynasties were massive, even though eligibility to the kingship was restricted. Secondly, the homicide rates are calculated from written sources, where the sample is heavily weighted in favour of the holders of power and the challengers for power.

Such systems could also be compared in respect of the number and duration of wars of succession. But two additional variables have to be taken into account. First, the extent of participation: Irish wars, although frequent, tended to concern only the dynasty itself, in contrast to the Merovingian wars of Gaul, the Plantagenet wars in France, and the English Wars of the Roses (Hogan 1932). Secondly, there may well be differences in the extent of violence. Although of all quarrels, those between kith and kin are often said to be the most unrelenting, and civil war more bloodthirsty than struggles with external enemies, in many of the simpler societies limitations are placed upon the weaponry used in combat between persons and groups who are close in a social sense.

While such measures may be of limited value, they at least offer some way of assessing the extent and incidence of conflict and disruption in a society. And this is needed if we are to draw more than philosophical comfort from discussions of the role of 'social conflict'. For a start, both 'social' and 'conflict' need to be given much closer semantic inspection than they have had in the past.

INTRODUCTION

(a) Ottoman Turks.

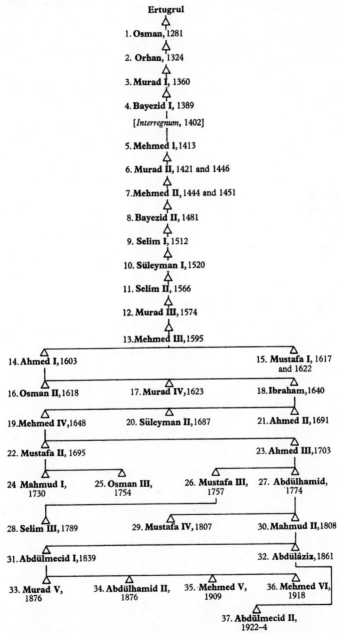

Ertugrul

1. Osman, 1281

2. Orhan, 1324

3. Murad I, 1360

4. Bayezid I, 1389

[*Interregnum*, 1402]

5. Mehmed I, 1413

6. Murad II, 1421 and 1446

7. Mehmed II, 1444 and 1451

8. Bayezid II, 1481

9. Selim I, 1512

10. Süleyman I, 1520

11. Selim II, 1566

12. Murad III, 1574

13. Mehmed III, 1595

14. Ahmed I, 1603 — 15. Mustafa I, 1617 and 1622

16. Osman II, 1618 — 17. Murad IV, 1623 — 18. Ibrahim, 1640

19. Mehmed IV, 1648 — 20. Süleyman II, 1687 — 21. Ahmed II, 1691

22. Mustafa II, 1695 — 23. Ahmed III, 1703

24. Mahmud I, 1730 — 25. Osman III, 1754 — 26. Mustafa III, 1757 — 27. Abdülhamid, 1774

28. Selim III, 1789 — 29. Mustafa IV, 1807 — 30. Mahmud II, 1808

31. Abdülmecid I, 1839 — 32. Abdülâziz, 1861

33. Murad V, 1876 — 34. Abdülhamid II, 1876 — 35. Mehmed V, 1909 — 36. Mehmed VI, 1918

37. Abdülmecid II, 1922–4

Dates are of accession. Source: Alderson (1956: 128–9).

JACK GOODY

(*b*) The Mossi of Wagadougou.

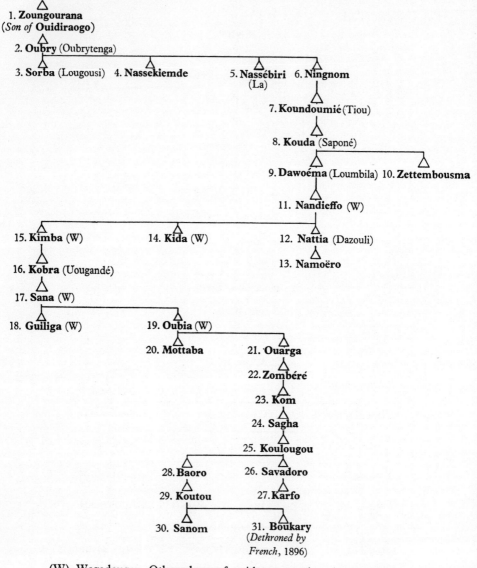

1. **Zoungourana**
(*Son of* **Ouidiraogo**)

2. **Oubry** (Oubrytenga)

3. **Sorba** (Lougousi)   4. **Nassekiemde**   5. **Nassébiri** (La)   6. **Ningnom**

7. **Koundoumié** (Tiou)

8. **Kouda** (Saponé)

9. **Dawoéma** (Loumbila)   10. **Zettembousma**

11. **Nandieffo** (W)

15. **Kimba** (W)   14. **Kida** (W)   12. **Nattia** (Dazouli)

13. **Namoëro**

16. **Kobra** (Uougandé)

17. **Sana** (W)

18. **Guiliga** (W)   19. **Oubia** (W)

20. **Mottaba**   21. **Ouarga**

22. **Zombéré**

23. **Kom**

24. **Sagha**

25. **Koulougou**

28. **Baoro**   26. **Savadoro**

29. **Koutou**   27. **Karfo**

30. **Sanom**   31. **Boukary**
(*Dethroned by French*, 1896)

(W), Wagadougou. Other places of residence are given in parentheses.
Source: Tauxier (1912: 461).

(c) The Mossi of Yatenga.

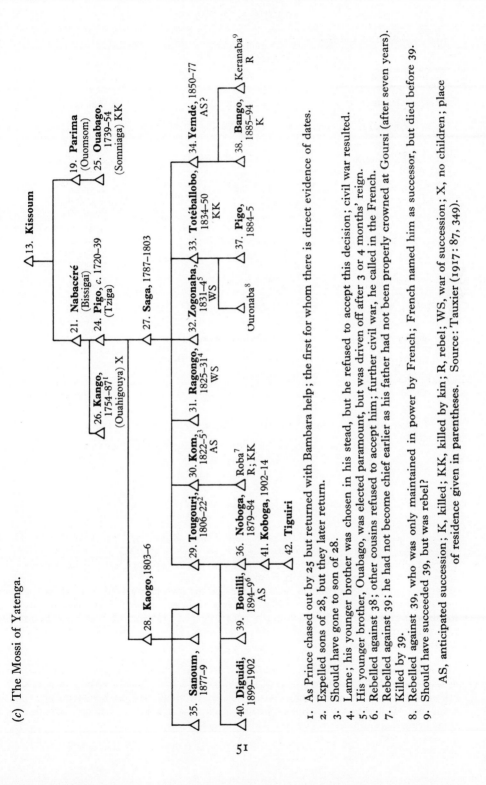

1. As Prince chased out by 25 but returned with Bambara help; the first for whom there is direct evidence of dates.
2. Expelled sons of 28, but they later return.
3. Should have gone to son of 28.
4. Lame; his younger brother was chosen in his stead, but he refused to accept this decision; civil war resulted.
5. His younger brother, Ouabago, was elected paramount, but was driven off after 3 or 4 months' reign.
6. Rebelled against 38; other cousins refused to accept him; further civil war, he called in the French.
7. Rebelled against 39; he had not become chief earlier as his father had not been properly crowned at Goursi (after seven years). Killed by 39.
8. Rebelled against 39, who was only maintained in power by French; French named him as successor, but died before 39.
9. Should have succeeded 39, but was rebel?

AS, anticipated succession; K, killed; KK, killed by kin; R, rebel; WS, war of succession; X, no children; place of residence given in parentheses.   Source: Tauxier (1917: 87, 349).

51

(*d*) The Irish of Leinster.

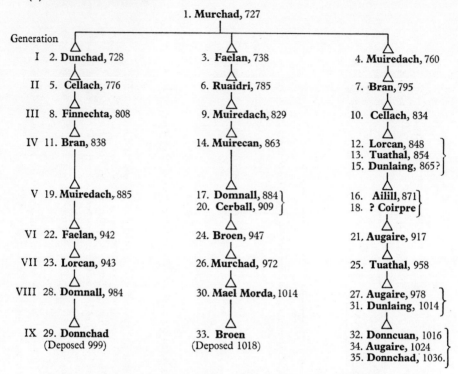

Dates are of death unless otherwise stated. Source: Mac Neill (1921: 126).

(*Note.* This genealogy is not consistent with the information on
Mac Neill, pp. 138–9.)

NOTES

[1] For a more extended discussion, see Goody (1962: 273–83, 329), and the appendix to 'Circulating Succession among the Gonja'. The classic sociological treatment of office is associated with the name of Max Weber (1947*a*; 1947*b*); for a more recent discussion, see Meyer Fortes (1962).

[2] So that I can distinguish between the various factors involved, I speak of the holder-heir (H-H) relationship when property is being passed down, and of the incumbent-successor (I-S) relationship when office is transferred. Since the latter phrase is rather cumbrous, I use the more customary 'heir' for 'successor' when the reference seems unambiguous.

In view of Gouldner's analysis of the 'successor' in an industrial organization, I should point out that I use the term for the designated 'heir', not the man who has already succeeded. Gouldner (1954) was dealing with the way in which the new man's relationship with his subordinates is influenced by their view of his predecessor; I am concerned with the relationship between successive office-holders and how this influences, and is influenced by, the wider social system.

[3] In Geoffrey's version, Lear divided his lands between Goriorilla and Regau, disinheriting Cordeilla with the words, 'In the way that thou lovest me in my old age, so will I love thee henceforth, for I will disinherit thee forever of thy share of ynys brydain...'. After being rejected by his two eldest daughters, he won back his kingdom a second time, and at his death, Cordeilla became queen. But the sons of her two sisters rebelled against her, claiming that it was disgraceful for a woman to rule the land. They defeated her forces and divided the country in two. Some time later, the elder tried to gain control of the whole realm but was beaten in battle by his cousin, who became ruler of all the original kingdom (Griscom 1929: 262 ff.).

[4] I do not wish to imply by the term 'archaic' that these institutions are neces-sarily functionless. Indeed, in pointing to the advantages of a monarch as head of the nation, Weber noted that besides providing a formal legitimation of an elected government, such an office also curbed the politicians' quest for power, because the highest position in the hierarchy is occupied once and for all. And this function, he notes, is associated with the system of succession itself, 'with the mere existence of a king enthroned according to fixed rules' (1947b: 264). It should be added that the tendency for the army to intervene in government may also be inhibited by its attachment to the monarch, a loyalty which places it partly outside the field of political activity.

[5] For an analysis of the importance of kinship in the control of British industry, see Wilson and Lupton (1959).

[6] In their study of social mobility in American industry, Lloyd Warner and James Abegglen note that 'the American system of rank is by no means an open one, and movement upwards is closely related to birth position and family prestige' (1955: 22). See also C. Wright Mills (1959: 30 ff.).

[7] The first English usage dates from 1670 and refers to the unfair preferment of 'nephews' and other kin by Popes and high ecclesiastics.

[8] Warner and Abegglen see one of the problems of industrialized societies as maintaining 'a sensible balance between the hereditary forces of the family and those of achievement and individual opportunity and equality' (1955: 225).

[9] I use the term 'electoral' to refer to the type of broad-based elective system found in 'democratic' states, distinguishing them both from the elective element associated with succession to Germanic kingship and the acclamatory procedures of one-party states.

I use the phrase 'dynastic succession' to refer to hereditary succession to high office, in particular to monarchical succession.

[10] However, fiefs were often partible among females, i.e. when a man had no sons but several daughters. This rule was widely applied to the inheritance of farm-land in the champion, open-field areas of England (Homans 1957: 190–1).

[11] *Post mortem* succession was obligatory among the Yoruba for there was a custom whereby the new chief or *oba* took unto himself the sacred powers of previous kings by eating the excised heart of his predecessor. They maintained that a man would die who did this without being of proper birth, and conversely that a rightful ruler who failed to perform these rites would be unable to withstand the magic potency of the charms incorporated in the royal regalia, and that he too would die. The late Awujale of Ijebu was said to have been improperly consecrated at his installation, because the previous *oba* was still alive, in exile, at the time. Added to this, his eligi-bility to the throne was dubious. His reign was marked by a series of political crises that disturbed the peace of the town and his people were apt to murmur, 'But what can we expect when we do not have a proper *oba*?' (Lloyd 1960: 227–8).

'Deposition could only be effected by death and never by exile or abdication, for only by the death of one *oba* could his successor perform the consecration rituals necessary to validate his own rule' (233). The chiefs, however, could ask their *oba* to die if he was felt to be acting in improper ways.

[12] The concealment of the king's death was practised by the Mossi, the Jukun, the Banyoro and the BaVenda (Skinner 1960: 405–6).

[13] A similar custom is found among the Mossi of Yatenga (Tauxier 1917: 352) and Wagadougou (Skinner 1960: 397), where the death of the Mogo Naba was kept secret until the war minister arrived; then the death was announced and chaos reigned. This custom persisted until 1942. It continues until the present day in some Ghanaian towns (e.g. Tema, *West Africa*, 1963: 132). The theme underlying these ceremonies is expressed in the Yoruba saying, 'Without the *oba* the town would cease to exist' (Lloyd 1960: 229).

[14] Richards has recently presented an excellent account of their functions, drawing upon much comparative material (1960).

[15] MacNeil 1921: 115, 142; Hogan 1932: 244–7. For Scotland see Stevenson 1927; Anderson 1928. It is the element of dynastic election that is given most prominence in English usage (e.g. in the *O.E.D.*), and it is in this sense that I have earlier employed the word as an analytic concept (Goody 1962: 281); the preliminary selection of the heir does not seem to have been the practice until after the Norman invasion (Hogan 1932: 244).

[16] A similar situation held for the inheritance of property (Field 1948: 113).

[17] The succession was, in effect, determined by the 'approbation of these men of war'; the allegiance of the nobles was given in the Biat ceremony where they kissed the hem of his robes and swore fealty to their Lord.

[18] The problem of indivisible office and polygynous households is discussed by Gluckman in 'Rituals of Rebellion' (1954) where he writes: 'A man who has two sons by his wife produces two rivals for a single position and property; and his wife is responsible for this dangerous proliferation of his personality. If he has two wives, each with sons, the cleavage, like the proliferation, is greater' (1963: 116). To this situation of conflict Gluckman links the accusations of witchcraft between co-wives. Clearly such proliferation is less likely to occur in matrilineal dynasties, where the king's sons are not members of the ruling estate. But they are available as an extra-dynastic force, whose loyalty and support are accorded to a particular monarch, their father.

[19] During various periods in the long history of the Ethiopian dynasty descended from the offspring of Solomon and the queen of Sheba, it was the practice to imprison the king's male heirs in a mountainous region to prevent rebellion against their father, for the same reason that the Turkish Sultan, Mehmed III, had refused to allow his sons to leave the court. This institution, which flourished in the tenth, fifteenth, and again in the seventeenth centuries, provided a variation on the theme of the 'banished heir' common in systems of vertical succession, although all the sons, not only the eldest, were so confined. From Bruce's observations at the end of the eighteenth century, it would appear as if the confinement of the dynasty weakened its hold on the government. If the king died and no heirs were at liberty, the choice lay with the chief minister whose inclination was to select an infant prince so that he might retain the reins of power (Pankhurst 1961: 133 ff.).

The third phase of the history of the Baganda kingship was marked by a similar institution of 'confining princes as a precautionary measure' (Southwold, below); indeed, during this recent period, princes were killed off for similar reasons. Once again, increasing autocracy and the butchering of princes were accompanied by an increase in the danger from non-royals, and in 1888 the *corps d'élite* of fusiliers 'expelled the Kabaka...and made themselves masters of the state' (Wrigley 1964: 26).

[20] The same idea crops up among followers of Christianity, although in a less institutionalized form (see Festinger 1956).

[21] The Swazi endeavour to promote this corporateness by refusing to name a successor until the king has died; 'the fiction of equality is studiously maintained until after the father's death, when the actual appointment is made' (Kuper 1947: 89).

[22] The difficulties of establishing birth order in the Mossi royal family arose partly from the fact that the wives of the king and his heir never gave birth in the palace, so that a message had to be sent to the king to convey the news that another royal child had been born. In one such case, the messenger was said to have been delayed and overtaken by one coming from another wife. 'Undoubtedly', writes Skinner, 'such allegations were sometimes used to foster and support dynastic rebellions' (1964: 45).

[23] In Zululand, 'the heir is born of the woman whom the king makes his chief wife' (Gluckman 1940: 35). Among the Tswana, the chief wife was selected by parents and councillors (Schapera 1955: 55). The Swazi also select the heir by means of a council who determine which of the wives of the king holds the highest rank; this is done after the monarch's death (Kuper 1947: 88).

[24] In using this example earlier (1962: 277), I wrote of Gloucester's efforts to become Richard III, urged on by his ambitious duchess. I confused the situation of Humphrey, duke of Gloucester, uncle, Protector, and heir apparent to King Henry VI, with that of the next duke of Gloucester, son of Richard Plantagenet. The former was a loyal man who resisted the prompting of his duchess, Eleanor, while the latter killed not only Henry VI and his son, Edward, but also his own brothers and their offspring in order to get himself crowned King Richard III, and in this he was opposed by his duchess, Anne, widow of Edward, Henry's son. Both dukes, then, were of the blood royal; but the roles of duke and duchess are transposed:

(Henry VI, ii): 'good' duke, 'ambitious' duchess.

(Richard III): 'ambitious' duke, 'good' duchess.

[25] Some ethno-historians have attempted to calculate dates from genealogies by assigning an average span to a reign; it is obvious that such a procedure has no validity unless one already knows the system of succession. The differences in the king-lists of the Mossi of Wagadougou and Yatenga, which have puzzled historians, is surely due to differences of this kind (Fage 1964). The average age of enthronement is just as necessary for calculating lengths of reign as the age of marriage in working out the lengths of generations.

[26] The diagram assumes binary increase, and, as I have noted, such an assumption seems reasonable for uterine and even monogamous dynasties; but it certainly under-states the case in polygynous agnatic ones. I would also emphasize the difference between a dynastic pedigree of this kind and the triangular form of ordinary genealogies among, say, the Nuer or the Tiv, a form that does not necessarily presuppose any major increase in the population, but refers to the disposition of relations between existing social groups.

[27] Susan Brown, personal communication. However, Rattray states that 'a son could not rise any higher than...his father' (1932: 552).

[28] See Professor Mair's account (1962) of the use of 'clientship' to accumulate followers other than kinsmen.

[29] Except in China, where eunuchs sacrificed themselves for the sake of the family. In Africa, no man was a eunuch unless he was first a slave.

[30] Weber saw acclamation as a mode of ensuring the transmission of charismatic leadership, which he also connected with representative government (Bendix 1960: 307-9). But Weber's concept of charisma, which is 'extraordinary and unstable' by definition and possesses 'an emergency character', is of rather limited use in the analysis of succession, even in relation to the discontinuities and changes.

[31] In the Roman Empire, the power of the Senate to elect the *princeps* gradually gave way to the deciding voice of the Army; the *consensus militum* replaced the

auctoritas patrum and the Senate became simply a legitimizing body, cloaking the direct military basis of imperial rule (Ensslin 1939: 369).

[32] Further genealogies of the Irish and Scottish systems are given by Hogan (1932). King-lists of this kind are usually constructed from oral and written traditions which may over-emphasize continuity. Moreover, the translation of words like *mac* or *levir* by 'son' or 'brother', and their delineation on the genealogy according to the usual English meaning of the word, may wrongly transform a distant ('classificatory') relationship into a close ('biological') one.

CHIEFLY SUCCESSION IN BASUTOLAND

By G. I. JONES

The Negro people of South Africa are divided into two main cultural and linguistic groups—Nguni and Sotho (Suto). The Sotho were originally grouped into a limited number of totemic non-exogamous dispersed patrilineal clans, the Nguni into a very large number of exogamous, non-totemic localized patrilineal clans. By the nineteenth century both peoples had become organized into a number of tribes of varying sizes, the basis of tribal unity consisting of allegiance to a chief, the head of the tribe. The office of chiefship was hereditary and was vested in a particular patrilineage and the tribe usually took the name of the clan to which this lineage belonged, though it also contained people from other clans as well who in many cases collectively outnumbered members of the dominant clan. Moshesh, the chief who founded the Basuto nation, was able to build up a larger structure which in addition to his own Kwena tribesmen included a number of other tribes, some of them as a result of conquest (tribal subjects), some of them through alliance (tribal allies), and his state took the pan-tribal name of Ba-suto. It now forms the state of Basutoland with a population of 624,000 people inhabiting a mountainous area of 11,716 square miles which forms the source of the Orange river, and which lies between the Orange Free State and Natal.

By 1868 the Basuto state consisted of ten primary political segments which the British Administration refer to as wards, and by 1940 these wards had increased to the twenty four shown in Fig. 4. Depending on its size, a ward was divided either into a number of ward sections and subsections, and these into village groups, or directly into a number of village groups; while a village group usually divided into a number of villages containing the huts and cattle kraals of from five to fifty families. Each of these units had a head or chief, called in Sesuto Morena. The Basuto distinguished the head of their state as Morena e Moholo, known to the British Administration as the paramount chief. The Administration also called the heads of village groups 'headmen' and limited the title 'chief' to the heads of higher political units, distinguishing when necessary between divisional chiefs, ward chiefs and subordinate chiefs.[1] In this paper I use the following terms for the hierarchy of chiefs: paramount chief, ward chief, sub-chiefs (heads of ward sections and subsections), headmen and village heads.

Villages varied considerably in size—from under 20 to over 1000 huts.

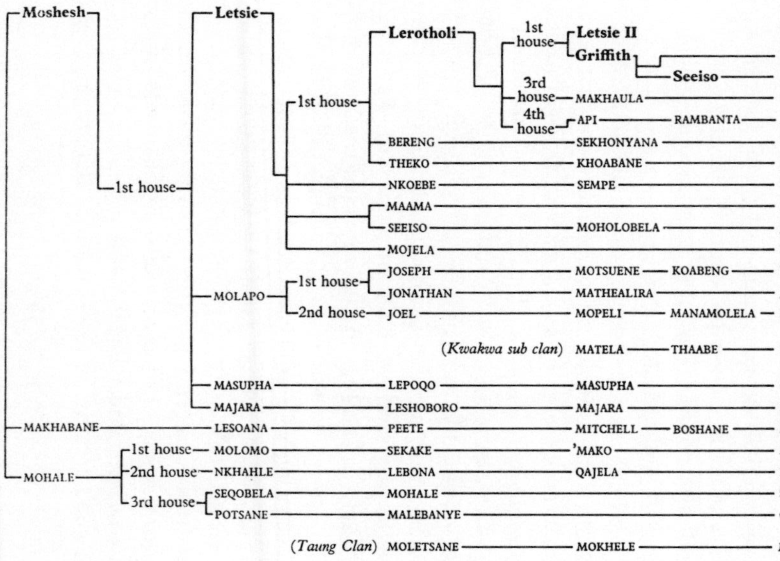

Ward chief	Ward	Taxpayers	Administrative district
The paramount chief	Matsieng	25,670[1]	Maseru
The paramount chief	Likhoele	9,200	Mafeteng
BERENG	Phamong	18,700	Mohale's Hoek
Bereng	Mokhotlong	10,300	Mokhotlong
THEKO	Ratsoleli and Mashai	14,300	Qacha's Nek
API	Kubake	2,300	Maseru
BERENG = 'MAMOHLALEFI	Masite and 5 other areas	7,240	Maseru, Mafeteng and Qacha's Nek
JACOTTET (alias LEROTHOLI)	Thaba Bosiu	10,700	Maseru
QEFATA	Quthing	16,900	Quthing
ALEXANDER (alias SEEISO)	Maama's	4,500	Maseru
JOEL	Matelile	4,800	Mafeteng
LEROTHOLI	Tebang	4,800	Mafeteng
LETSIE	Leribe	20,400	Leribe
JONATHAN	Tsikoane	15,100	Leribe
KUINI	Butha Buthe	6,900	Butha Buthe
TUMANE	Makhoakhoeng	3,800	Butha Buthe
GABASHANE	'Mamathe's	14,200	Teyateyaneng
DANIEL (alias LESHOBERO)	Majara's	2,600	Teyateyaneng
MAKHABANE	Koening and Mapoteng	7,700	Teyateyaneng
MOHALE	Tajane, Ramoetsana's and Mohale's	4,300	Mafeteng and Mohale's Hoek
PHAKISO	Thaba-Tsoeu	1,400	Mohale's Hoek
SOLOMON	Senqunyane	1,200	Mafeteng
GOLIATH	Likoeneng	2,200	Mohale's Hoek
MOEKETSI	Taung	5,900	Mohale's Hoek

Genealogical diagram (left side):

Moshesh
Letsie (1st house)
  Lerotholi (1st house)
    Letsie II (1st house)
      Griffith (3rd house)
        Seeiso
    MAKHAULA
    API — RAMBANTA
  BERENG — SEKHONYANA
  THEKO — KHOABANE
  NKOEBE — SEMPE
  MAAMA
  SEEISO — MOHOLOBELA
  MOJELA
  JOSEPH (1st house) — MOTSUENE — KOABENG
  JONATHAN — MATHEALIRA
  JOEL (2nd house) — MOPELI — MANAMOLELA
(Kuakua sub clan) — MATELA — THAABE
MASUPHA — LEPOQO
MAJARA — LESHOBORO
LESOANA — PEETE — MITCHELL — BOSHANE
MOLAPO
  MASUPHA
  MAJARA
MAKHABANE — SEKAKE — 'MAKO
  MOLOMO — LEBONA — QAJELA
MOHALE
  NKHAHLE — MOHALE
  SEQOBELA — MALEBANYE
  POTSANE
(Taung Clan) MOLETSANE — MOKHELE — MOEKETSI

Fig. 4. Basutoland political structure: wards and administrative districts.

1 Includes figures for thirteen ward sections (4170 taxpayers) usually shown as 'independent chiefs and headmen' in the Mafeteng district.

Those of sub-chiefs were usually larger than those of headmen or village heads, while those of ward chiefs were larger still. The focus of village unity was allegiance to its head not kinship, as the members of the village could be drawn from a number of Sotho and even Nguni clans, while members of a single extended family or minimal lineage were very often distributed in a number of villages and even in different wards.

The Nguni clans are exogamous and the marriage of cross-cousins is forbidden. The Sotho permit marriage of parallel as well as of cross-cousins. This results in a considerable modification of the mother's brother's/sister's son situation described by Junod and Radcliffe Brown as a mother's brother is frequently a 'father' and quite as frequently a father-in-law. It also provided a means not available to Nguni chiefs of linking together rival, or potentially rival, chiefly dynasties through the intermarriage of parallel cousins, as can be seen in Fig. 5. For example the most serious potential rival of the Paramount Chief Letsie I was his brother Molapo, the chief of the largest ward in Basutoland. But Molapo's heir, Joseph, and Joseph's full brother, Jonathan, who later acted as regent for him, were both married to a daughter of the paramount. Thus when Letsie I and Molapo died, Lerotholi, the new chief, was able to intervene very effectively in the internal politics of the Molapo ward as his sisters were married to its ward chief and to its regent and were the mothers of their respective heirs.

Among the Sotho and Nguni ordinary people usually had only one wife but chiefs, particularly the higher chiefs, were polygynous to a high degree. Following local usage, a chief's patrilineal descendants are collectively referred to as his 'house' (e.g. the house of Moshesh) and they are further subdivided according to the particular wife from whom they are descended (e.g. the house of 'Mantai). These houses, like the wives themselves, are ranked in the order in which the marriage occurred. Owing to the productivity of these royal marriages, the dynasty was faced with the twin problems of how to provide for the progeny and how to regulate the succession to office.

A way of dealing with the first problem, which found favour with both Sotho and Nguni (particularly in Swaziland and Basutoland), was for the chief to settle a portion of his chiefdom upon the eldest sons of his various wives while he was still alive. The son became the chief of this territory and subordinate to his father, or to his father's successor in office, and he took with him his mother and his full brothers and their dependants, whom he was now responsible for supporting. This was the institution known in Basutoland as the 'placing system'.

The second problem was met both in Swaziland and Basutoland by a system of agnatic succession. The choice of which son was to succeed lay in the hands of a council consisting of members of the chiefly lineage that met on the death of the chief.

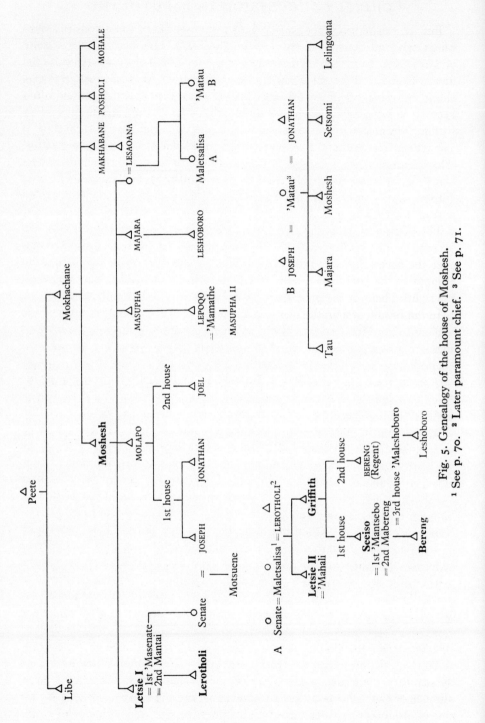

Fig. 5. Genealogy of the house of Moshesh.
[1] See p. 70. [2] Later paramount chief. [3] See p. 71.

But the conventions regulating the succession which these councils were called upon to interpret differed strikingly. Sotho custom stressed seniority of birth. The heir should be the eldest son of the senior wife (that is, the first wife married by the chief). Ideally (and very frequently in fact) this eldest son was built up by his father as his deputy, so that the son had often been acting as chief for several years before his father died and he succeeded without question.

Swazi custom went to the other extreme. Like the Zulu the paramount and other chiefs shared a fear of the rivalry between the heir and his father. If the Swazi heir was indicated at all, he was distinguished late in his father's life.[2] This obviously meant that the lineage council was able to play a considerable part in determining who succeeded.[3]

The Basuto system was the opposite to the Swazi and, to judge by the example of other Southern Bantu systems,[4] was remarkably efficient. Trouble over the succession was rare; when it did happen the causes were either the attempt of the late chief to alter the succession in favour of a son other than the rightful heir, or the premature death of the chief or of his eldest son.

In the Basuto system the heir was defined very early, though the choice was subject to confirmation by the lineage council after his father's death. The succession was defined beyond the immediate heir, as far as his son or even his grandson, and when the heir succeeded to his father's office, his own heir was already defined. A chief was thus able to build up his heir as a strong chief; in the case of the paramountcy, he was made a ward chief during the father's lifetime.

At the same time the attempt of a chief to build up a favourite son as against his rightful heir was restricted by deferring the jural recognition of the heir until after the father's death and by vesting this function in a council in which all the elder male descendants of the founder of the dynasty or the chieftainship had a voice. The larger the chieftainship and the longer the line of chiefs, the greater the number of men entitled to attend the council.

My aim in this paper is to examine the ways in which paramount chiefs and ward chiefs sought to regulate the succession to their own and to subordinate chieftaincies during the period 1868–1920.[5] Their two principal instruments were marriage and the placing system.

THE PLACING SYSTEM

In 1868 when the boundaries of Basutoland with the Orange Free State along the Caledon river were finally defined, the lowland and foothill area of the country contained a considerable population which included a large number of Sotho formerly resident in the Orange Free State. Behind lay an area of mountain pastures three to four times the size, very suitable for cattle in summer but considered too cold for residence in winter. The introduction of European crops (winter wheat) and livestock (Angora goats, Merino sheep and horses) and the development of cross-bred cattle more resistant to cold facilitated the gradual expansion of population into this mountain area. At first the main lowland wards extended their settlements and boundaries into the central mountains and later new wards were established by paramount chiefs for their principal sons along the Natal and Cape Colony border.

The placing system, as it developed in Basutoland, must be viewed against this background of peaceful territorial expansion. The system itself originated at an earlier date. Moshesh found it convenient to administer the massive number of heterogeneous fragments of tribes and villages that had attached themselves to his leadership by dividing his territory up into the primary units which later became known as wards. The central area (which became the wards of Matsieng and Likoele) he retained directly under his control, but the outlying parts to the north and south of this were portioned out into a number of wards over which he placed as subordinate chiefs his senior sons, his brothers, and some of his 'tribal allies'. Within the central area Moshesh also placed other sons, as well as loyal commoners and allies, over smaller portions of territory, that is, over ward sections and village groups. Each of the ward chiefs did the same in their own wards. This process was continued by subsequent paramount chiefs and ward chiefs, as well as by any subordinate chiefs whose territory was large enough to permit such division.

As it originally functioned during the nineteenth century the system was to some extent a process of decentralization; but it also enabled the paramount and ward chiefs to group together scattered communities by giving them as a chief a son, a close relative or an unrelated councillor. The superior chief was thus able to reward the more able of his relatives and followers, while at the same time the people gained by acquiring as their local head a person who was in favour with their lord and in touch with his capital.

There were also economic as well as administrative advantages. As long as they remained at the superior chief's court, sons and councillors had to be supported from the farming and grazing lands attached to his capital. On his placing a son or supporter took with him a number of personal followers and their dependants and settled in his new placing, either in an existing or more usually in a new village. Thus considerable economic relief was afforded not only to the chief who made the placing but also to the land attached to his capital which no longer had to accommodate the holdings of these sons and their followers.

In the period of Letsie I and Lerotholi, the second and third paramount chiefs, this system of placing greatly facilitated the redistribution of population between the lowland and highland areas. The paramount chief and principal ward chiefs could 'place' a commoner and his people or a junior son and his following in a sparsely populated area either by specifically sending him out there or by officially recognizing him as a village headman if he had already settled there of his own volition. As more village settlements were established in the area, the same chief or his successor could consolidate the territory by placing there a more senior son over the whole area as a sub-chief, or if the area was a large one, as a ward chief.

There was, however, another aspect of the system which, as the population became more evenly distributed, came into increasing prominence; this was known as 'displacing'. The sub-chief or headman over whom another man was placed was not completely dispossessed of his chiefly authority, but he was reduced in rank and normally in territory. From being a subordinate chief directly subject to a ward chief, he became a subordinate of the sub-chief who was placed over him and who now became the direct subordinate of the ward chief. From being a headman of a group of villages, he became headman of a single village and subordinate to the new headman of the whole group. Again when a new placing was created, those sub-chiefs or headmen of adjacent areas, even though they were not themselves placed under the new sub-chief, very frequently found themselves shorn of part of their territory so that it could be included in the new chiefship. Examples of the system of placing and displacing as it affected the wards created for chiefs Makhaula and Molapo are summarized in Figs. 6 and 7, and detailed in Appendices I and II.

FACTORS REGULATING THE PLACING SYSTEM

There was no appeal against displacement but there were a number of conventions by which placing and displacing was regulated and to which the paramount, ward chiefs and other chiefs conformed, or professed to conform.

The weakest of these was associated with the Basuto belief that it was unlucky to 'cross the hand', i.e. to exceed five. Thus it was felt that the major placings made by a chief should be limited to this number. But this convention seems to have been so consistently ignored that it can hardly be considered more than a pious hope.

On the other hand two other conventions were as consistently respected. One of these was that the paramount should not displace a ward chief, other than a tribal subject, nor should he place any nominee of his in a ward chief's territory, nor should he reduce the boundaries of a ward once these had been properly defined.

The other was that no chief or headman should be displaced by a person of lower rank. Conversely a person of lower rank (unless a ward chief) must expect to give way to a person of higher rank and had no right to resist displacement by him. With this went the corollary that a person of high rank should be placed in a 'caretaking' commensurate with his rank.

GENEALOGIES

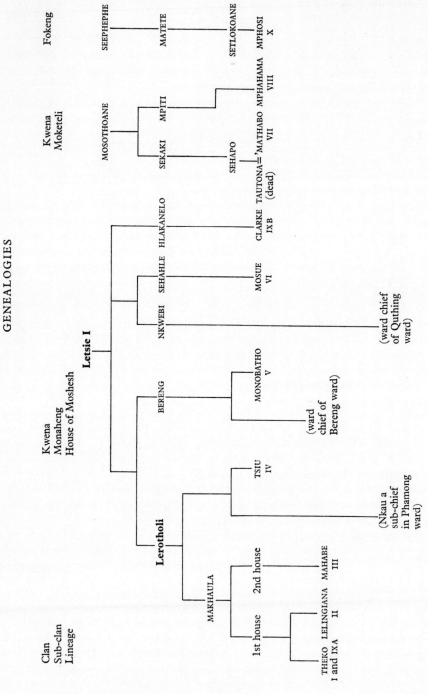

	Before Makhaula's placing	In 1938–	Remarks
Central area	At least 7 local communities (namely: five under Puthi headmen; 1 under a Fokeng (Chamela), 1 under Maluke (Posholi) and the sub-chiefdom of Sehahle (subordinate to his brother Nkwebi the ward chief of Quthing)	I Section of Ratsoleli directly under Ward chief THEKO	Containing 20 local communities 4 of which subdivide into 10 sub-communities. Population approximately 2,413 tax-paying males
		II Section of Matebeng under sectional chief LELINGOANA	Containing 6 local communities. Population 1,145 tax-paying males
		III Section of Matsaile under sectional chief MAHABE	Containing 5 local communities. Population 946 tax-paying males
		IV Section of Mohlana Peng under sectional chief TSIU LEROTHOLI	Containing 4 local communities. Population 352 tax-paying males
		V Section of Tsoelike under sectional headman Kotonyane acting for sectional chief MONO-BATHO BERENG	Containing 2 local communities. Population 406 tax-paying males
Southern area	Chiefdoms of Sekaki and Mpiti Mosothoane	VI Section of Souro under sectional chief MOSUE SEHAHLE	Containing 11 local communities. Population 2,011 tax-paying males
		VII Section of Patlong under 'Mat-habo widow of TAUTONA SEHAPO SEKAKI	Containing 5 local communities. Population 1,770 tax-paying males
Northern area	Chiefdom of Hlakanelo Letsie	VIII Section of Pheelong under sectional chief MPHAHAMA MPITI	Containing 3 local communities. Population 594 tax-paying males
		IX Section of Mashai subdividing into A. Subsection of Mashai under ward chief THEKO	Containing 10 local communities. Population 1,594 tax-paying males
		B. Subsection of Sehonghong under subsectional chief CLARKE HLAKENELO	Containing 6 local communities. Population 1,520 tax-paying males
Extreme north	—	X Section of Linakeng under sectional chief MPHOSI MATETE	Containing 4 local communities. Population 637 tax-paying males
	—	10	76 — 13,388 tax-paying males

Fig. 6. The structure of Makhaula's ward.

Genealogy

Title	Position on map	Tax-paying males	Notes
Ward chief	A1 and A14a	4523	
	A2	219	
	A3	1028	Placed over Selebalo Jobo Moshesh
	A4a	1705	Placed over Joang Khethisa
	A5	523	Shown as headman in 1938
	A6a	1790	
	A6b	642	Subordinate to Tau junior house
	A14b	1090	Subordinate to A14a
	A7	2175	
	A8	1843	
	A9	525	Shown as headman 1938–
Ward chief	B1 and 14	4084	
	B2	895	
	B3	2224	
	B4	956	
	B5	1896	
	B6	248	
	B7	449	
	B8	596	
	B9	2148	
	B10	551	
	B11	492	
	A10	410	Placed in area of sons of Joseph
	B12	163	Shown as headman in 1938
Ward chief	C1	1274	
	C2	929	
	C3	645	
	C4	390	
	C5	383	
	C6a		
	C6b	1535	Chief subordinate to Molapo (C6a)
	C6c		
	C7	357	Chief subordinate to Molapo (C6a)
	C8	373	
	C9	248	
	C10	346	
	A11	710	
	A12	1047	
	A4b	2118	Subordinate to Masupha Joseph A4a
	C11	420	
	B13	398	
	A13	1159	

Names appearing in the genealogical tree:

Moshesh

MOLAPO

JOSEPH — 1st house — Motsuene — 1st house: KOABENG — LETSIE; Shpheseli — Motsuene; Mapapi — Masupha; Moliboea = o 'Mamasupha; Makhobalo — Sekhooana
2nd house: Teketsi; Tau — Khetisa, Sheshote, Letsie
? house: Mosheh; Majora; Setsomi; Leligoana
4th house: MATHEALIRA — 1st house: JONATHAN II, Makoae
2nd house: Motsarapane, Mokokoana
3rd house: Tumo, Moramang
4th house: Mahlomola = o Anna; Matsoete; Tumahole = o 'Marosa; Ntseke; Paulo — Malefetsane = o 'Mampoi; Lejone; Kotsana — Lepoqo

JONATHAN — 1st house: MOPELI — 1st house: Majara — MANAMOLELA, KUINI, Hlasoa; Sekhobe; Malilekefane
2nd house: Molapo — 1st son Joel; Jameson; Cartwright
Qhobela — 2nd house: Selomo; Lepekola; Talimo; Morhuntsane

JOEL — 2nd house
3rd house: Moliboea — Thasi, Enoke
4th house: Seetsa — Molapo, Halekhethetloe
5th house: Khethisa — Joang
6th house: Hlasoa — Mutlanyane, Mopeli
7th house: Manama — Khethisa

Jobo

Motsoane = o 'Malibe

66

STRUCTURE

A, *Leribe ward* = 4 major sections I–IV namely:

I, Leribe under Letsie and including ward sections A1, 2, 3, 5, 7, 8, 9, 10, 11, 12, 13;

II, Matlakeng under Letsie and including ward sections A14a and 14b;

III, Pitseng and Matsoku under Khetisa Tau and including ward sections 6a and 6b;

IV, T'hakoli and Thaba Phatsoa under 'Mamasupha wife of Moliboea Masupha (deceased) and including ward sections 4a and 4b.

Total tax-paying males 20,400 approx.

B, *Tsikoane ward* under Jonathan II and including ward sections B1–14.

Total tax-paying males 15,100

C, *Butha Buthe* ward under Kuini and including ward sections C1–11 of which no. 6 divides into three subsections.

Total tax-paying males 6900

Fig. 7. The structure of the Molapo wards.

The various criteria of the Basuto ranking system are complex and in some cases contradictory. Those which affected the placing system were the ranking order of a chief's wives, that is, of their 'houses', seniority of birth within such a house, and the rule of 'looking forward' and not 'backward' when reckoning seniority; thus persons of the highest rank were those most closely related by agnatical links to the ruling chief and among these his son ranked higher than his brothers, and these brothers ranked higher than his father's brothers and their descendants. Again, all the sons of the ruling chief's first house ranked higher than those of any other house; the eldest son of this house ranked higher than any other person and was subordinate in rank only to his father. At the ward level both these conventions favoured the ward chief as against the paramount chief, and even more as against the sub-chiefs in his ward any of whom could rightfully be displaced to make way for one of his sons. But the ward chief himself could not be displaced. In theory (and this was strongly supported by the British Administration) the paramount is the owner of all Basutoland and all other chiefs are 'caretakers' of the territory over which they have been placed by him; they and any of their successors in office must be installed at a special ceremony by an emissary of the paramount chief. In fact, the ward chiefs were in administrative control of their wards; until recently they decided whom they would place and displace in them and they pleased themselves whether or not they referred to the paramount at all. They usually did so in the case of major placings in order to strengthen the position of the person placed. The paramount always seems to have agreed to a placing. But he had other more effective ways of influencing ward politics.

The result of the anomaly which left ward chiefs free from any fear of displacement meant that every ward (except the three that remained directly under the paramount chief, namely Matsieng, Likhoele and Mokhotlong) had its own ruling dynasty derived from the original ward chief. The ruling ward chief came from the senior line of descent and most of the subordinate chiefs in the ward traced their descent to the original ward chief by collateral lines, and the higher a chief's rank the greater the number of ward chiefs through whom he traced it. The senior line of descent kept proliferating at the expense of the collateral lines whose chiefs were gradually depressed in the course of a few generations from sectional chiefs to subsectional chiefs, and then to headmen and eventually village heads. For this process of placing sons over father's brother's sons was used by the subordinate as well as by ward chiefs. It should be realized, however, that this process of displacement of collateral and of other lesser chiefly houses by the ruling dynasty depended on too many conflicting factors, and was in operation for too short a time for it to have become completely systematized. In almost every ward there still survive as sectional and subsectional chiefs, men who are only very distantly related to the ward chief, while in quite a number of wards there are still sub-chiefs and important headmen whose descent is from lineages other than that of the house of Moshesh, and from clans other than the Kwena. Again the tendency has been not to eliminate altogether these collateral lines, but to increase the number and decrease the size of ward sections, subsections and headmanships so that some kind of caretaking, however small, could be found for the heads of displaced collateral lines. Thus no less than 1330 chiefs, sub-chiefs and headmen became gazetted as subordinate native authorities following the Basutoland Native Administration proclamation No. 61 of 1938,[6] and many more claimed that they should have been included.

A legal marriage in Basutoland was one in which marriage cattle, *bohali*, had been paid by the house of the husband to the house of the bride. The issue of the marriage belonged to the house that had paid *bohali*. Where a man had more than one wife, the senior ranking wife (the 'great wife', *mabatho mofumahali*), was the first in order of marriage. The great wife was the mother of her husband's heir. If she bore no sons, the heir was the son of the next senior wife in order of marriage. She became the mother of the heir though the great wife still took precedence over her in all other matters. But a wealthy and powerful son could not marry anyone he pleased and make her his first wife. The marriage had to be sanctioned by the head of his house, that is, the marriage cattle had to belong to the head of the house, who was either his father or grandfather. This right to arrange the great marriages of his sons, and if he lived long enough, of his grandsons, gave a ruling chief considerable control over the succession not only to his own chieftaincy but also to the lesser chieftaincies which he had established for his other sons. During the period we are studying (1868–1920), when the marriages of chiefs and their sons were of crucial political importance, the definition of the great wife and the ranking order of other wives was affected by the ranking order of the fathers of these wives. It was held, for example, that the daughter of a paramount chief took precedence over the daughter of a lesser man, and that a chief's daughter took precedence over a commoner's. Later the Laws of Lerotholi restored the original custom, that the first wife was the first in order of marriage regardless of her rank.

There was also a number of other customs affecting the seniority and positioning of wives which a chief or his sons could hope to manipulate to their political advantage; these institutions were those of the 'associated wife' (*moetsi*), the 'broom wife' (*lefielo*), the sororate (*seantlo*), the levirate (*kenela*) and, more rarely, of adoption. A junior wife was not normally given her own hut until she had borne a child but was attached to the huts of a senior wife and was known as her *moetsi*. The senior wife looked after her until just before the birth of the *moetsi*'s first child. This normally happened in its maternal grandmother's hut and before the expectant mother left to go there, a special ceremony was performed in which the senior wife anointed her with ochre and fat. When the junior wife returned, she had her own hut and her children belonged to her own house; but a close bond existed between the two houses and if the junior one received no patrimony of its own, it could claim a share in that given to the senior.

Lefielo (literally a broom) was the name given to a girl whose marriage cattle had been paid by a rich man on behalf of his daughter, who thus became the legal husband of the 'broom'. The latter accompanied her as a servant and the children she bore (who were supposed to be conceived by a man other than her mistress's own male husband) belonged to the mistress's own house, and took the name of her male husband.

The sororate and levirate need no explanation except to point out that the levirate came into operation not only on a husband's death, but also in the event of his becoming permanently mad or otherwise incapable of performing his normal political and social roles.

It was also customary, though not very frequent, for a senior house which had no son to adopt one from another house. However, should this adoption be into a great house, the lineage council preferred to recognize as heir the son of the house next in seniority rather than the adopted son of the senior house.[7] Some of the traditions of the Leribe district provide interesting examples of these institutions and their manipulation, particularly those associated with Moshesh's grand daughter, Senate.

SENATE AND HER MARRIAGES

Reference to Fig. 5 will show that Senàte, who is now regarded as the first wife of Joseph Molapo, was the daughter of Letsie I, Moshesh's heir, by Letsie I's first wife, 'Masenate. According to these stories, Moshesh wished the succession to pass through the house of 'Masenate, but Letsie favoured 'Mantai, his second wife, the mother of Lerotholi; so Letsie procured the death by sorcery of 'Masenate's only son whom he suspected of having been fathered by another man. Moshesh, however, planned that in default of sons the succession should pass through 'Masenate's daughter, Senate, and he made Joseph come to his capital to marry her. He accepted no Molapo cattle for the marriage and thus her sons by Joseph could be claimed as being the heirs of Letsie I and not the legal sons of Joseph. If this legend were accepted, then Joseph's own heir should have been Teketsi, the son of 'Mateketsi who is now ranked as his second wife.

To take care of any accidents, Moshesh also paid marriage cattle to Lesoana for his daughter, Maletsalisa, who became the 'broom' of Senate and whose children would therefore belong to Senate's house. Letsie I countered this by seeing that Lerotholi became the actual 'husband' of Maletsalisa and father of her children. Maletsalisa's younger sister, 'Matau, was betrothed to Leshoboro, son of Majara, the fourth ranking son of Moshesh. However, Joseph's brother Jonathan, the second ranking son of Molapo, eloped with her and hid her in the mountains until the anger of Moshesh and Molapo had subsided and they had agreed to her marriage to him. A variant of this legend maintains that Moshesh arranged for 'Matau to be married into the Molapo house as a substitute for Senate, since Senate's children were to belong not to the Molapo house but to the first house of Letsie I. Thus 'Matau's house was to rank as the first house of Joseph and her eldest son Tau should have been Joseph's heir. The fact that 'Matau was married to Jonathan, not Joseph, is of no significance as Joseph went mad soon after his marriage to Senate and it could be claimed, as Jonathan subsequently did claim, that she was Joseph's wife whom Jonathan had taken in levirate marriage.

Moshesh died in 1870 and Molapo soon after, during the 'Gun War'. Letsie I became paramount chief and Moshesh's plans for Senate, if they ever existed, were disregarded. Senate was accepted as the great wife of Joseph, and Maletsalisa as the great wife of Lerotholi; and her sons, who later succeeded as paramount chiefs, Letsie II and Griffith, were regarded as belonging to the house of Lerotholi's mother 'Mantai, and not to the house of 'Masenate.

POLICY AND PRACTICE OF SUCCESSION

In the case of the paramountcy, of ward chieftaincies and to a lesser extent of sub-chieftaincies, the succession was thus a matter which could be planned by the chief and continued (or modified) by his successors. In his declining years, the chief would ideally have, as heir apparent, a married son of middle age who had numerous sons of his own. This heir was built up as the chief's successor and he came to act more and more for his father as the latter's power declined. This was what actually happened in the case of the first three paramount chiefs who succeeded Moshesh. Thereafter the succession was complicated by the premature deaths of two paramount chiefs. The first, Letsie II, lacked the health of his predecessors and died within a few years of his succession and the only son who survived him, a young boy, died soon after. Letsie's full brother, Griffith, who should have become regent (for his brother had many wives) refused to act in this capacity and declared that if they wished him to rule, they should offer him the paramountcy. The succession council agreed to this and he succeeded his brother. When Griffith died in 1939, the succession was disputed by his two senior sons, Bereng, his eldest and favourite son, and Seeiso, the son of his first house. Bereng's position had been greatly strengthened by his father, Griffith, who had placed him as ward chief of the paramount's own personal ward of Phamong. However, the succession council preferred Seeiso and when Seeiso died a year later, it rejected Bereng's claim to act as regent for Seeiso's heir, preferring Seeiso's first wife 'Mantsebo. Bereng was subsequently found guilty of a medicine murder and executed, and Seeiso's heir, who is also called Bereng, has now (1960) succeeded as paramount chief.

However, the succession to his own chieftaincy was not the only one in which a paramount or ward chief was concerned. He had other sons, some his favourites and all of them potential founders of subordinate lines, whose fortunes he could found, and whose lines he could establish, by judicious placings and by judicious marriages. Thus he was able to control the succession in the senior line and the fortunes of its subordinate lines to a very considerable extent. But his will was by no means absolute and he was bound by custom; he might have favourite sons, but he could never make a favourite his heir unless the favourite's rank entitled him to this position; he might indicate which son or grandson he considered should succeed but the final word lay with the lineage council that met after his death. Similarly the placings of other sons made during his lifetime could be changed by his successor in office—not immediately for that would arouse too much resentment, but in course of time when the senior sons of this successor became ready for placing.

Thus one finds a systematic pattern of placing which characterizes practically all Basuto dynasties whether of the paramount chief or of ward chiefs. Each successive chief provided a substantial placing for two or more sons of his first house. He also provided reasonably large placings for the eldest sons of his second and other senior ranking house, out of which they could make provision for themselves, for their full brothers and for other dependants of their house. Sons of junior houses could not expect placing as of right but only through the favour of their father, or in the case of junior sons of a paramount, through the favour of an elder half-brother who had been newly placed as a ward chief.

A study of the successive placings in the principal Basuto wards also shows a regular pattern of the sons being placed at the expense of their father's brothers, and of their father's father's brother's sons. During his reign, a ward chief, and a sub-chief, as far as he was able, placed his sons at the expense of those sub-chiefs and headmen placed by his father or grandfather. But apart from the one who succeeded to the chieftaincy, these sons and their descendants had to make way for the sons of the new ward chief in the next generation. The only exceptions were the few who were able to win the support of the paramount to the partition of the ward between the heir and his dissident brother, who then became recognized as ward chief of the part that split off. This was only likely to happen, and only did happen, in wards which might present a threat to the supremacy of the paramount because of their size or position, notably in the wards of Molapo in the north and of Mohale in the south. The history of the Molapo succession is given in Appendix II; in the case of the Mohale dynasty, an early rivalry between the sons of his first and second houses resulted in a division into two wards, under Molomo (first house) and Nkhahle (second house). Seqobela of the third house married a daughter of Letsie I and was placed in additional territory in the central mountains where he was helped to establish his independence of Molomo and his recognition as a ward chief directly subordinate to the paramount. Letsie's successor, Lerotholi, completed the process of fragmentation by marrying his daughter to Malebanye, a grandson of this third house, and by recognizing his claim to the status of ward chief. The large original ward established for Mohale had thus broken down into the four rival wards shown in Fig. 4.

The pattern is very similar at the higher level of the paramountcy. A son placed as a ward chief by a paramount could expect his descendants to continue as chiefs of that ward, but once the father who has placed him was dead any further expansion of his territory was blocked by wards created for the sons of the new ward chief. For example, Nkwebi, the son of Letsie I, was placed in the Quthing ward. When Nkwebi's brother, Lerotholi, became paramount the boundaries of the Quthing ward were firmly and finally delimited by the establishment of Lerotholi's two sons, Griffith and Makhaula, in wards to the west and north. When Griffith became paramount, any possible expansion northward of Makhaula was similarly ended by the placing of Griffith's heir, Seeiso, in the new ward of Mokhotlong on Makhaula's northern boundary.

By placing a number of sons of the first house in large caretakings, a paramount or a ward chief secured for his heir a predominance of power as against other less senior lines. Full brothers might quarrel amongst themselves but in any dispute between a chief and his half-brothers he could count on the solid support of his full brothers. That is what happened for instance when chief Maama Letsie challenged the authority of his half-brother, Lerotholi, on the latter's accession to the paramount chieftaincy. He immediately found himself threatened by the combined forces of Lerotholi's full brothers, the ward chiefs Bereng Letsie and Theko Letsie. In this and in subsequent conflict with his uncle Masupha of the Berea ward, Lerotholi had no difficulty in mustering overwhelming force against them. Not only were other ward chiefs hopelessly divided against each other, but those in charge of the larger wards had more than enough to occupy them in maintaining order in their own wards and in keeping in check the rival ambitions of their own sons and half-brothers.

For the ideal pattern whereby the chief of a ward was able to plan the succession during his maturity and, in his declining years, to watch his plans develop gradually under the active direction of his heir, was not necessarily the usual one. Quite often a ward chief's sons developed plans of their own as soon as they reached maturity, or even earlier if their mothers' were persons of political ability and determination. By playing off their father against their rivals, they endeavoured to secure as many advantages as they could during their father's lifetime against the day when their father's position passed to his heir. Such advantages included, for example, a definite pronouncement by their father as to the rank of their house, or a placing in a populous and fertile area. If they failed to obtain adequate recognition from their father, they could at least seek to win the support of his heir-apparent, particularly if, as often happened, he was unpopular with his father who was trying to advance the fortunes of a favourite son. Thus, as his sons reached maturity, the head of a dynasty in his later years might very well find himself compelled, first to intervene to keep the peace between rival sons and other subordinate chiefs in his ward, and later, as his powers declined, to fight a losing battle to make his wishes prevail against the rival ambitions of those of his sons who, having managed to win his favour and confidence, were using their position to defeat his policy and to advance their own ends. In such situations there was always the superior authority of the paramount to whom he could appeal for support when he was no longer able to maintain order. This dependance on the paramount was also accompanied by a close relationship through continual intermarriage between the paramount's family and those of his ward chiefs, a relationship which not only kept the paramount in close touch with the ward chief and his principal sons, but also enabled the paramount to play what was often a decisive role in the internal politics of the ward.

These are probably the main reasons why despite its size and decentralization, the Basuto state remained so remarkably free from civil war and rebellion during this period.

APPENDIX I: THE WARD OF MAKHAULA

The ward founded for Chief Makhaula Lerotholi, and now known as Ratsoleli and Mashai, lies in the south-western part of Basutoland, in a mountainous area drained by the Sinqu river. In the last quarter of the nineteenth century, it was largely uninhabited except in the lower parts of the Sinqu valley which formed the domain of the Puthi chief, Moorosi, a 'tribal ally' of Moshesh. Moorosi was defeated and killed by the Cape Colony forces during the 'Moorosi War' and during the ensuing 'Gun War', Nkwebi, an ambitious and active son of the paramount, Letsie I, established himself in that part of Moorosi's former territory now known as the Quthing ward and proceeded to extend his territorial claims over the adjacent country. Lerotholi, Letsie's heir and his deputy in the central and southern part of

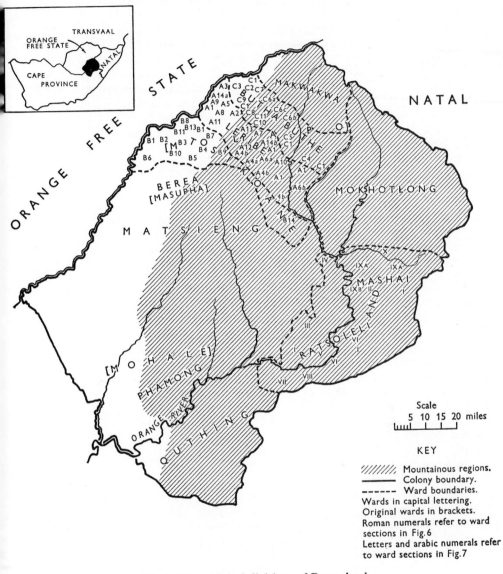

Fig. 8. The political divisions of Basutoland.

Basutoland, could do nothing to check the expansion of his brother's ward while their father was alive owing to the favour Nkwebi enjoyed. But as soon as Lerotholi became paramount, Nkwebi found his expansion halted and his boundaries defined by the placing of Lerotholi's second ranking son as chief of a new ward, Phamong, on the western side of Quthing, and of Makhaula, the first son of Lerotholi's third

75

house, in a new ward to the north of it. His other boundaries were with Cape Colony.

Makhaula's area was still sparsely inhabited and in addition to a number of local communities under Puthi headmen, contained various Basuto groups whose headmen or chiefs had settled there with their followers after the Gun War and who had been recognized by Letsie I. The most important of these were Sekaki and Mpiti Mosothoane, who were Kwena of the Mokoteli subclan, and Hlakanelo, a 'junior son' of Letsie I; his mother is said to have been attached to Letsie I's fourth wife as a 'broom' (*lefielo*) in the manner described on page 70. Hlakanelo's chiefdom seems to have been an important and sizeable one as with him two elders of the Fokeng clan were placed as headman to act as his councillors. Nkwebi had established his full brother Sehahle in the centre of this area and between the Mokoteli headmen and Hlakanelo. Any hope that this might lead to the extension of the Quthing ward northward to include these areas, disappeared with the placing of Makhaula there, and with his recognition as ward chief of the area north of Quthing. Sehahle became subordinate to Makhaula with these other sub-chiefs and headmen, and the ward was divided into five sections of varying size. Three were respectively under Sekaki, Mpiti and Sehahle, one, a large part of the central area formerly under Sehahle and now called Ratsoleli, was now directly under Makhaula and one, the area which had formerly been under Hlakanelo and which was now called Mashai, was also directly under Makhaula. This was divided into two ward subsections, one under Makhaula and the other under Hlakanelo, who thus became reduced to the rank of a subsectional chief under Makhaula, the chief of the Mashai ward section. Three Fokeng councillors who were sent to advise Makhaula were placed as headmen in various parts of the ward.

As they came of age Makhaula placed the two sons of his first house, namely Theko and Lelingoana, and the eldest of his second house as ward section chiefs, Theko at Mashai, the others in sections taken out of the Ratsoleli section. He also placed his half-brother, Tsiu Lerotholi, and the second son of his father's full brother, Monobatho Bering, in smaller areas taken from Ratsoleli. In 1938 these were regarded as separate ward sections, like the area in Mashai section over which the Fokeng councillor, Matete, had been placed; the structure of the ward at this time is shown in Fig. 4.

Makhaula's ward is of more recent origin, situated in an underpopulated area with plenty of room for expansion and one where the first ward chief had few wives and his successor only one wife. Thus a larger number of original sub-chiefs and their descendants escaped displacement. The pattern, however, is clear. The piecemeal expansion of population up the Sinqu valley under a number of locally autonomous petty chiefs or headmen was consolidated by the creation of a new ward for a son of the paramount chief under whom all these local communities and their heads were placed. Nkwebi, who was the son of the former paramount and till then dominant in the area, had to make way for a new generation of paramount's sons and to see his own full brother, Sehahle, made subordinate to one of them. The other petty chiefs, who had been directly subordinate either to the paramount or to the ward chief of Quthing, now came under Makhaula; while one of them, Hlakanelo, was reduced to the status of a subsectional chief.

APPENDIX II THE MOLAPO WARDS

Apart from Matsieng, which was directly under the paramount chief, the ward in which Molapo was placed was the most heavily populated in Basutoland and it was later divided into the three wards of Buthe Buthe, Leribe and Tsikoane. According to tradition Masupha, the third ranking son of Moshesh, was first placed in this northern area of Basutoland, while Molapo, Moshesh's second son, was placed south of him in territory bordering on the Matsieng ward. Later, because of the enmity which developed between Molapo and his eldest brother, Letsie I, Moshesh reversed these placings so that Molapo should be as far away as possible from Letsie I who remained in Matsieng.

Molapo's two most important sons were Joseph, by his first wife, and Joel, by his second. Wishing to strengthen his own and Molapo's influence in the Buthe Buthe area, Moshesh arranged for Joel to marry as his first wife the daughter of the chief of the neighbouring Makholokwe, a small tribe of Kwena origin. Joel objected, saying that he did not like the ways of his bride and her tribe, particularly their habit of eating tadpoles. Moshesh insisted, and it was only after Joel's first son, Mopeli, was born that Moshesh, on a visit to Buthe Buthe, had publicly recognized this child as Joel's heir, that he permitted his son to marry other wives.

On Molapo's death, Jonathan, his second ranking son, became regent for his elder brother Joseph, who was mad, and acted as head of the first house of Molapo (i.e. as chief of the Leribe ward) and of the whole Molapo lineage. The history of this part of Basutoland in the early days of the British Administration is mainly an account of the feud between the two redoubtable chiefs, Jonathan, head of the first house, and Joel, who was the head of the second house and chief of the northern section of this ward. During the Gun War when Jonathan was 'loyal' and Joel therefore a 'rebel', Joel was able to drive his brother out of the area and force him to seek British protection in the British camp. When peace was made, Joel was recognized as chief of the territory over which Moshesh and Molapo had placed him. At this settlement those sub-chiefs of the other houses of Molapo who had taken a prominent part in the fighting were allowed to elect which chief they wished to join. Most stayed where they were, but Hlasoa, Molapo's sixth house, moved from Jonathan's area into Joel's, and Khetisa, of the fifth, did the opposite. The reasons given for their association in each case was that their respective mothers had been 'associated wives' (*moetsi*) in Molapo's first two houses, Khetisa in the first house (Joseph and Jonathan's), Hlasoa's in the second (Joels').

Thus, as far as can now be deduced from annual reports and local traditions, in 1884 the rival ambitions of Joel and Jonathan produced a division of Molapo's chiefdom between his first and second houses. Joel's area became known as the Buthe Buthe ward and was subdivided into five sections: one directly under Joel, one under his half-brother, Hlasoa, one under the chief of an immigrant Ndebele (Nguni) group, one under Molopi, chief of the Kholokwe tribe (Kwena), and one in the extreme north under Matela, chief of the Kwakwa tribe (another Kwena offshoot). All these chiefs were at first considered subordinate to Joel. In the course of the next decade Joel placed various sons at the expense of Hlasoa, Molopi and the Ndebele; so that today the first four sections of the ward of Buthe Buthe have subordinate chiefs, all but one of whom are sons or grandsons of Joel. The exception, Mutlanyane, son of Hlasoa, continues as a sub-chief only because Joel made the mistake of joining the losing side during the Anglo-Boer War in 1901, primarily because Jonathan was again 'loyal'. While he was once again a 'rebel', Joel drove out Hlasoa and burnt down his village. This attack gave the paramount chief and the British Government an opportunity to intervene and compel Joel to restore to Hlasoa his lands and his status.

Joel was even less fortunate with the Makwakwa area. According to Leribe tradition the paramount chief encouraged Matela to approach the paramount chief direct and not through Joel, thereby indicating that he no longer considered himself subordinate to him. Joel immediately endeavoured to reassert his authority by going to war with Matela, but the Government intervened to restore order and Matela was made subordinate only to Jonathan, the head of the Molapo house. Today the Makwakwa area is gazetted as a separate ward, that is, its chief is directly subject to the paramount.

CHIEF JONATHAN AND THE LERIBE WARD

The rest of the Molapo area was under Jonathan and became known as the Leribe ward and district. In theory Joel himself was subordinate to Jonathan who represented the head of the house of Molapo, but as long as Joel lived this was ignored, anyhow by Joel who dealt directly with the paramount. Jonathan's territory contained the following important chiefs or headmen who had either been placed over particular areas by Molapo or had been found there by him when Moshesh had placed him over this part of Basutoland. They were: (i) Moliboea, son of Molapo's third house; (ii) Seetsa, son of his fourth house; (iii) Kethisa, son of his fifth house; (iv) Selebalo, son of Jobo, a son of Moshesh by a junior wife; (v) Ramapepe, a Fokeng headman. The rest of the area was directly under Jonathan as regent for his brother Joseph. From about 1904 when the eldest of his sons reached maturity, the paramount chief, Jonathan, and the British Administration were fully extended trying to keep the peace between these many sons and in trying to restrain Joseph's heir, the unbalanced and violent Motsuene, son of Joseph and Senate. After his father's death, Jonathan had found it advisable to bring Motsuene from Matsieng and recognize him as Joseph's heir; he thus strengthened his position against Joel and Molapo's other sons, who, it is said, were supporting Joel against him. Motsuene was placed by Jonathan on Joel's border, where in his early years he spent much of his energy in boundary fights and disputes with Joel's Ndebele sub-chief, and, in his later years, in demanding a larger caretaking as well as permission to succeed his father. His unsuitability for such a position was so patent that neither the British Government, the paramount chief nor any chiefs of the house of Molapo were prepared to support his claim.

Jonathan's main worries were caused by his own sons. The two protagonists were Mathealira, son by his second wife (the first being without issue), and Tau, son of his favourite wife, 'Matau, who if she was considered as married to Jonathan ranked as sixth wife. It was known that Jonathan favoured Tau as his heir rather than Mathealira. However, Mathealira's mother was a daughter of Letsie I, the paramount chief, and could not lightly be passed over. In 1898 Tau was placed in the Pitseng Plateau, largely at Khethisa Molapo's expense and with consequent friction between them and between Khethisa and Jonathan. In 1905 the annual report on the Leribe district states that 'the two eldest sons of Jonathan' (i.e.

Mathealira and Tau) 'are now grown up and are bad friends'. The 1906 report remarks upon the rising tension in the ward saying that trouble is being caused by Jonathan's refusal to declare which is senior. The 1907 report says that 'Jonathan has made an ambiguous pronoucement which although it has failed to allay the tension is probably better than a definite statement in favour of one or the other as this might precipitate a crisis'. This 'ambiguous pronouncement' was that 'Matau had been married not for Jonathan but for Joseph; her house therefore ranked as a Joseph and not as a Jonathan house. This made Tau senior to Mathealira since Joseph was senior to Jonathan. But it recognized Mathealira's mother's house as Jonathan's senior house, and it could not give 'Matau's house a particularly high rank amongst the houses of Joseph. The tension between Mathealira and Tau continued to mount until the paramount chief intervened with the support of the British Administration and in 1907 Griffith, son of the paramount Chief Lerotholi, and acting as his deputy, made a boundary between them which the annual report describes as being 'very satisfactory' as it left 'the sons of Joseph to the north, the sons of Jonathan to the south and their uncles (Moliboea, Seetsa and Khethisa) in between them in the centre'. Also, in case of further trouble on this point, Motsuene was officially recognized as Joseph's heir on the day this boundary was announced.

Mathealira's policy was clear and the settlement of 1907 gave him what he had been working for. Not only was his status unambiguously defined as head of the line of Jonathan and therefore of all Jonathan's legal sons, but the agreement also made a clear territorial division between the legal sons of Joseph and those of Jonathan. Thus on the death of Jonathan, Mathealira could expect to succeed his father as chief of this division, while Motsuene (or his heir) would succeed as chief of the rest of the district. (This is in fact what happened.) It was therefore in Mathealira's interest that this settlement should be adhered to.

Tau's line of action was less obvious. He could no longer claim to be the heir of Jonathan or Joseph and therefore his only course was to extend his own territory and establish himself as chief of as large an area as possible. He could not hope for much support from his own brothers each of whom had been made a chief in his own right by Jonathan, for they had probably more to gain by supporting whoever succeeded to the chieftainship of the Joseph or the Jonathan division. Tau seems to have adopted the policy of trying to prevent his father placing anyone else in what he considered to be his special territory. He died not many years later, leaving his great wife 'Mathe to act as regent and continue his policy.

Neither could Motsuene derive much advantage from his recognition as Joseph's heir. This fact had already been accepted for some time in Leribe but he could do little to advance his own interests as long as Jonathan was acting as regent, for the only interests that Jonathan served were his own. Pressed by his numerous other sons to find places for them, Jonathan ignored the Matati river boundary line and placed those that found favour with him wherever he could. This led to further trouble. Mathealira demanded the removal to the northern division of all those 'sons of Joseph' who had been placed in the southern division, namely Tau's younger brothers. The sons of Joseph and 'Matau counter-claimed that all sons of Jonathan should be moved from the northern division. In 1922 the paramount chief had to intervene again to relieve the tension, and sent ward chief Makhaula as his deputy to readjust the boundary. This he did by arranging for Moshesh and Setsomi, of the house of 'Matau, to change places with Motsarapene, Tumo and Moramang.

Moramang had originally been placed by Jonathan near the Sehonghong river. This change produced a dispute with Tau who claimed the area as his own, and Jonathan agreed to remove him and placed him in the area of his brother, Tumo. When they were moved into the southern division, Tumo found his new placing (the area formerly given to Moshesh) too small for the two of them and Mathealira placed Moramang in the south of his own area. About the same time, or possibly a little later, 'Mathe brought another dispute to a conclusion by a court action which ordered Jonathan to remove Kotsana and Khethoa from her territory, since they were his sons and did not belong to the house of 'Matau.[8] They had both been placed in Tau's area on the grounds that their respective mothers were both 'associated wives' (*moetsi*) of 'Matau's house. 'Mathe claimed that they were not, and the court upheld her claim. Jonathan arranged for Kotsana to be placed in the southern division but placed Khethoa in the northern, albeit as a headman under Masupha.

Before he died Jonathan had succeeded in placing no less than fifteen of his sons as sub-chiefs, that is: the eldest sons of his five senior houses with male issue, namely Mathealira (second house), Motsarapane (third house), Tumo (fourth house), Mathlomola (fifth house) and Tau (either sixth house of Jonathan or fourth house of Joseph): the eldest sons of six junior houses, Paul, Matsoete, Tumahole, Lejone, Kotsana and Ntsekhe: and the four younger sons of 'Matau's house, Moshesh, Majara, Setsomi and Lelongoana. Their placings are roughly indicated on the sketch map. In addition no less than ten other eldest sons of junior houses had been given subordinate placings as headmen as well as one younger son of a senior house, Moramang, who is now ranked as a sub-chief.

Thus of the twenty-eight subordinate chiefs in the original Leribe ward nineteen were actual sons of Jonathan, and the ward itself has been split into two, that is, Leribe which contains the chiefdoms of five sons of Joseph, of six sons of Jonathan claiming Joseph as their legal father, and of three other houses of Molapo, and Tsikoane which contains exclusively the chiefdoms of the legal sons of Jonathan. On Jonathan's death, Motsuene's heir succeeded as ward chief of the Leribe ward and also as head of the whole house of Molapo (which included the wards of Buthe Buthe and Tsikoane), while Mathealira succeeded as ward chief of the Tsikoane ward.

The structure of the Molapo wards in 1949 is given in Figs. 7 and 8. It will be seen that of the original chiefs and headmen placed by Molapo or already established there, only five of their successors survive and these in much smaller subchieftaincies. The expansion of the reigning chief's line at the expense of collateral lines has continued, particularly in the Leribe ward where it was at the expense mainly of Khethisa Molapo and Khethisa Tau, who have had to make way for Letsie, the heir of Koabeng Motsuene, and his cousin Moliboea of the same first house of Joseph. In all three wards the tendency has been to increase the number of sub-chieftaincies rather than to displace sub-chiefs who were of the houses of Joel, Jonathan and Joseph. But in the largest ward of Leribe this has necessitated a regrouping into four major sections.

NOTES

[1] Some government administrative districts contained more than one ward, in which case the senior ranking chief might be given the title of district chief or principal chief.

[2] By defining his mother as the main wife. See also Kuper (1947: 88–9).

[3] This point has not been adequately studied.

[4] E.g. Schapera (1956: 157–68).

[5] After 1920 most chiefs became Christians and this has resulted in their becoming virtually monogamous. They have thus far fewer sons in need of placing and the placing system as described in this paper no longer functions as it did in the period under review.

[6] Vide schedule attached to High Commissioner's Notice, No. 171 of 1939.

[7] For example Motsuene, the heir of Joseph Molapo (ward chief of Leribe) married Senola his great wife and she was barren. He also married as a junior wife, Selahleo, a granddaughter of his grandfather Molapo. Selahleo's son, Makakamela, was a favourite of Motsuene, who is said to have wished him to be adopted as a son of Senola and thus become his heir. However, the lineage council that decided the matter on the death of Motsuene chose Koabeng of the next senior house. Those who support Makakamela's claim like to believe that this was engineered by Masupha, Motsuene's full brother, who was acting as regent after Motsuene's death and who had quarrelled with Makakamela.

[8] I have been unable to trace records which would give the precise date.

SUCCESSION TO THE THRONE
IN BUGANDA

By MARTIN SOUTHWOLD

INTRODUCTION

Under the British Protectorate (which lasted from 1894 to 1962) the Kingdom of Buganda formed the central and most important province of Uganda, in British East Africa. It had an area of 17,295 square miles (excluding open water), and at the Census of 1959 its African population was 1,834,128 persons (of whom 1,006,101 were Baganda by tribe).

The irruption of British power into this area in the 1890s was turned to advantage by the Baganda, who used their alliance with the British greatly to expand the area of their kingdom. I estimate that the area of the kingdom proper (excluding, that is, autonomous but tributary chiefdoms) in earlier decades was around 10,000 square miles. The population at that time was probably about 1,000,000 persons.

It therefore seems likely that in 1880 as today the overall population density was about 100 per square mile. This is well below the carrying capacity of the land, even with the existing rather simple technology. In general therefore, land is not scarce, though an artificial scarcity is created by the tendency to concentrate settlement around the capital.

At earlier periods of Buganda history the kingdom was still smaller; it began indeed as a very small principality in the area of Kampala, the principal town today (near which is located the royal capital at Mmengo). We are dealing therefore with a nation which has expanded greatly over the centuries, at first but slowly and with many rebuffs, but from about 1750 rather fast and generally irresistibly. This expansion was based on military strength, which in turn was related to a remarkably effective political organization.

Buganda, which lies along the north-western quadrant of the shores of Lake Victoria, is intersected by the Equator, and most of the country is about 4000 feet above sea level. The temperature is warm but equable, and the rainfall moderate, reliable, and well distributed throughout the year. In these conditions the plantain flourishes, and it is the principal subsistence crop of the Baganda. The fecundity of the plantain enabled the Baganda to support themselves with relatively light demands on land and on labour; food production in fact was almost entirely in the hands of the women. Men were little employed in the processes of production, and their labour was therefore available for investment in other sectors of life. It was employed in warfare, mainly in order to obtain plunder (principally women, slaves and cattle) from neighbouring tribes, but also to conquer new areas to be added to the kingdom. It was employed in building and maintaining the compounds of the King and the chiefs; the abundance of labour made it possible to build large royal capitals,[1] and to shift them frequently, which was necessary on sanitary grounds, and useful on political grounds. Labour was also employed in keeping open the impressive network of roads[2] which linked the compounds of all the chiefs to the royal capital, and which contributed to the power of the central government and its ability rapidly to muster large armies. The very business of government made considerable demands on manpower, for chiefs of high and low degree were numerous, and employed substantial bodies of assistants, retainers and servants. In government the Baganda to some degree offset the handicaps of poor technology and ignorance of writing by utilizing their abundance of manpower.

The kingdom has often been described as a despotism, and in fact the political system was probably as despotic as it is possible to be without fire-arms or writing. It was extremely complex, sophisticated and efficient, and highly centralized; though it is clear that the centralized autocracy of the last century was only achieved as the result of centuries of political development.

The supreme political authority was the Kabaka or king, whose office was, in the Baganda sense, hereditary; the present Kabaka, Muteesa II, is the 35th in the supposedly unbroken line stretching back to Kintu, who is generally regarded as the first real king and the founder of the dynasty. The Kabaka is greatly revered, though in no sense a divine king; and, especially before the establishment of the British Protectorate, he was exceedingly powerful.

The king's mother had the title of *Namasole*[3] (or Queen Mother); she was regarded as another *Kabaka*, and had her own palace, estates, and body of chiefs. She was an important person, especially because of her personal influence over her son; but she was very much less powerful than he. She was less powerful in fact than the commoner chiefs, who might (if they were able) pursue a quarrel with the king to the point of deposing him: for if her son lost the throne she was unlikely to be mother to the next king.

The half-sister with whom the king went through the ceremonies of succession[4] had the titles of *Lubuga* and *Nalinnya* (or Queen Sister); she was also a *Kabaka*, with her own palace, estates and body of chiefs. She appears to have been politically unimportant, though she might have had personal influence with the king. The relative unimportance of the *Nalinnya*, a princess, compared with the *Namasole*, a person of commoner blood, is a sign that among the Baganda, as contrasted for example with the Basuto and the Bemba, political power was not the property of the royal descent-group, corporately or distributively, but belonged rather to the kingship, to the one royal who had 'eaten' it, and to those whom he chose to favour.

The senior political officer under the king was the Katikkiro, or prime minister, who was always a commoner. The day-to-day business of government was generally left in his hands, though the Kabaka was free to intervene, and if he chose, to overrule him. He was formally subordinate to the Kabaka, though in practice his power rivalled and sometimes exceeded that of the Kabaka. He was chosen and appointed by the Kabaka, and could be dismissed by him; but on the other hand he took the leading part in choosing the Kabaka when the throne fell vacant.

The next most senior official was the *Kimbugwe*, also a commoner, who was in charge of the royal compound, and has been aptly described as the *aide-de-camp*[5] of the Kabaka. He was concerned with the Kabaka personally, and was employed by the Kabaka when he wished to move against his Katikkiro.[6]

Below the Katikkiro were the *ssaza* chiefs, ten in number at the time of the arrival of British Government. Each of them was responsible for the government of a territorial division of the kingdom, a *ssaza* or 'county'. Below them were sub-chiefs (for whom there is no specific term in Luganda), each of whom ruled a division of a county.

The Katikkiro, *Kimbugwe*, *ssaza* chiefs, and sub-chiefs were known generically as *bakungu*[7] (singular *mukungu*). All *bakungu* were appointed directly by the Kabaka himself (or in practice sometimes by the Katikkiro), and not by their superiors in the hierarchy. Most of these posts (including those of Katikkiro and *Kimbugwe*) were non-hereditary; though some of the *ssaza* chiefships and sub-chiefships were hereditary in a sense (see Southwold 1961: 5–6).

The chiefs of lowest level having territorial jurisdiction were the village chiefs; and between them and the sub-chiefs there might be one or more chiefs of intermediate level. I shall refer to these people as minor chiefs. Some of them were *batongole* (see below) and therefore appointed directly by the Kabaka; some were appointed by chiefs senior to themselves; and some were *bataka* (see below p. 85) and therefore hereditary.

Another category of chiefs was that of the *batongole* (singular *mutongole*), who were more narrowly servants to the Kabaka, and 'his men'. Most of them had specific duties to perform for the Kabaka; and each had an estate, usually a single village, on the lands of the Kabaka which were distributed throughout the country. The *mutongole* had political authority over the people living on his estate. Many of the *batongole* were grouped into departments (*bitongole*, singular *kitongole*) and in such cases the estates of members of the department were usually in a compact block; the senior *mutongole* who was head of the department thus exercised authority over a considerable tract of territory, and was an officer of importance comparable to that of the *bakungu*. *Batongole* posts were never inherited, at least of right; in fact the term *mutongole* is often used to mean a non-hereditary officer in contrast to a *mutaka*, an hereditary officer.

Although the *batongole* were originally created partly in order to act as a check on the *bakungu*, over time the differences between these two categories of chiefs seem to have diminished. *Batongole* were subordinate in most matters to the chiefs of the counties in which they held their estates, and they were fitted into the administrative hierarchy within the county. Thus, for example, the fourth sub-chief in a certain county would be the head of a department of which the estates formed a division of the county. Many of the minor chiefs were *batongole*. In the course of promotion or demotion, men were frequently transferred between the categories of minor chiefs, *bakungu* and *batongole*. I therefore use the word 'chief' to apply to the officers of any of these categories; it must of course be remembered that the transferable and usually non-hereditary chiefs of Buganda are notably different from the chiefs of some other African societies.

CLANS

Every Muganda, other than a prince or princess, is a member of one or other of the totemic clans. These number about fifty, though many of these are politically insignificant.[8] The clans are agnatic, and a person belongs to the clan of his genitor—a rule which provides one of several means of becoming accepted as a member of another clan if it proves convenient. A man who cannot persuade any clan head to acknowledge him as a member is not a Muganda, and is therefore ineligible for any senior political office. This responsibility for validating citizenship was one of the more important functions of the clan system—though there were others. As will be suggested below, clanship was one of the most important bonds utilized in the formation of political factions—and as clans were largely dispersed, this had characteristic effects on the political system.

In general, a person may not marry into his own clan, nor into that of his mother—though a few clans do permit in-marriage.

The clans are segmented; three levels of segment are recognized below the clan itself. Each clan and recognized segment thereof has a head, whose office is hereditary; these heads are known generically as *bataka* (singular *mutaka*). On behalf of his clan or segment, each *mutaka* held an estate (usually a single village) attached to his office and known as a *butaka*. He had political authority over persons living on this estate, and authority on matters of clanship over the members of his clan or segment, most of whom were dispersed. Many religious and ceremonial offices, and some political offices, were the prerogative of some *mutaka*, and hence hereditary.

Few *bataka*, except probably in the earliest times, wielded great power; but as a group the *bataka* were an important element in the nation. Although the king, as *Ssaabataka*, was the head of all *bataka*, relations between king and *bataka* were often strained, and the *bataka* tended to form an opposition to the State machine of the king and his chiefs. Part of the opposition seems to be related to the fact that the offices of the *bataka* were hereditary, and in this important respect challenged the uniqueness of the royal office.

I have not space here to analyse the rules of succession to the offices of *bataka*; though as the rules were similar to those governing succession to the kingship, I sometimes cite them as illuminating the latter.

THE ROYALS

Any male descendant in a male line from a Kabaka is termed a prince (*mulangira*); a female is a princess (*mumbejja*). We may speak of princes and princesses together as 'royals', though there is no Luganda equivalent for this term.

The princes are divided into the 'Princes of the Drum', who are the sons and grandsons of any Kabaka, and who are alone eligible for the throne; and the 'Peasant Princes' or 'Princes of Lineages (*Mituba*)', whose descent from a king is more remote, and who are ineligible. The latter are divided into lineages, with hereditary heads, which function largely as do the lineages of commoner clans. Peasant Princes at all remote from the throne are generally almost indistinguishable from everyday commoners; they nevertheless retain some of the special status and honour belonging to royal blood.

It is an important principle, which has been maintained to this day with very few exceptions, that no prince, not even a Peasant Prince, may hold any senior chiefship (probably they were not favoured for junior chiefships either, though evidence for this is scant). Though the fear of giving political power to likely rivals would explain the exclusion from chiefship of Princes of the Drum, it is less easy to see why Peasant Princes were excluded. The meaning may be to assert restriction of the privilege of royal blood, in favour of the commoners; or to emphasize the uniqueness of the kingship.

The royals are frequently spoken of as constituting the clan (*kika*) of Princes. Good informants, however, like to qualify the use of the word 'clan': and they give as reason the fact that the descent-group of royals, unlike all the commoner clans, has no totem.

Nsimbi (1956: 219) relates a legend that Kintu (K1, i.e. the 1st king) had the Dog as totem, and this totemic allegiance was passed on to his sons. Ccwa I (K2), however, saw a dog eating something foul, so decided he could no longer respect it as a totem, and would leave that clan. He did not like to enrol himself in any other clan, and this is said to be why royals have no totem.

Nsimbi (1956: 167–8) also recounts how Muteesa I (K30; 1856?–84) decided he would like to have a totem, as his chiefs did, and enrolled himself in the Lion Clan. He had the head of the clan build his compound near to the royal compound, and bestowed high dignities on him. 'But when the senior chiefs saw that the Kabaka wished to break the custom of the Princely Clan, which ought not to be broken, they explained to him that kings and royals of the Drum of Buganda from the most ancient times have had no totem. And Kabaka Muteesa at once heeded what his senior chiefs told him, and abandoned the Lion totem.'[9] This is the more striking, inasmuch as Muteesa was a powerful king who by fiat altered a number of important customs.

I was told that Ccwa II (K34; 1897–1939) wished to pass on his totemic allegiance (Bushbuck, through his mother) to his sons and daughters, as he thought that royals, like commoners, should inherit their father's totem; and that he was prevented.

The point is an important one: there is an insistence that the royals should not form a clan homologous with others, but more privileged than they. The kingship does not belong to one clan to the exclusion of others; but rather to a group which is not a clan, and in a way which offers all the commoner clans an equal interest, over time, in the kingship.[10]

Seen from another side, the absence of a royal totem asserts that the descent-group of royals is not a body bound together by a common interest. In practice, as examination of the history will show abundantly, relationships between princes were usually characterized by intense rivalry. This is natural, when we consider how great a prize the kingship was[11]—and that it was the only substantial prize open to any prince.

If relationships between princes were typically those of fear and hatred, a prince, unlike a commoner, would hardly trust his agnates, or turn to them for support. Naturally, therefore, he would look to his matrilateral kin for support; and them he would be able to trust, since by the rule of exogamy they were necessarily commoners, who could not be rivals in competition for the throne. And equally, the men of his mother's clan, as commoners, could never place one of their number on the throne; the closest kinsman of theirs who could hold the throne was a sister's son. Hence, if a prince could look to no kinsmen other than his 'mother's brothers'[12] to support him, in their loyal and ardent support he could have every confidence. And, as lack of solidarity between a prince and his agnates found expression in their lack of a common totem, so the solidarity between a prince and the people of his matrilateral clan found expression in their sharing a common totem.

Princes, then, taboo the totems of their mothers; and since to assert 'I taboo the totem A' is the usual way of asserting membership of the clan which has totem A, this virtually amounts to saying that the prince is a member of his mother's clan. Some Baganda do indeed say just this; more careful informants say rather that he is very closely associated with that clan without being fully a member.[13]

Nsimbi (1956: 167) writes 'In the old days the princes greatly trusted and greatly loved their "mother's brothers" and the people of that descent-group (*sc*: clan) more than their "brothers" (*sc*: agnates) themselves, because it was the people on their mother's side who hid them when their "brothers" sought to slay them. And when they (the princes) went to make war on their fellow who had succeeded to the throne, they mostly recruited the army to fight with from the clans of their mothers.' Kaggwa names some of the chiefs who supported rebel princes (and also those princes who held the throne) in rebellions both successful and unsuccessful; in about half the cases I find that the prince was supported by at least one chief who was his 'mother's brother', together usually with chiefs of other clans. Even if one hesitated to suppose that in the other cases the prince had support from maternal kinsmen not named by Kaggwa, it would be evident that the attachment of a prince to his maternal clan was of great political importance. I shall argue below that it may be assumed to have been important in the peaceful election of a successor to the throne.

Naturally, the prince who held the throne relied no less on his maternal kin to help him keep it. Various offices, of which the principal duties were to protect the Kabaka against potential rivals, were the perquisites of the Kabaka's mother's sisters and mother's brothers; the latter are described as constituting a corps of Security Police (Kaggwa 1905: 121; Nsimbi 1956: 51–2). These offices were doubtless rewarding to their recipients; and the office of Queen Mother, held by the king's own mother, was particularly important to her clan, since she usually had considerable influence over her son. The king was also expected to reward his 'mother's brothers' with other favours, including chiefships; the record shows, however, that they were never given more than a few of the major chiefships.[14]

Besides those already alluded to, other measures were taken to keep watch on the Princes of the Drum, and to hinder them from rebellion. Roscoe (1911: 188) writes, correctly: 'No prince was allowed to become the guest of any chief, or to attach himself to his retinue, because it was feared that in such a case the chief might espouse his cause, and try to place this prince upon the throne....' Kaggwa (1901: 111) and Mukasa (1934: 119) refer to a practice, by implication customary, by which the chiefs were commanded to revile the assembled princes, in terms indicating that they had no wish to see any of them as king; this was done, Mukasa says, so that the king could trust the chiefs not to have friends among his children.

The Princes of the Drum were under the charge of the *ssaza* chief *Kasujju*, who was responsible for their good behaviour, and in an interregnum for advising the Katikkiro which of them was in his opinion most suitable to be chosen as king. Most informants (including Nsimbi 1956: 46) state that the *Kasujju* kept these princes in a prison (*ekkomera*); but the mere frequency of rebellions would make this seem improbable. Kaggwa (1905: 120) tells us that when a son of the king reached the age of ten he was given his own estate to live upon (under the care of a guardian); and the history reveals that at least a few princes who were brother to the king lived on estates of their own. Kaggwa relates that Sssemakookiro (K 27) was advised by an oracle to confine his sons in prison, and did so; and that Sssuuna II (K 29) confined his sons, and Muteesa I (K 30) his brothers. But the way Kaggwa relates each of these as a separate event indicates that he did not regard them as instances of a custom. Each of these three kings also killed large numbers of princes as a precaution; but again Kaggwa's manner of narration implies unawareness of a custom. Even though Kamaanya (K 28) is not described as having done either of these things, it would seem that killing and confining the princes were becoming in some sense customary with the later kings; but, particularly as the evidence points firmly to Ssemakookiro as having been a radical reformer (see below, pp. 114–17), it seems a fair inference that neither practice was customary in earlier reigns.

Kaggwa (1905: 120–1) does state it as a custom that when the wife of a brother or father's brother of the king was with child, she was brought to the royal compound to be delivered of the royal midwife (a mother's sister of the Kabaka), who, if the babe was a boy, promptly throttled it. As I remark below (pp. 97–8), there is nothing in the historical record to refute this.

SOURCES

In this paper, I am concerned to determine the customs governing succession to the throne in Buganda. Since the customs have certainly changed under the influence of Christianity (and other factors), it is necessary to distinguish between the pre-Christian and the modern eras. My analysis deals with the former era, which ends with the accession of Kabaka Mwanga II in 1884. (I describe briefly the present practice in Appendix 1.)

In general, the best authorities on customs are the Baganda authors Kaggwa and Nsimbi, who wrote in Luganda and (mainly) for Baganda readers. Neither of them, however, attempts to set out explicitly all the rules and customs governing succession to the throne; though they do state some, and imply others. This is surely because they assumed that the rules were familiar to their readers.

It is not difficult to obtain from Baganda informants statements about the rules; but as these statements are often contradictory, or are refuted by the historical record, it is not possible to rely on them alone.

I have judged that the best evidence of the customs of succession is what is embodied in the historical record of the kings. The traditional history of Buganda, for which Kaggwa (1901) is the best but not the only source, tells of thirty-one kings, from Kintu, who is generally accepted as a conqueror who founded the dynasty, to Mwanga II, the last of the kings who succeeded to the throne in the pre-Christian era; consequently it gives us thirty cases of succession. I have treated as hypotheses the statements of informants—both those explicitly concerning succession to the throne, and those concerning succession to headships in clans, which are said to follow the same rules—and have related them against the historical record. This has enabled me to decide which statements of custom can be accepted as correct. I have also deduced from the historical record some rules which were not stated by any of my informants.

With only thirty cases to handle, there remains a certain area of doubt. It seems clear from the historical record that some of the customs have altered over time; this still further reduces the number of cases that can be cited in support of a supposed rule. I became confronted with the problem of how many cases can be taken as sufficient to establish a regularity; and with the further question, how far a regularity can be regarded as evidence of a rule. I have therefore felt it necessary to cite and discuss the evidence bearing on each supposed rule.

In general, I have not set out those statements given by informants which I have judged to be erroneous; but as many of Roscoe's statements fall into this category, and form the basis of the received account in English, I have given them more explicit refutation.[15]

CHARACTER OF THE HISTORICAL RECORD

The basic facts: the names of the kings, their clan-affiliations, their order of succession, and their genealogical relationships: are unanimously agreed. Since various groups are intensely concerned with such details, the absence of dispute indicated that the record is historically accurate; and there are other substantial grounds for accepting that, in Buganda, such facts would be accurately and permanently preserved. The traditions also record much more detail about the historical circumstances, on which I have also drawn in my analysis; although we cannot have the same degree of confidence about the accuracy of such details, I do regard the account as essentially reliable.[16]

The historical record shows that a considerable number of the kings acquired the throne by force rather than by peaceful succession. Five (whose names are indicated on my king-list (Appendix II)) were straightforward rebels. Kayemba and Tebandeke are said to have killed their predecessors by sorcery: while Kyabaggu was so annoying his predecessor by sorcery that the latter abdicated. I class these three as rebels by sorcery. Jjunju won the throne by his victory at the end of a period of fighting among princes, some others of whom had murdered the previous king. Kamaanya fought a rival for the throne; he had earlier been nominated by his father to succeed, but since such a nomination was not binding, we are open to consider him either as an elected successor who defeated a rebel, or as a prince who won the throne by force of arms. Nakibinge also had to fight a rival at the beginning of his reign; but Kaggwa's phraseology seems to imply that he had already been elected king. Hence we have nine—or with Kamaanya, ten—cases, which it would seem wise to exclude if we are seeking to establish the normative rules which determined the choice of a successor.

If we plot the consanguineal relationships between kings and their predecessors, we find essentially the same pattern when we examine the kings who acquired the throne by force as when we examine only those who were peacefully chosen to succeed; and this remains true even when we distinguish the three periods exhibiting different patterns (see below, p. 99). It is therefore unnecessary to handle separately the cases of forceful accession. As I shall argue below (pp. 107, 109–10, 113), the successful rebels appear to have been princes who either had a particularly good claim to the throne, or else had a good claim to succeed together with reason to expect that they might in fact be passed over. If this is true—and there are of course too few cases to be certain—then we are still further justified in accepting the rebels as providing evidence of the rules of succession.

But a rebel needed more than a plausible claim to ensure success; the kings normally resisted, and Kaggwa describes a number of rebellions which in fact failed. The successful rebels owed their success to their military strength, which in turn rested on their political support. The fact that successful rebels were the same kind of people as those who were peacefully elected as successors indicates that the strength of political support also had a part in determining peaceful election—a conclusion I have already suggested, and shall develop.

CATEGORIES OF CUSTOMS GOVERNING SUCCESSION

The Baganda lay much stress on the fact that their kingship is an hereditary office; and analysis of the data shows that the pattern of succession to the kingship can be analysed in terms of a set of rules concerning consanguinity—what one would normally understand as rules of hereditary succession. These can be divided into two categories, prescriptive rules and preferential rules. But, as has just been suggested, other factors also played a part in determining the selection of a successor; and it would be unrealistic to omit consideration of these. I distinguish five main categories of rules, customs, and principles, which together determined the choice of a successor:

(1) Prescriptive (consanguineal) rules of hereditary succession.

(2) Preferential (consanguineal) rules or principles of hereditary succession.

(3) Personality factors, i.e. the personal characteristics of candidates, consideration of which might lead to the preference of one candidate over another.

(4) Political factors, i.e. those which operated in a distinct and regular way to weight the preference given to one candidate over another.

(5) The electoral institutions, i.e. what categories of persons expressed opinions which were taken account of in choosing a successor, how discordant opinions were assessed and amalgamated to produce one choice, and how this choice was proclaimed and ratified.

Empirically, these categories sometimes merge into one another. I shall argue, for instance, that relative age and youth appears to have affected an important preferential consanguineal rule; and also that political factors had a serious consequence for the preferential consanguineal rules.

Since, for comparative purposes, I judge the first two categories to be the most important, I shall examine their contents most fully, after first handling the other three categories.

ELECTORAL INSTITUTIONS

Those eligible to succeed to the throne were the Princes of the Drum, those men of whom the father or father's father had reigned. I expand this statement below (pp. 97–8); here it serves to make plain that at any one time there was a significant number of men who were eligible.[17] It was therefore necessary to have a procedure to choose one from the many princes eligible.

Roscoe (1911: 189) says that the responsibility for choosing the successor lay with the Katikkiro, the *Kimbugwe*, and the *ssaza* chief *Kasujju*: they then called a meeting of the *ssaza* chiefs, and informed them of their choice and sought their concurrence—which failing, 'there would in all probability be civil war'. Kaggwa's version (1905: 4) is somewhat different: 'The Kingship (*or* Kingdom) of Buganda was succeeded to thus: when the Kabaka had died, the Katikkiro summoned the leading chiefs, *Kimbugwe*, the *ssaza* chiefs, and a few of those who were heads of large *bitongole*. Then they discussed which prince should eat the kingship, and when they had chosen him, the Katikkiro commanded *Kasujju* who had charge of the princes, saying 'It is Prince So-and-So whom we have chosen to be our king".' In another work, Kaggwa (1908: 50) says that *Kasujju* was asked to inform the Katikkiro which prince he considered on grounds of personal character to be most suitable to be made king.

But Kaggwa (1901: 110–12) gives one very detailed account of the choice of a successor; this was the choice of Muteesa I (*c.* 1856), and reads as if it were taken from an eyewitness. Here we find that important chiefs come singly to the Katikikro and tell him who they think should succeed; the Katikkiro makes up his own mind after examining the mother and mother's brother of a recommended prince. He then informs the *Kasujju* of his choice, and with *Kasujju* publicly proclaims the choice, telling the chiefs who dissent to mind their own business. Now it is true that this Katikkiro was remarkably powerful; nevertheless I would judge that this is most likely to have been the normal procedure. There were no constituted councils in Buganda. The king, the Katikkiro, and every chief, made use of a *lukiiko*, which consisted of those people he had summoned or who chose to come along and speak; but he was not obliged to heed even the unanimous decision of a *lukiiko*. Obviously, in choosing a successor, the Katikkiro would have been imprudent not to discover the preferences of those powerful enough to cause trouble; and doubtless he often found it expedient to have the matter discussed in a *lukiiko* of leading chiefs. But it would have been anomalous in the Ganda pattern of government for responsibility to have been formally vested in a body of persons, rather than in the senior officer, the Katikkiro.

The day after the choice had been decided and announced to the *Kasujju*, all the leading chiefs assembled. *Kasujju* brought the princes, and lined them up. He then walked up and down the lines, and taking the chosen prince by the hand, he presented him to the Katikkiro saying 'This is your king'. The Katikkiro then addressed the gathered people, and said of the rejected princes 'Those are commoners (*or* peasants): if any one fights, just kill him'. *Kasujju* then led the rejected princes away to give them a feast in the Katikkiro's compound; while the Katikkiro accompanied the king-elect to Budo, where he began to go through his protracted accession ceremonies (Kaggwa 1905: 5—fully confirmed in the account of Muteesa's choice).

Roscoe (1911: 190) gives a somewhat garbled version of this, and adds that the Katikkiro challenged any dissentients to fight: whereupon any dissatisfied chief stepped forward, carried off the prince he favoured, and called upon his allies to fight: civil war then ensued. This seems an unlikely arrangement; Mair (1962: 209), who bases her account on Roscoe without reference to Kaggwa, surmises that an armed challenge to the choice of successor was more likely to have occurred some time later. In fact Kaggwa's account of Muteesa's election shows just this. A powerful body of chiefs had supported another prince, and thought the Katikkiro had agreed to choose him. When Muteesa was proclaimed, their leader protested and was snubbed. Their reaction was to spread sedition, but they raised rebellion only considerably later.[18] This account also reveals why an immediate challenge to the proclaimed prince was unlikely: the Katikkiro brought to the ceremony his own retainers, armed and charged to fight if there was any trouble. Examination of the historical record shows that only three kings (Nakibinge (K8), Jjunju (K26), and Kamaanya (K28)) had to fight a rival at the very beginning of their reigns: and in each case it is evident that the challenge was not made at any ceremony of proclamation.

Roscoe (1911: 189) also writes: 'The reigning king generally made his wishes known to the Katikkiro and the *Kasujju*, and his wishes were adhered to, if possible; but if these chiefs thought that there was another prince who would make a better sovereign, they did not hesitate to appoint the latter.' Such indication of a successor was known as *kulamira* (the word now used for making a will), and I shall term it 'nominating a successor'. It was a common custom among the people generally—with the same proviso, that it was not obligatory to heed the wishes of the deceased. In the historical record, however, the first king[19] who is described as indicating in advance his successor is Ssemakookiro (K27). Each subsequent king did so, though the facts sometimes emerge only indirectly from Kaggwa's account. I shall argue below (pp. 115–16) that this seems to have been an innovation, part of a set of radical reforms introduced by Ssemakookiro. I doubt if Roscoe's statement is really true of earlier periods.

PERSONALITY PREFERENCES

In making their choice among the princes, the electors considered the personal characteristics of the candidates. Mukasa (1934: 119) says that they avoided a prince who was in the habit of torturing mice and small birds, lest as king he might prove equally cruel to his people; and secondly, that it was taboo to choose a prince whose mother was dead, as his grief might lead him to be cruel to his people, and he would have no one to check his excesses of wickedness. This latter point underlines the importance of the Kabaka's maternal connexion (see above, pp. 87–8), and it is probably correct.[20]

Kaggwa (1908: 50) says that the *Kasujju*, the chief in charge of the princes, was asked to name to the Katikkiro the prince he considered to be 'a restrained man meet to be given the kingdom'. The word I have translated as 'restrained' is *muwombeefu*. Le Veux's Vocabulaire renders this word as 'retenu', 'calme', which seems much more apt than the 'humble', 'docile' of the Luganda–English Dictionary. I suggest that the quality looked for resembled what the closely related Banyaruanda call *itonde*, and expect to find in a Tutsi: '*Itonde* could be translated by self-mastery...' (Maquet 1961: 118).

The electors did not always succeed in getting a *muwombeefu* prince: of several cruel Kabakas it is recorded that *yeesala akajegere*—literally 'he cut from himself the small chain', or as we would say 'he kicked over the traces', 'he abandoned all restraint'. The rebel Ssemakookiro (K27) appears to me from Kaggwa's account (though he does not use the word) to have been *muwombeefu*: as a prince, when he endured much ill treatment from his brother until their mother provoked him to rebel; and as a king, when, as Kaggwa (1905: 59) writes: 'he became a good king, and trade increased to the enrichment of his people, and he hearkened to his chiefs when they forbade him to slay his people, so he became a Kabaka of peace who paid heed to his council (*lukiiko*) until the day he died.'

Roscoe (1911: 232) suggests that the electors might reject a prince as too young, and that it was for that reason that brothers were sometimes chosen to succeed. I discuss this point below (pp. 104–7) in the context of fraternal succession, and conclude that it seems plausible at least for the period during which Buganda was most engaged with her military rival Bunyoro. I show also (p. 116) that later young princes were in practice favoured—though it is worth noting that it was on the grounds of his youth that many people objected to the choice of Muteesa I (Kaggwa 1901: 118).

A. I. Richards[21] reports that when choosing a Kabaka the Katikkiro consulted the *Kasujju* to learn of the conduct of the princes, and which of them had 'mother's brothers' who might make trouble if their nephews were not elected. This latter point must now be taken up.

POLITICAL FACTORS

I described above (pp. 87–8) how a prince was closely associated with the people of his mother's clan; and how such association between a prince and a body of commoners had an important part in the organization of rebellions—as in the king's own organization to repel them. It was clearly important also in the choice of a successor to the throne.

The following facts are clearly described in Kaggwa's account of the election of Muteesa I (Kaggwa 1901: 110–13). (1) A leading chief, the *Mukwenda*, came to the Katikkiro and proposed the choice of Prince Kikulwe, who was the son of his sister Zawedde. The Katikkiro assented. (2) Then another chief (the sub-county chief *Namutwe*, who was not a clansman of either Kikulwe or Muteesa) pointed out to the Katikkiro that he, the Katikkiro, had had a hand in the killing. by the previous king, of the father of Zawedde and *Mukwenda*, and he would suffer if Zawedde became Queen Mother and *Mukwenda* the senior royal mother's brother. He advised the choice of Muteesa, pointing out that in two ways the previous king had indicated his preference for him (which the Katikkiro later blandly remarked he had forgotten). (3) The Katikkiro immediately asked 'Who is his mother? And who is his mother's brother?' and was told their names and the fact that they were of Civet-cat clan.[22] (4) The Katikkiro sent for them at once, and after examining them, told them that he would choose their 'child'. (5) The Katikkiro, in charging his men to fight if there was trouble at the ceremonial proclamation, told them 'Tomorrow I will give the kingdom to Muteesa, of Civet-cat (clan)'. (6) When Muteesa was led out from the line of princes, *Mukwenda* objected, and was told by the Katikkiro that his nephew was his own affair. (7) As we learn from Mukasa (1934: 118), a number of leading chiefs, of various clans, were joined in supporting the choice of *Mukwenda*'s nephew. After Muteesa had been chosen, these chiefs, with *Mukwenda*, went about sowing disaffection. (8) Kaggwa and Mukasa relate that Muteesa later arrested *Mukwenda* and some of the other dissidents; those remaining at liberty then organized a rebellion. (9) *Mukwenda*'s nephew appears to have died (of plague) by this time; the rebels secured two other princes, one of them also of *Mukwenda*'s clan, the other the own sister's son of one of the dissidents still at liberty. The rebellion was, however, nipped in the bud.

In view of the many advantages which the king bestowed on people of his mother's clan, and also of the fact that precautions were taken to prevent princes from befriending chiefs, it is natural that this matrilateral link should have been of central political importance. Nevertheless, since there were many clans, and the major chiefships were in practice spread among them, it is unlikely that the chiefs of any one clan acting alone could have secured the election of their own 'sister's son'. As the above case shows, chiefs of several clans, doubtless connected to one another in various ways, had to ally to create a party strong enough to win. It is characteristic of the Baganda to hedge until they see where victory will go, and then to join the winners; I imagine therefore that elections were often virtually unanimous. When this was not so, consideration of the logic of coalition building would suggest that the rival factions eventually sorted themselves into two parties, and that these were nearly balanced in strength.

Now analysis of the record shows that the Katikkiro never put through the election of a prince of his own clan.[23] I assume that there was at least a tacit convention which forbade it; just as there seems to have been one forbidding the Kabaka from appointing a Katikkiro of his own clan (see Southwold 1961: 6). To this important extent, therefore, the Katikkiro was neutral in the political competition for the choice of rival candidates. But the Katikkiro had his own retainers, and, as Kaggwa shows, brought them armed to the ceremony at which the elected prince was proclaimed. I consider therefore that the Katikkiro and his forces acted as a balancer in the process; and that the party which received his support thereby achieved an advantage sufficiently decisive to discourage an immediate challenge by the losers.

It can be seen then that both the paternal and the maternal affiliations of a prince were important in bringing about his selection: the former gave him the status which made him eligible. for the throne, the latter the political support which gave him victory. The rules, *strictu sensu*, of hereditary succession concerned paternal affiliation, and left a wide range of choice; within this area, the specific choice was determined by political factors, which were to some extent canalized through maternal affiliation. A king required both the rank, received through his father, which enabled him to reign, and the political support, received through his mother, which enabled him to rule; the system employs the intersection of the two possible kinds of affiliation to determine the one man who maximizes the essential qualities.

If we consider paternal affiliation alone, Buganda had an hereditary monarchy; if we consider maternal affiliation alone, bearing in mind that the rule of exogamy made it impossible for father and son (among royals) to be of the same clan, the system of selecting a ruler has something in common with the elective presidential system of the United States. In fact it combined some of the virtues of both a monarchy and a republic.

However, despite the importance of political connexions in narrowing down the choice of the successor to the throne, it is possible, to a large extent, to analyse the pattern of succession entirely in terms of rules of hereditary succession which are wholly concerned with patrilateral links—the same rules which governed succession among commoners, among whom maternal affiliation was not considered at all. I now proceed to do this.

PRESCRIPTIVE RULES OF HEREDITARY SUCCESSION
TO THE THRONE

In this and the next section I deal with the various rules and preferences which defined eligibility, and its degrees, with reference to consanguinity. Since for comparative purposes these may be singled out as the rules of succession, I shall state each as a rule, and give it a number. (The whole set of rules are restated together, for reference, in Appendix III.)

Rule 1. Only a prince, that is any male descendant in a male line from any Kabaka, was eligible to succeed to the throne. This is so axiomatic as hardly to require comment. Details imperfectly digested in the historical record arouse strong suspicions that Mawanda (K 22) have may been a commoner, and Kimera (K 3) a Munyoro prince. But the vigorous attempt to explain these details away both shows the force of the rule, and forbids us to suppose that any exception would have been plainly recorded.

Rule 2. Among princes, only the Princes of the Drum were eligible. These were defined as men who were the sons, or son's sons, of any Kabaka.

This rule is stated by good informants, and conforms to the evidence of the historical record; they also state that a similar rule governed succession to headships of clans and clan-segments, which case-material supports. Roscoe (1911: 187) appears to have had it in mind when he wrote 'The heir apparent was a son or grandson of a king...'.

Other statements on the point by Roscoe (*loc. cit.*) are false. He writes 'The brothers [of the king]...were themselves still eligible for the throne; their sons, however, were debarred therefrom.' But Kayima (K 7) was the son of a brother (who did not reign) of the previous king; and Mwanga I (K 23) and his two brothers Namugala (K 24) and Kyabaggu (K 25) were in a similar position. Moreover, Kaggwa (1905: 120–1) tells us that it was the custom to throttle at birth the sons born to brothers and father's brothers of the reigning Kabaka; it is clear that this was done because such sons would have been eligible, since Kaggwa, in telling us that sons of a grand-uncle of the reigning Kabaka were not throttled, says that they were spared because they were ineligible to succeed (see Rule 4). He also says that sons of the sons of the reigning Kabaka were not throttled 'because their [fathers'] father was on the throne'—this accounts for the survival of Kayima and the others mentioned above, as it can be demonstrated from the historical record that they were almost certainly born during the reigns of their grandfathers.

Roscoe also writes 'Princes in the direct line of succession were called "Princes of the drums", having been born while their father was king, and while he had the royal drums (*mujaguzo*); the others were called "Peasant princes", because their father was not in possession of the throne and the drums'. But in reality the Princes of the Drum (*sic*) were all those eligible to succeed, and, as the above paragraph demonstrates, these included those whose father was never king.[24]

Rule 3. The first-born son of the Kabaka had the name/title of *Kiweewa*, and was barred from the succession (Nsimbi 1956: 54)—a similar bar on first-born sons applied also, until altered by Christian and Moslem influence, to all cases of succession among commoners. If the first-born son died, he would, like all other mature people, have had a personal successor appointed to his name; this would usually have been one of his brothers, probably the eldest, who would thereby have succeeded to the exclusion. Even if the *Kiweewa* died in infancy, I suppose a successor would have been appointed to the title, since it carried significant duties. Hence in practice it would normally have been the eldest son who was excluded by this rule. Probably sons of the *Kiweewa* were also excluded, though I have no statement to this effect. In fact, one *Kiweewa* did become king (K 32); but he was enthroned by Christian and Moslem rebels who claimed that as they 'had turned their backs on heathen customs, they need not regard this old superstition' (Ashe 1894: 104).

Rule 4. Princes of any generation above the reigning Kabaka (i.e. classificatory 'fathers', etc.) were ineligible. Though I find no definite statement to this effect, it is implied by the fact that 'fathers' are never mentioned as eligible in statements about the rules of succession to any position. I do in fact find two cases of 'fathers' succeeding to clan offices, but in both cases the circumstances appear to be sufficiently odd for the cases to be regarded as anomalous. This rule seems the best way to account for the exclusion (see above) of sons born to a grand-uncle of the reigning Kabaka (who would have been eligible under Rule 2), though Kaggwa does not offer this explanation.

Rule 5. A grandson of the late king could be chosen only if all his sons were dead or otherwise not available to succeed.

This is apparently[25] what Roscoe (1911: 187) meant when he wrote: 'The heir apparent was a son or grandson of a king; but grandsons were only accepted when there was no son living who could succeed.' It is agreeable to the historical facts: only two kings, Kimera (K3) and Ttembo (K4) directly succeeded their grandfathers, and in both cases the father of the successor was already dead, and had no surviving brothers.

I think this rule receives some indirect support from the fact (see above, p. 98) that sons born to sons of the reigning Kabaka were not throttled at birth. Kaggwa's own explanation of this—'because their [father's] father was on the throne'—itself demands further explanation; when we consider the matter in its context, it seems natural to suppose that such infants were spared because they would not be considered eligible.

I remain with some doubt whether this can firmly be stated as a prescriptive rule. I have no statement from an informant that grandsons would be considered as successors only in the absence of sons; and I do have some cases of succession among commoners where a grandson has been chosen when a son was alive. But in most of these cases, at least, there was some special circumstance which debarred the son from the succession.

PREFERENTIAL RULES OF HEREDITARY SUCCESSION

These rules are mostly concerned with fraternal succession. For a number of reasons this is an extremely difficult topic to analyse.

None of my informants stated directly that fraternal succession was practised in relation to the kingship; many of them, by saying the succession went always to a son, implicitly denied it. Mair's informants seem to have been of like mind, as she writes: 'The kingship went in direct descent from father to son' (Mair 1934: 180). But the king-list shows at once that fraternal succession was common. I have abundant evidence that this was the preferred mode among commoners; and the informants who stated that this was one of the rules governing succession to clan-offices also stated that these rules were the same as those governing succession to the throne.

More careful examination of the king-list (Appendix II) reveals a further complication: although fraternal succession was practised during the middle period of the pre-Christian era, this was preceded and followed by periods in which it was not practised. It is of course possible that the rules themselves changed, conceivably as a result of varying cultural influences from outside Buganda. But, by Occam's Razor, I prefer to assume that the rule remained the same throughout, but the practice changed with circumstances. I shall attempt to determine what these circumstances were.

Moreover, it would appear that within the period marked by fraternal successions, there was a shift in the definition of the kind of brother preferred as successor. At first half-brothers and ortho-cousins (also 'brothers' in Luganda) succeeded; after a time, we find it is full brothers who succeed. This presents especial difficulty, since even the best informants (Kaggwa and Nsimbi) do not speak of full-brother succession, but implicitly deny, if not its occurrence, at least its frequency and regularity. I shall show that in fact full-brother succession created profound difficulties, which may account for the fact that Baganda prefer not to notice it. It seems the more likely that full-brother succession developed unintentionally out of a broader type of fraternal succession; it can also be argued, with some plausibility, that it was the latent pattern throughout, and was prevented by special circumstances from emerging earlier in practice.

These shifts in the pattern of succession seem to arise from a conflict within the Ganda system of values. On the one hand there was a principle, certainly among commoners, that the succession should be given to an agnate of a remote collateral line, in order to keep alive the bond of kinship. On the other hand, people naturally liked to pass on the advantages attached to the succession to a son or other close kinsman. One may suppose that this latter tendency was reinforced among royals by the consideration that to maintain a wide range of collaterals as eligible for the succession was to maintain also a wide range of potential rebels.

It will clarify matters if I begin by explaining the rules of succession among commoners. Kaggwa (1905: 198) writes of choosing a successor to a dead chief:[26]

Even if there were very many children of the deceased chief, the successor did not come from among them so long as there were brothers [of the deceased] still alive. So they chose a kinsman, a son of the father [of the deceased] and he succeeded. Or if they did not choose him, they could choose from another sub-clan with which they always succeeded together (*kusikirana*), with which they did not repudiate kinship (*kuboolagana*) as they had a common ancestor of long ago, and he succeeded. What prevented them from choosing a child [of the deceased] was fear of repudiating kinship, for they thought 'If we make his own child the successor, later there will be repudiation of kinship'...But the custom of succession by an agnate [*sc*: brother] when there were sons, Kabaka Muteesa [I–K 30] swept it away; then one of the children of the deceased was chosen to succeed his father.

The word *kusikirana* means literally 'to succeed among one another'; another expression which is used means 'to exchange successors'. Informants use these expressions to describe the preference for choosing a remote agnate; and some (like Nsimbi 1956: 5) go so far as to say that any member of the same clan (of the same sex and appropriate generation) might be chosen to succeed. In practice, as I suppose on the basis of the few relevant cases I have, the choice of successor was limited to a restricted group of fairly close agnates, or to members of a collateral clan-segment with which a specific link was recognized.

With regard to succession to headships of clans and clan-segments, my informants told me that the eligible successors were restricted to a group analogous to the Princes of the Drum—that is, to sons and grandsons of a former head. Within such a group the operation of the principle of *kusikirana* implied the preference for a rather more remote collateral over a member of the same line. It emerges that a conscious consideration was to postpone the exclusion of a collateral line from eligibility, as it would become excluded after two generations had passed without holding office. Hence, if the succession were to pass to a junior generation, it would go to a brother's son rather than to an own son of the deceased. Otherwise, the principle itself would explain the preference for choosing a brother of the deceased. It ought also to lead to preference of a cousin over a brother, and I have cases illustrating this. Further, it should lead to the preference of a second cousin (if otherwise eligible, as he might be) over a first cousin. But I have no clear cases of this, and I failed to pursue the point; and I have the impression that a second cousin was unlikely to be favourably considered. However much people wished to avoid 'repudiating kinship', collateral lines were bound to become excluded in time; and I think serious efforts to preserve eligibility were made only within the minimal lineage (*enda*) descended from the grandfather of the most recent incumbent.

Hence we have the rules, clearly stated by informants, that the preferred successor for a clan office was a 'brother' (including first cousin), or when the time came to move to a junior generation, a brother's son. These rules, and their underlying logic, are paralleled among the closely related Basoga (Fallers 1956: 86–92).

I can now state the preferential rules, some of them tentative, which appear to have governed succession to the throne.

Rule 6. By the principle of *kusikirana*, if the succession remained in the same generation a first cousin was the preferred successor.

In fact, I have considerable doubt whether this rule was applied: there are only two cases which can be cited in illustration, and in both there is a suggestion that the circumstances were peculiar, so that the successor was chosen on personal grounds rather than as a cousin. There is, however, one case which indicates that the principle of *kusikirana* could be appealed to with reference to succession to the throne. According to Kaggwa (1901: 18), immediately Nakibinge (K 8) came to the throne he was challenged by Prince Jjuma, who was a cousin (though of what degree there is not enough information to say). Jjuma said to Nakibinge 'Come and succeed my father Kyabayinze, and let me succeed your father Kayima (K 7), because he nominated (*kulamira*) me as successor when he was alive...'. But it may be more significant that Jjuma's claim was given short shrift.

The first king who succeeded a cousin, possibly by Rule 6, was Kimbugwe (K 13). There is no evidence that his succession was challenged, and in fact he reigned peacefully for a long time (I would deduce, from what Kaggwa says about his son (Kaggwa 1901: 27 and 29), for not less than fifteen years). Nevertheless, there is a concatenation of odd facts about his and the two previous successions. Kimbugwe's cousin Ssekamaanya (K12) had full brothers; and, as I shall show below (pp. 110–11) it is unusual for a full brother to have been passed over, and indeed that he should not have rebelled to ensure his own succession. The succession of Kimbugwe's father Ssuuna I (K11) also seems odd. He is the only third of a set of brothers to have succeeded peacefully; indeed I shall suggest below (p. 107) that there may have been a preferential rule against allowing two fraternal successions in one generation. When Ssuuna was elected, Ssekamaanya was most probably old enough to have been made king, and I therefore seek a reason why he should have been passed over. It is odd too that Ssekamaanya himself did not protest by rebelling; apart from Kagulu (K20) he is the only king of a junior generation who waited to succeed peacefully after there had been fraternal succession in the senior generation (Kamaanya (K28) rebelled, but his rebellion was crushed). If we suppose that Ssekamaanya and his brothers were for some reason in disfavour, and therefore lacked support, all these facts would become explicable.

It will be seen that Ssekamaanya is the only king who came from the Civet-cat clan. It seems plausible that this clan may not have been considered suitable to provide kings. According to Nsimbi (1956: 194), before Kintu, the first king, came to Buganda, the head of this clan was ruling the other clan heads in Buganda. Nsimbi (1956: 195) also writes 'When Kabaka Ccwa I (K2) disappeared from Buganda, and the throne remained (vacant), Walusimbi [head of Civet-cat clan] ruled as Kabaka'. Kaggwa (1908: 26) says simply that he took care of the kingdom; but also says that Nakku, the daughter of Walusimbi and widow of Ccwa I, met Kimera (K3), (who was probably an invader from Bunyoro), 'and informed him of all the matters to do with ruling the Kingdom of Buganda'. There is, then, at least a tradition pointing to Walusimbi as some kind of autochthonous ruler; and this would probably have made it seem impolitic to choose a prince of his clan to become Kabaka.

We are told also that Kayemba, full brother of Jjuuko (K16), proposed to marry a daughter of Walusimbi (Kaggwa 1901: 34). Diviners told Jjuuko that if this went ahead 'you (plural) will die', so he sent to Kayemba saying 'Don't marry the woman Nakku: the gods forbid her to us.' Kayemba disobeyed, and Nakku bore him a limbless child, Prince Kawumpuli, who became the god of bubonic plague—and as such caused Jjuuko and other kings much trouble.

There is thus a good deal of circumstantial evidence to suggest that the title of Ssekamaanya (and his full brothers—he had no half-brothers) was a dubious one; and if this is so, Rule 6 is not required to explain the succession of Kimbugwe.

Similarly, when we examine the only other case of succession by a cousin (Ndawula, K19) we find signs that it was the succession of the senior of the cousins, Tebandeke (K18), whom he succeeded, that was dubious.

The father of Tebandeke, Mutebi (K15), is specially noted for having built shrines for all the gods (*balubaale*); and, comments Kaggwa (1901: 32), 'he loved the gods greatly, he was very evil that Kabaka'. Kaggwa of course was a first-generation Christian, and all that he says about the pagan gods has to be treated with suspicion. There is, however, a good deal of evidence that the typical relation of the Kabaka to the gods was one of some hostility; and at least the fact that Muteesa I (K30) encouraged the teaching of both Islam and Christianity cannot be attributed to prejudice in the sources. Even if such evidence were lacking, it could be predicted on structural grounds that Kabakas were likely to be in opposition to the gods and their priests.[27] Hence, if there were any reason to suppose that Tebandeke and his brothers were likely to continue their father's indulgence towards the gods, this might well have counted against them.

Now Mutebi's brother Jjuuko would appear from Kaggwa's account to have had a long reign; and the third brother, Kayemba, is definitely stated to have reigned long (Kaggwa 1905: 44). Hence Tebandeke must have been a mature man before he eventually achieved the throne. Kaggwa (1901: 41) states that for a long time after he came to the throne (as by implication before) all the children born to him died. In itself this would have been a good reason for not choosing him as king. Moreover, in Buganda it is childless men who are particularly apt to associate with the gods, and even to become their mediums.

In fact, just this happened: Tebandeke first employed a medium of a god to remove his childlessness, and then quarrelled over payment and had all the mediums killed and the shrines of the gods destroyed. The leading god retaliated, as was his wont, by making his enemy mad; and to recover from his madness Tebandeke was obliged to become a practising medium of the god. Kaggwa, naturally, describes him as a very bad king.

When Ndawula succeeded Tebandeke, he refused to have anything to do with the mediumship: he declared that he had not inherited (*or* succeeded to) the god, and had Tebandeke's son Jjuma Kateebe made successor to the mediumship side of Tebandeke's *persona*.[28] It may therefore reasonably be conjectured that Ndawula was chosen as king not so much because he was a cousin as because he was a more suitable person than the sons of Mutebi; once again, Rule 6 need not be invoked.

I conclude, therefore, that there is no good evidence that Rule 6 was ever applied; though, since it was certainly applied among commoners, it was probably recognized in theory.

Rule 7. A brother was preferred to a son.

Roscoe (1911: 232) writes: 'In some instances the succession was carried on through a brother of the king, in cases when the king's sons were too young to rule, or when, for some reason, a prince was rejected.'

At first sight, this seems ill-phrased, since there are no fewer than eleven instances (including rebels) of fraternal succession; and the regularity is the more striking when it is observed that these instances all occur within a restricted period. Among commoners, as I have observed, a brother was the preferred successor; and this preference follows, as in Busoga, from the principle of *kusikirana* which seeks to maintain the unity of the 'succession lineage'. It therefore seems likely that in succession to the kingship a brother was chosen, not *faute de mieux* as Roscoe would have it, but by rule.

Nevertheless, we saw above that it was doubtful if the principle of *kusikirana* alone ever singled out a cousin as successor to the throne; it may be that Roscoe was right, and brothers were preferred as mature men rather than as collaterals.

We are not, of course, usually told how old the sons of previous kings were on occasions of fraternal succession. But from statements about the age of a king, the length of his reign, and sometimes about the birth of his sons in sequence with other events, it is usually possible to form a rough estimate. At the accessions of Jjemba (K 10), Jjuuko (K 16), Mawanda (K 22), Namugala (K 24) and Kyabaggu (K 25), the sons of the last king (as of any of the set of brothers) probably were young. This is clearly true of the accession of Kimbugwe (K 13) also, since we are told (Kaggwa 1901: 26) that shortly before the death of Ssekamaanya his son Kateregga was 'a mature lad' (*mulenzi mukulu*), i.e. about twelve years old.

The sons, at least of the eldest eligible line, probably were mature at the accessions of Ssuuna I (K 11) and Kayemba (K 17); but I observed above (pp. 101–3) in another context that the sons concerned, Ssekamaanya and Tebandeke, seem not to have been in favour. When Kikulwe (K 21) succeeded, the sons of his predecessor Kagulu had been killed with their father when the nation rose in revolt (Kaggwa 1905: 47). The sons of Jjunju (K 26) were probably old enough to have succeeded him; but as Ssemakookiro (K 27) won the throne by military action, the point hardly requires discussion.

The evidence, therefore, appears to support Roscoe's statement. Much will turn on what meaning is to be given to his phrase 'too young to rule'. Further understanding will emerge from analysis of the apparent reasons why fraternal succession was confined to the middle period of the pre-Christian era.

This middle period began in the generation of Mulondo (K 9). His father, Nakibinge (K 8), was killed in battle against the Banyoro, presumably as a young man: at any rate the children he left were 'very young' (Kaggwa 1901: 21). Although Nakibinge is recorded as having a brother (Kaggwa 1905: 32), he may reasonably be presumed to have died in the same battle. Mulondo, the eldest of the eligible children, was chosen to succeed; and vivid stories, reminiscent of those related of James VI of Scotland, are told of the ways the chiefs indulged the child-king. Mulondo himself died when he was 'mature but not aged' (Kaggwa 1901: 23); probably his son Ssekamaanya was still young —apart from any other disqualifications he may have had (see above, pp. 102–3). A brother, Jjemba, was chosen to succeed.

Now the Baganda concede that with the death of Nakibinge their army was routed by the Banyoro; Banyoro traditions claim, with much plausibility, that the Banyoro overran Buganda, and omitted to annexe it to their own kingdom only because of a taboo. It is evident, therefore, that the middle period of Buganda history began in a situation of great military difficulty; and it is evident too from the record that for generations the Baganda were pre-occupied with defending themselves against the Banyoro and other enemies, and in expanding their kingdom by conquest as they were able. Hence it may be supposed that brothers, as mature men, were preferred to succeed because of the military responsibilities of the king. Such considerations would have been especially evident initially, when the Baganda had just undergone the experience of attempting to recover from military disaster under a child-king (Mulondo).[29]

Many of the traditions recorded of the earliest period of the history have a legendary character; clear facts are scarce. Nevertheless they suggest conclusions consistent with the argument.

Apart from a few cattle-raids initiated by the Baganda, there is no reference to wars in the reigns before Nakibinge (K8). Banyoro traditions suggest that at this period Bunyoro, then much the greatest power in the region, was engaged further west; the little kingdom of Buganda, in an area relatively unfavourable for cattle-keeping, was perhaps beneath her notice. Nsimbi (1956: 74) records that in Nakibinge's reign the Baganda conquered a considerable part of Ssingo county from the Banyoro; as most of Ssingo is cattle country, it may well have been this that provoked Bunyoro to crush her southern neighbour.

In this earliest period the relative power of the Kabaka in the nation is said to have been much less than it later became. Kaggwa recounts that even as late as the reign of Mutebi (K15) several clan heads had virtual autonomy on their own lands, styled themselves Kabakas, regarded the king as their peer or equal, and were outraged when he made good his supremacy over them (Kaggwa 1905: 51; cited in Southwold 1961: 10. In that paper I outline the development of the royal supremacy in Buganda, as evidenced in the traditional history.) Such a pattern is consistent with a state of affairs where military organization was not of pressing importance.

I find no reference to very young kings in this earliest period; there is, however, evidence that kings were frequently old men. The history describes vividly how horribly withered with age Kigala (K 5) was before he died; and that Kintu (K 1) was also an old man. It relates that the reigns of Ccwa I (K 2) and Kimera (K 3) were very long; and the fact that both men were succeeded by grandsons also indicates that they reigned to an advanced age. It appears therefore that it was not important that a king should be in the prime of life, which is understandable if his tasks as ruler were relatively undemanding. It may be suggested, too, that if a king reigns into old age, there is little reason for choosing as successor his brother, presumably only a little less aged.

Thus what little we know about the first period, in which there was no fraternal succession, is consistent with the reason we have suggested for its practice in the second period. We are on firmer ground when we examine the third period, in which again fraternal succession was not practised.

The third period begins with the reforms of Ssemakookiro (K 27), who killed his brothers and most of his sons, and appears to have taken pains to make clear his nomination of a favoured successor. His measures seem to have been designed to reduce the dangers of rebellion; I prefer to deal with them below (pp. 114–17), after I have shown how the practice of fraternal succession led to frequent rebellions.

Here I wish to relate the third period to the external situation. From about the middle of the eighteenth century Bunyoro, under a succession of weak kings, went into a period of relative decline. This would have become evident to the Baganda when, under Jjunju (K 26), they conquered from Bunyoro the large, populous, rich, and strategic province of Buddu, on the west. Kaggwa, in his judgment on Ssemakookiro (K 27) quoted above (p. 94), remarks a great development of trade in this reign. This would have been a consequence of the conquest of Buddu, by which for the first time the Baganda obtained access, uncontrolled by Bunyoro, to the salt, iron, and cattle products of Western Uganda; and, still more importantly, to the Arab trade goods which at this time were beginning to reach the west of Lake Victoria, having come up by way of Tabora from the coast near Zanzibar. The growth of trade is of course conventionally taken as an index of peace. It does not appear from the record that in these later reigns the Baganda ceased to go to war; but their wars appear mainly to have been concerned with conquest, plunder, and the enforcement of tribute from weaker neighbours. The military pressure from a dominant neighbour, with which the second period began, no longer existed; and it is significant that three of the nominated successors of this period (Ssuuna II, Muteesa I, and Mwanga II) all came to the throne as notably young men. Though the direct cause of the change in the pattern of succession was surely a consideration of internal politics, the easing of the external situation may be cited as a contributory factor.

However, to argue that it is the relevance of the ages of possible successors that leads to fraternal succession involves a certain paradox. If a king's son is passed over in favour of a brother who is in the prime of life, then by the time the son eventually succeeds he will be a mature man. By the time he has reigned and died, *his* brothers are likely to be elderly, and his sons of a more suitable age to carry the burdens of kingship. Hence fraternal succession might be expected to occur at most in alternate generations. Yet in fact it is found in each of the five successive generations from that headed by Mutebi (K 15) to that headed by Jjunju (K 26). It will be seen that there is a marked tendency after fraternal succession for the succession to pass to the junior generation as a result of rebellion. Tebandeke (K 18) and Mwanga I (K 23) were successful rebels; Kamaanya (K 28) rebelled unsuccessfully; Jjunju (K 26), though not a rebel himself, became king after defeating his half-brothers who had killed their father Kyabaggu. In these generations, only Kagulu (K 20) is an exception. The real cause of these rebellions was probably impatience to get the throne—the kings killed by rebellion of a junior generation were all the third of their own generation to reign. Another cause may have been the fear that a father's brother would pass the throne to his own son rather than to his nephew—both the successful rebels were not sons of the previous king. Equally, we can see that these filial rebellions had the function of facilitating the repetition of fraternal succession. To a large extent fraternal succession was both cause and effect of filial rebellion.

A variety of lines of argument tend to confirm the justness of Roscoe's association of fraternal succession with the relative ages of the candidates. In so far as this is accepted as the crucial factor, the case for supposing that the principle of *kusikirana* was invoked is weakened. In fact I doubt if the military situation in the latter part of the second period was such that the age of the king was a crucial consideration. Here it will be seen that fraternal succession is largely succession by full brothers, which is related to yet other factors: I deal with it below under Rule 12.

Rule 8. After one fraternal succession, subsequent succession by a third brother was disfavoured.

I have no statement to this effect; but my limited material on succession in clans seems to show that an office is not usually held by more than two men of one generation. Apart from Ssuuna I (K 11), the peculiarities of whose situation have been noted above (p. 102), each of the third brothers to hold the throne (Kayemba (K 17), Mawanda (K 22), and Kyabaggu (K 25)) obtained it as a rebel. Kayemba and Kyabaggu were rebels by sorcery; and I shall argue below (p. 109) that a rebel by sorcery is typically a person who has a formally valid title which is likely nevertheless to be disfavoured— the sorcery arises in a situation where norms conflict. If it is true that third brothers were likely to be disfavoured by the electors, this may well be related to considerations of age.

Rule 9. An elder 'brother' was, other things being equal, preferred to a younger.

I have no statement to this effect; and my informants, in discussing succession among commoners, insisted very strongly that a younger brother was preferred to an elder if he was the better man. The very strength of their insistence makes me suspicious;[30] and in fact I found that in modern cases of succession among commoners, when an elder brother was passed over, which was rarely, it was normally thought necessary to specify a reason.

With every case of fraternal succession, Kaggwa describes the first king as 'elder brother' (*mukulu*) or the second as 'younger brother' (*muto*). As the same words also mean 'senior' and 'junior', their applicability might perhaps be more a consequence than a cause of the order of succession. But in some cases, at least, Kaggwa's phraseology definitely refers to age or to birth-order.

I think it is probably true that, between brothers for whom other things were sufficiently equal for each eventually to hold the throne, the elder held it first.

Rule 10. By the principle of *kusikirana*, a brother's son was preferred to an own son.

This rule is definitely stated by informants to have applied to succession among commoners. With regard to the throne, it did not lead to the succession of men whose fathers never reigned.[31] I discuss its application in other situations under the head of the next rule.

Rule 11. When the succession dropped to a junior generation after passing through a set of brothers, a son of the senior of the brothers was preferred.

This rule would normally follow from a combination of Rules 9 and 10; or, if 'senior' be substituted for 'elder' in Rule 9, it would follow from that alone.

This rule is stated by Roscoe (1911: 232); after having mentioned that a brother might succeed, he continues: 'Yet in such cases the sons of the first brother ultimately succeeded to the throne, and not the sons of the second brother who had stepped in as king during their minority.'

The succession did indeed return to the sons of Mulondo (K9), Ssekamaanya (K12), and Mutebi (K15). It did not return to the sons of Tebandeke (K18), but this is probably explicable in terms of the special circumstances described above (p. 103).[32] The sons of Kagulu (K20) also did not succeed; they were killed when the nation rose in revolt against their father (Kaggwa 1905: 47). The fact that the sons of Kikulwe (K21) did not succeed, though their deaths are nowhere recorded, seems contrary to at least the spirit of these rules. The sons of Mwanga I (K23) and of Namugala (K24) should have been preferred to those of Kyabaggu: but as Jjunju (K26) won the throne in a civil war, their failure was probably due to weakness. It seems likely that when Ssemakookiro (K27) killed most of his own sons, he included those of Jjunju also, so they had no chance to succeed.

Hence Roscoe's statement is not true as a description of a regularity. It would appear that Rules 10 and 11 were originally effective, but were later overridden by other considerations.

One case seems to emphasize the weight of Rules 10 and 11 in earlier times. It will be seen that Kateregga (K 14) was a rebel; in fact the first rebel other than Ttembo, whose case is exceptional in at least two ways. Kateregga rebelled against his father's 'brother' Kimbugwe. I remarked (p. 101) that it was typical to rebel against a father's brother; but also that those who did so successfully rebelled against the third brother of the set. As Kateregga was only a lad (p. 104) when Kimbugwe became king, he had less reason than most to plead impatience as a reason for rebellion: by Rules 10 and 11 he could have expected to receive the succession in good time.

Now Kaggwa (1901: 27) specially notes that Kimbugwe had a son, Prince Kamyuka, whom 'he loved greatly'. Kateregga ought to have succeeded before Kamyuka; but if he did, Kamyuka was unlikely to have succeeded at all. I suggested above (p. 101) that second cousins do not appear to be seriously considered as successors. If Kamyuka *had* succeeded Kateregga, a large step towards a dynastic type of succession would have been taken; and this, together with Rule 8, would have left no scope for fraternal succession. In the circumstances, Kimbugwe might have been tempted to nominate Kamyuka as his successor; or worse, to have followed Kigala's (K 5) example, and abdicated after first persuading the electors to choose his son (on Kigala—Kaggwa 1905: 30). This would have been contrary to the principle of *kusikirana*; and since, by the argument just stated, it would probably have excluded Kateregga permanently, it would have justified a charge of 'repudiating kinship'. But in Buganda what the king is strong enough to achieve counts for more than the right.

Kaggwa (1901: 28-9) says that the occasion for the rebellion was this: Kateregga asked Kimbugwe to perform a kinship ritual for him, and Kimbugwe refused on the grounds that Kateregga had broken a relevant taboo. Kateregga was enraged, and raised rebellion, saying to his men, 'Kimbugwe has repudiated kinship with me, I am not his agnate.' I suggest that the repudiation of kinship that was really causing trouble was the prospective succession of Kimbugwe's son.

On the king-list I have classed Kateregga as a simple rebel, since he raised an army and fought; but as it was his sorcery that actually killed Kimbugwe, he may equally be classed as a rebel by sorcery. On theoretical grounds we might have anticipated sorcery in a situation where kinship threatened to become attenuated or repudiated; particularly as the situation was the product of contrary norms. In one of my few detailed histories of succession in a clan, I find a case where a man of a collateral line kills an office holder by sorcery because, my informant said, he saw that his line was being left out though fully entitled to succeed.

Two more of the rebellions by sorcery—those of Kayemba (K17) and Kyabaggu (K25)—may be explained in a similar way. Both were third brothers (in succession order) who might have been disfavoured by Rule 8; but if they had been passed over for a son, they would then have become ineligible under Rule 4, and their sons would also have had little chance of succeeding. (A simpler explanation is that these men were attacking their full brothers—see below, p. 113.) The remaining rebellion by sorcery, that of Tebandeke (K18), can be assimilated to the same pattern: by Rule 11 he should have been the preferred successor, but he might well have been passed over on account of his personal characteristics (see above, p. 103).

Rule 12. The king's full brother, if any, was the preferred successor.

This rule, which of course involved the same clan being attached matri-laterally to two successive kings, is nowhere stated. On the contrary, the regularity which resulted from it is implicitly denied by the best sources.

Kaggwa has a chapter in which he describes the duties given to the close maternal kin of the Kabaka; of one of the most important he writes: 'On account of its importance, that duty was given to the maternal kin of the Kabaka, because they are the most diligent in taking care of him, and *the female parentage is not wont to bear twice*' (Kaggwa 1905: 121; my italics). The words in italics appear to be a proverb; and the reference must be specifically to princes, since matrilateral affiliation is of no formal significance among commoners. They clearly imply that full-brother succession is exceptional.

Nsimbi (1956: 251) makes a similar point still more strongly. He remarks that Nanteza was the mother of two kings, Jjunju (K26) and Ssemakookiro (K27), and says that this is the origin of the proverb 'The wild banana does not fruit twice, except for that of Nanteza'.

Examination of the king-list, however, shows that five kings came to the throne in succession to full-brothers: Jjuuko (K16), Kayemba (K17), Namugala (K24), Kyabaggu (K25), and Ssemakookiro (K27). Mawanda (K22) should be counted as a sixth case, since, although he did not have the same mother as his brother Kikulwe, their mothers were sisters, daughters of one father (Kaggwa 1908: 63): in Ganda terms, Kikulwe and Mawanda would be reckoned as full brothers. Full-brother succession was therefore common: indeed the instances of it outnumber those of succession by half-brothers and cousins (five instances).

Since the Baganda are evidently unwilling to recognize the occurrence of full-brother succession (and with good reason, as I shall show), it may be that the practice developed unintentionally, in which case it may be said to have originated in the generation of Mutebi (K15). On the other hand it can be argued that it was in some sense normal, and failed to occur still more frequently only through special circumstances.

Ccwa I (K2) had full brothers, and it cannot be positively said why they did not succeed.[33] Kigala (K5) had a full brother who, significantly, rebelled: he was defeated and killed by Kigala's sorcery (Kaggwa 1901: 14–15). No other king of the first period is shown to have had a full brother; though, for this first period, negative evidence cannot be given much weight.

The sons of Nakibinge (K8) are not shown as having had full brothers; as they were very young when their father died, and there was a three-years weaning taboo, this is probably correct. Ssekamaanya (K12) had full brothers; but I suggested above (p. 102) that they may have been disfavoured because they belonged to the Civet-cat clan. No subsequent king is shown as having had full brothers, other than those who were in fact succeeded by them. Negative evidence is of course inconclusive; but at least it cannot be argued that Kaggwa distorted the evidence in order to make it fit the rule.

Four of the six kings who succeeded full brothers did so as rebels. As we have seen, some rebels (like Kateregga) had a particularly good title to succeed; others seem to have rebelled because their claim was not good enough. Hence the mere fact that these four men obtained the throne cannot be interpreted unambiguously. But Jjuuko (K16) and Namugala (K24) succeeded peacefully, presumably by election; hence it may be supposed that the claim of a full brother was good.

In another connexion, I mentioned above (p. 102) that Jjuuko (K16) was warned by diviners that his full brother Kayemba should not marry the woman Nakku. It may have been observed that the diviners said 'if he marries her, you (plural) will die', and that Jjuuko told Kayemba 'the gods forbid her to us'. Jjunju (K26) wanted to sleep with a wife of his full brother Ssemakookiro; she refused, saying she was pregnant, and Jjunju replied 'Sure, the pregnancy is mine' (Kaggwa 1901: 67). When Namugala (K24) abdicated in favour of his full brother Kyabaggu, he said 'all that is ours is thine: I have relinquished the kingdom for thee, therefore eat it' (Kaggwa 1901: 59). Such phrases surely imply that there was virtual identity between full brothers. In describing the quarrels between Jjuuko and Kayemba, and between Jjunju and Ssemakookiro, Kaggwa remarks several times how bad it was that full brothers should hate one another; on the former case he writes (1905: 43): 'Now those two kings...were born of one mother, Namutebi; on account of which they reckoned themselves to be twins in the womb of their mother: if the kingship had not caused them to be seized by jealousy they would have been the closest friends—but they did not love one another.' As the identity of twins is very heavily emphasized in Buganda, there could hardly be a stronger statement of the identity of full brothers.

Full brothers, of course, should not have killed one another. The only prince reported to have killed his full brother in a straightforward way is Mawanda (K22). The soldiers of Ssemakookiro (K27) killed his full brother Jjunju; but he was very angry with them, saying he had wanted him taken alive, and he punished them (Kaggwa 1901: 69–70).[34] Kayemba (K17) killed his elder full brother by sorcery, and Kyabaggu (K25) attempted to do so.

Except for Kigala (K5) of an earlier period, who killed his rebel (and presumably younger) full brother by sorcery, no elder full brother killed a younger even by sorcery. This is remarkable, since the elder brothers generally hated the younger and/or knew that they were plotting against them. Namugala (K24) knew that Kyabaggu went constantly to sorcerers seeking medicine with which to kill him; he reproached him with this, said he did not wish to fight him, and abdicated. Jjunju (K26) was jealous of his brother Ssemakookiro, and killed his wife and unborn child; he then sent him to live in the Mabira forest, hoping that the *mbwa* flies might kill him,[35] but otherwise left him free to recruit soldiers.

Kikulwe (K21) heard that the nation preferred his younger brother Mawanda, and made a plot to kill him: he invited him to be his guest, and had a game-pit dug, hoping he would fall into it. But Mawanda was informed, and passed on one side of the trap; Kikulwe was seized with shame, and fled.

After Kayemba had defied Jjuuko (K16) by marrying Nakku, Jjuuko made a plot to kill him. He gave him command of a fleet sent to attack islands in the lake, and provided him with a clay canoe which he hoped would sink and drown him. Kayemba was warned in time, and embarking instead in a wooden canoe he took the islands and refused to return. Jjuuko eventually deceived him into returning to the mainland, and summoned him to the capital to explain himself. Kayemba said forthrightly that he had rebelled because Jjuuko had tried to kill him: 'And when the Kabaka heard the words of Kayemba, he did not abuse him, nor did he do him any harm, because their mother and their father were the same; he said to him "Well, return to your estate which you left to go to the war".' Kayemba did so, and straightway began to make a kind of sorcery to kill Jjuuko, having been so advised by diviners 'if you want to eat the kingdom soon'. Jjuuko was warned of his danger, and took tedious (and eventually ineffective) precautions against the sorcery; but he did nothing directly to check Kayemba (Kaggwa 1901: 33–9).

Such bizarre manœuvres may in part be attributed to the norms demanding solidarity and love between full brothers. But on this interpretation younger full brothers should have been as reluctant to kill as elder; and typically they were not. It seems more exact to say that a king was inhibited from simply killing his full brother, no matter what the provocation, nor how much he desired his death.

The ramshackle plots by which Kikulwe and Jjuuko sought to bring about the accidental deaths of their younger full brothers find a parallel in another relationship. Ssemakookiro (K27) was informed that certain chiefs were plotting to rebel and enthrone Kamaanya, their 'sister's son' and Ssemakookiro's son. Ssemakookiro executed the chiefs, together with Kamaanya's mother. He confined Kamaanya in a hut in which people had died of plague; as he survived this, Ssemakookiro sent him to beat barkcloth, hoping that the sap would kill him; and when he survived this, he took no further measures against him (Kaggwa 1901: 72). Now it was not because he was his son that Ssemakookiro had refrained from executing Kamaanya; for he had recently put all his sons but three to death merely on information that they wanted to rebel. Kaggwa does say, however (1901: 77), that when Ssemakookiro killed the mother and 'mother's brothers' of Kamaanya he said to him 'You will eat Buganda as an orphan (*munaku*)'. This implies that he regarded Kamaanya as heir-apparent; and I suggest that the curious reluctance simply to kill younger full brothers also derived from their being heirs-apparent. There is some evidence in the narrative that they were.

When Jjuuko wanted to lure Kayemba back to the mainland, he put the nearer part of the country into mourning for the death of a king, and sent the Katikkiro to say he was dead. The Katikkiro said to him 'I have come to fetch you: the Kabaka is dead: come and eat the kingdom.' Kayemba was suspicious enough to send out scouts to investigate; but when they reported that the country was in mourning, he left with insufficient force to put up a fight. The diviners who told him how to kill Jjuuko also seem to have assumed that his object would have been to *hasten* his succession. Later, Namugala (K24) seems to have found it natural to abdicate in favour of his full brother.

Even if full brothers were not formally nominated as heirs-apparent, their virtual identity, to which I referred above (p. 111) would have had the same effect—as Namugala, in abdicating, implied when he said 'all that is ours is thine'. The Baganda firmly maintain that it is dangerous to publish in advance the choice of a successor, as he will surely commit murder to hasten his succession. The rebellions of full brothers may be attributable to such logic: the title of a full brother to the throne was not only good, it was equal to that of the brother who actually held the throne. It is true that two full brothers, Jjuuko and Namugala, waited peacefully for the throne; but even this is weakened by the fact that Namugala had only nine days to wait (Kaggwa 1901: 57).[36]

Thus the mere existence of full brothers tended to produce rebellions; and rebellions which the king was hampered from crushing effectively, even when forewarned. Moreover, if I had space to analyse the narrative in further detail, I could show that the quarrels between full brothers were frequently marked by horrible acts or events which symbolically blasphemed against the values attached to blood and the womb.

The possibility of full-brother succession also destroyed the balance in the political system which should have been produced by using both paternal and maternal affiliations in designating a successor. When it occurred, the circulation of the kingship among the clans was interrupted, and one clan received an undue share of power. At the same time, because of it a king was less able to trust in the loyalty of his mother's people: Jjunju (K26) in fact lost the throne through trusting in his mother's advice when she was actually plotting in favour of her other son Ssemakookiro (Kaggwa 1901: 67–8). The cross-cutting of the two lines of affiliation should have designated a unique choice: the prince who, because he combined royal rank and the strongest political support, was best qualified to reign in peace.[37] But if there were full brothers, the unique choice was a set of princes, of whom only one could be king at a time, yet between whom it was hardly possible to distinguish: and the outcome was not peace, but unmanageable strife.

So full-brother succession produced rebellions against which the king was relatively helpless; it exposed a fallacy in the basic logic of the political system; and it led to blasphemy against basic norms at their deepest level of embodiment. It is little wonder that the Baganda prefer not to notice it.

The third period of the pre-Christian era, in which there were no more fraternal successions, begins after the accession of Ssemakookiro (K27), and clearly as a result of measures he introduced. Many informants say that he started the custom of killing the Princes of the Drum, even if they know nothing else about him.

Roscoe (1911: 188–9) gives the following account of his reforms: 'To avoid the danger which was often caused by princes rebelling, King Ssemakookiro allowed his mother to put all his brothers except three to death as soon as he had several sons born to him, and thus the succession to the throne was secure...The custom thus established of putting princes to death as soon as a new king had secured the succession was carried out until Mutesa's reign.' This makes the basic points rather well, though Roscoe has got the details badly garbled.

Kaggwa does not say that Ssemakookiro's mother had a hand in the executions; but he does relate (1901: 130) that the mother of Muteesa I (K30) had all *his* brothers except two killed—and this was in 1875, i.e. nearly twenty years after Muteesa's accession. He also relates (Kaggwa 1901: 93) that Ssuuna II (K29) had all sixty of his brothers, except two, burnt, and adds: 'The reason for killing the princes was this: the Kabaka had begotten sons of his own, and was told "Kill these, they want to rebel and eat the kingdom".' As it was Kaggwa who supplied Roscoe with most of his informants, it is evident that Roscoe only imperfectly understood what he was told. Except for one of his sons, Kamaanya (K28) did not kill any princes (though his father had already killed all his brothers, except for one who fled to Bunyoro, and another who was killed fighting Kamaanya for the throne). Kaggwa nowhere speaks of a *custom* of killing the princes; and in fact by narrating the executions under Ssuuna and Muteesa as separate events (the latter with an exclamation mark), he shows that he was not consciously aware of the regularity. We have in fact here an excellent example of the way repetition passes over into custom.

Kaggwa (1905: 58) writes 'Immediately after Ssemakookiro had eaten the kingdom, he was a very cruel Kabaka; although afterwards, when he had been on the throne some time, he reformed. Because, as soon as he ate the kingdom, he arrested three of his sons, and others of his agnates, and burnt them as he thought they wished to take the kingdom from him.' This hardly supports Roscoe's statement, particularly as we know (Kaggwa 1901: 67) that Ssemakookiro had many sons even before his quarrel with Jjunju had begun.

In his book of history (Kaggwa 1901: 70–1) Kaggwa says nothing about Ssemakookiro's executing his brothers; he does say, however, that at a time which was evidently several years after his accession, he was told that his *sons* wanted to rebel, so he had them all arrested and burnt except for three, who are named. Elsewhere (Kaggwa 1905: 217) he gives a further variant: the medium of the principal god came and delivered Ssemakookiro an oracle "If you wish to live long, arrest all your sons the princes, confine them and keep them in a prison, and thus you will obtain peace."[37] So he did this, and arrested all his sons and put them in fetters, and some he killed, till at length there was no peril in the land.'

It is incredible that Ssemakookiro would have spared his brothers when he killed his sons; considering also the different attributions of date, there are probably two, if not three, separate incidents referred to.

Kaggwa (1901: 110) tells us that, after some heart-searching, Muteesa I (K 30) in the early part of his reign had his brothers confined in a prison. He also implies (Kaggwa 1901: 111) that Ssuuna II (K 29) had his sons arrested.

It therefore appears that Ssemakookiro began the practices of killing and of confining princes as precautionary measures, and that neither was recognized by Kaggwa as a custom. There remains some doubt exactly what Ssemakookiro did; but the essential points are clear enough.

In saying to his son Kamaanya 'You will eat Buganda as an orphan', Ssemakookiro appears to have nominated him as successor. Kaggwa (1901: 86) writes 'Ssuuna (II, K 29)...succeeded his father Kamaanya...as a boy of about twelve years old. When Kabaka Kamaanya was dying, he said to...the Katikkiro and the leading chiefs "When I am dead, don't fight, but look out the young prince to eat Buganda", and therefore Ssuuna ate the kingdom as he had been nominated (*kulamira*) by his father.' It emerges also that Ssuuna II indicated his preference for Muteesa to succeed him, though sufficiently obscurely for the Katikkiro to have forgotten and agreed to choose another prince (see above, p. 95). According to the missionaries, Muteesa I in turn nominated, on his deathbed, his son Mwanga to succeed. As we saw above (p. 94), nomination of a successor is provided for in custom; but it seems to be implied that as an effective practice it began with Ssemakookiro.

Kaggwa scrupulously remarks that Ssemakookiro's period of cruelty was temporary (see p. 115); and I quoted earlier (p. 94) his judgment that Ssemakookiro became a notably good king. His tribute is the more striking when it is considered that Kaggwa's own great-grandfather was one of the rebels supporting Kamaanya whom Ssemakookiro executed. Unlike that of some other kings, Ssemakookiro's bloodshed cannot be attributed to cruelty of character, but must rather be viewed as a matter of policy. The considerations which led to it can be imagined from Ssemakookiro's previous experiences.

His father Kyabaggu (K25) had announced that he meant to abdicate, and invited the princes to fight for the throne. Two of them, sons of Mawanda (K22), were defeated by others, and brought to Kyabaggu under arrest. Them he executed, and turning to the other princes he told them that if they showed insolence they would be treated likewise; he then continued his reign without further suggestion of abdication (Kaggwa 1901: 62–3). This was clearly but a strategem to cull and cow the princes; and we may reflect that the pattern of fraternal successions and filial rebellions had by this time grossly inflated the number of eligible princes.

Later, Kyabaggu was murdered by three of his sons, who then went to attack Jjunju (another son), who was lying in wait for them: after two battles, he defeated and killed them. Jjunju was then attacked by another group of princes, including two sons of Kyabaggu (K25) and one of Namugala (K24): these too he defeated after two battles, the second described as a big one in which many people were killed. Jjunju then became king, but was shortly attacked by yet another prince, and would have been defeated had not Ssemakookiro come to his assistance. Some time later, as we have seen (p. 112), Jjunju quarrelled with Ssemakookiro (partly because of jealousy arising from this incident), and Ssemakookiro was persuaded by their mother to raise an army and depose Jjunju, again after heavy fighting.

No one, then, would have known better than Ssemakookiro the dangers that princes, both brothers and sons, presented to both the peace of the nation and the reign of the king. His imprisonment and killing of princes, as those carried out by later kings, were hardly superfluous.

What, however, was the point of nominating a successor? We may note that none of the nominated successors had a full brother; but it seems more significant that Ssuuna II was only twelve years old, both Muteesa I and Mwanga II under twenty, and all three specially noted for their youth. If one son is nominated as successor, this would tend to weaken the support of chiefs for others, and make them less likely to rebel successfully against either their father or their brother. On the other hand, the nominated successor would be all the more likely to rebel against his father (see above, p. 113)—as Kamaanya did. But a young prince would be less capable of successfully organizing a rebellion. These considerations would hardly weigh with a king on his deathbed; but since, apart from them, nomination of a stripling was most impolitic, I suggest that these young princes had in fact been favoured earlier.

CONCLUSION

When we examine the pattern of succession to the throne in Buganda, as witnessed by the historical record, it becomes evident that within the pre-Christian era we need to distinguish three periods, of which the second was marked by frequent fraternal succession, and the first and third by its absence. We have therefore to account for two different patterns of succession, and, if possible, for the two historical changes in the pattern.

It is possible that there occurred a change in culture, related perhaps to an ethnic change in origin or orientation of the royal house, involving a change in the basic rules of succession, between the first and second periods. The evidence for this is tenuous and conjectural; and the explanation has the further demerit of putting a full stop to further analysis. No such explanation appears possible for the change between the second and third periods. I prefer to assume that the basic rules remained the same throughout, but produced different results as a consequence of different circumstances.

A possible hypothesis is that the rules always indicated a son as the preferred successor, and that the succession of brothers in the second period was in breach of the rules. But it is difficult to suppose that eleven cases of fraternal succession in eight generations can all have been illegitimate, especially as fraternal succession was the preferred mode among commoners.

I therefore take it as my hypothesis that by the rules a brother was generally the preferred successor; and that it is the absence of fraternal succession in the first and third periods that requires special explanation. Such explanation is to be found by analysing the implications of fraternal succession, that is, its preconditions and its consequences, and by examining the circumstances in which the two changes in the pattern of succession occurred.

Among commoners, fraternal succession is preferred as an application of the principle of *kusikirana*, by which the succession is given to collaterals in order to maintain the solidarity of a group of agnates. But the principle of *kusikirana* should also lead to preference for a cousin over a brother; yet we find only two cases of succession by a cousin, and both invite explanation in other terms. Again the principle of *kusikirana* should lead to preference for a brother's son over an own son; yet such a rule was only imperfectly realized. It therefore appears doubtful whether this principle was as effective among royals as it was among commoners. Among commoners, the principle was annulled by royal decree giving preference to sons over brothers, in the latter part of the last century. The Baganda say that this change was a response to the fact that the value of the property to be inherited by the successor increased with the development of trade with the outside world; and Fallers (1956: 90–2) employs a similar explanation for a parallel change among the neighbouring Basoga. But the value of the succession to the throne was always very great, and it seems reasonable that this should have led to a comparable derogation from the principle of *kusikirana* among royals very much earlier. We observed that, because of the value of the throne, there was a marked lack of solidarity among agnates of the royal descent-group; and without a desire for solidarity among agnates, the rationale for *kusikirana* disappears.

This suggests the hypothesis, indicated by Roscoe, that brothers were preferred as successors not because they were collaterals but because they were more mature than the sons. Naturally, the evidence concerning the ages of potential successors on each occasion is inadequate; but such as it is, it appears to support the hypothesis.

If it was indeed considerations of relative age that led to the choices of brothers to succeed in the second period, then the absence of such choices in the first and third periods might be attributed to such demographic factors as the ages at which kings died. Some, but not all, of the kings in the first period died when they, and presumably their brothers also, were notably old men; but such an explanation seems irrelevant for the third period, where in fact the sons who succeeded were typically very young. Alternatively, the changes may be associated with changes in the circumstances which placed a premium on maturity. We find that the second period began in circumstances of dire military need. It seems reasonable that when the nation is under military pressure, the king ought to be an effective general, and ought also to be capable of organizing the nation under him.

Although information on the first period is scarce, it does appear that at that time Buganda was under relatively little military pressure. A king long past the age of warriorhood, and a segmentary political organization giving a large measure of power to clan heads, and so making relatively light demands on the king, would then have been acceptable.

We find, too, that the change to the third period corresponds with a decline in the strength of Bunyoro, Buganda's most formidable military rival.

But if the change *to* the practice of fraternal succession can reasonably be related to a sudden need for military vigour and political dominance in the king, it is less plausible to attribute the change away from fraternal succession simply to a decline in that need. After that change, Buganda continued to go to war; and, for generations before it, her situation can hardly have resembled that of dire military necessity with which the second period began.

Our argument so far explains the introduction of fraternal succession, but hardly its continuance over eight generations. We now observe that over the latter part of the second period fraternal succession was in fact succession by full brothers. The choice of a full brother depended not on preference for a collateral, nor necessarily on preference for a mature man, but rather on the fact that the manner of designating a successor was unable to distinguish between full brothers.

Roscoe suggests that the measures by which Ssemakookiro initiated the third period were motivated by a desire to curb rebellion. Their effect would clearly have lain in this direction; and consideration of the turmoil through which Ssemakookiro had lived makes it easy to believe that he had such a desire, intensely.

All the (successful) rebellions, save one, occurred in the second period; and we educed a number of reasons why the practice of fraternal succession should have tended to increase rebellion:

(1) To maintain brothers as potential strong successors was also to maintain strong and able rivals.

(2) Succession through brothers may not have been a result of the principle of *kusikirana*, but its effect was the same, to inflate the number of persons eligible to succeed, and eligible also to lead rebellions.

(3) A younger full-brother, because his claim was no less good than that of the elder, was especially jealous of the throne: indeed all the successful fraternal rebels were younger full-brothers. But it was virtually impossible for the king to protect himself effectively from such a threat. And, although royal agnates were expected to hate one another, for uterine kin to do so was especially horrible.

(4) Third brothers, probably because their claim to succeed was relatively poor, seem to have been particularly prone to rebel.

(5) Succession by brothers (or cousins), especially third brothers, appears to have provoked rebellion by the filial generation.

Apparently a brother was chosen to succeed in order to secure a mature and therefore strong king; and to secure a series of strong kings was to strengthen the kingship. But the practice of fraternal succession tended to foster rebellion. Gluckman has argued that rebellions strengthen kingship; and this was true in Buganda, at least to the extent that after a rebellion the strongest prince was in possession of the throne. But on the other hand rebellion, and the fear of rebellion, tend to weaken a king; and if a series of kings are weakened in this way, the kingship itself is weakened. Moreover, even for the intensely monarchical Baganda, the kingship was not simply an end in itself, but existed for the sake of the nation. Incessant conspiracy, spying, execution, fratricide, patricide, and civil war—such as Ssemakookiro especially saw—were not conducive to peace and good government.

The measures adopted by Ssemakookiro, and largely followed by his successors, did in fact eliminate successful rebellions. Clearly they were in the interest of those kings themselves; but also in the interest of the nation. Their effect was to produce a series of remarkably strong and secure kings; and if this strength was sometimes employed cruelly and tyrannously, on the whole these were beneficial, even good kings. No one, except that egregious hagiologist Sir H. M. Stanley, ever thought of Muteesa I as a saint; but he was undoubtedly a wise and able king, to whom largely the kingdom of Buganda owes its healthy survival through the period of European dominance.

Yet these strong kings were produced against the odds; the overall tendency of Ssemakookiro's reforms was to weaken the kingship. If Kamaanya (K 28) had died soon after his accession, there would apparently have been only four eligible princes: his three infant sons, and his brother Kakungulu who, as he had long been in league with the Banyoro, would not have been acceptable. In the Christian era, the Moslem king Kaleema (K 33) so effectively butchered the royals, that the Christian chiefs could find no other prince with whom to replace him than Mwanga—whom but a year earlier they had themselves deposed as unmanageable and insufferable. When he made it necessary for him to be deposed again, in 1897, of the handful of princes technically eligible the only one politically acceptable was his one-year-old only son, Ccwa II. The violence of those times was in part a function of the incursion of European power; but in the policy of killing potential rebels there was always inherent the danger of eliminating all suitable candidates for the succession.

The apparent policy of nominating young sons to succeed also put the strength of the kingship in jeopardy. After his election, Muteesa I found himself overshadowed by his Katikkiro, whom he had the greatest difficulty in removing from office. Mwanga II disliked and feared his older chiefs, and put power into the hands of youths of his own age; it was this, together with other youthful follies, which led to his deposition four years after his accession. The throne then passed to brothers, whom Mwanga had been unable to kill, since, partly because of his youth, he had failed to beget sons. Events might have taken a different course but for the impending intervention of European powers; nevertheless, it is clear that, at least in the early years of their reigns, kings were still vulnerable to fraternal rebellion.

When Ccwa II succeeded as an infant, the powers of the kingship were vested in regents, dominated by the Katikkiro, Sir Apolo Kaggwa. After his coming of age in 1914, it took Ccwa twelve years of trouble to free himself from Kaggwa's domination. After Ccwa's death in 1939, there was again a regency, and it was, in part, Muteesa II's struggles to establish a policy of his own which produced a clash with the British in 1953. This in turn led to the Constitution of 1955, by which the Kabaka became formally a constitutional monarch, and political responsibility was vested in the Katikkiro.

It would be absurd to overlook the effect of British overrule on these developments. But, no less, it is necessary to see that they were inherent in the reforms made by Ssemakookiro, which in fact produced young kings, and were likely in the process of time to produce incompetent ones. Sooner or later there was bound to be a king who could not shake off his Katikkiro's initial domination; and once this occurred, the balance of power was likely to shift decisively in favour of the Katikkiroship and the commoner chiefs generally.

Anthropologists have often supposed that social change in Africa must be attributed to the impact of the colonial power, as a *deus ex machina*. In Buganda it is evident that the practices concerning succession to the throne changed without any intervention from outside the Interlacustrine region. Even with respect to those changes that occurred under British overrule, the British were not the sole begetters of change, but rather the midwives of change inherent in the indigenous system. The structure of the Buganda kingdom was always remarkable in the extent to which it treated the kingship as an object of competition among commoner clans, and not the exclusive possession of one royal clan. Through military necessity the kingship was strengthened, but yet consequentially weakened through the profusion of rebellion; but the policies, intended to preserve the king from royal rivals, could only end by subordinating the kingship to the power of commoner chiefs. These realities underlie and shape the changing patterns of succession to the throne.

APPENDIX I. THE CURRENT RULES

Since the establishment of the British Protectorate in 1894, the successor to the throne is formally elected by the Great Lukiiko, a constituted parliament. But in practice it seems that the choice is predetermined. Only recognized sons of the late king would be considered, unless of course there were none. As the Kabaka is a a Christian monarch, he has officially only one wife, and only her sons would be seriously considered. Since Mwanga II, Ccwa II, and so far Muteesa II, have each had only one son by their Christian wives, the issue of choosing between them has not arisen. If it did, it seems likely that, as among commoners, the eldest son would be chosen. When Prince Kiweewa, the son of the present king by his official wife, was born, he at once began to be written of as the heir-apparent. This assumption appeared to be inspired by the British Protectorate Government; and Dr Goody had pointed out to me that it was generally Colonial Office policy to have the succession to thrones clarified in advance. Some Baganda had reservations.

Now that British overrule has been removed, there may ensue modifications. Many Baganda felt that sons of the king by other wives than the official Christian one ought to be considered as eligible; but many others would be reluctant to see Christian monogamy set at naught. I should guess that the rule will remain what it now is among commoners, that the eldest son of the church-married wife is the preferred successor, unless there are special reasons for passing him over.

MARTIN SOUTHWOLD

APPENDIX II. GENEALOGICAL KING-LIST

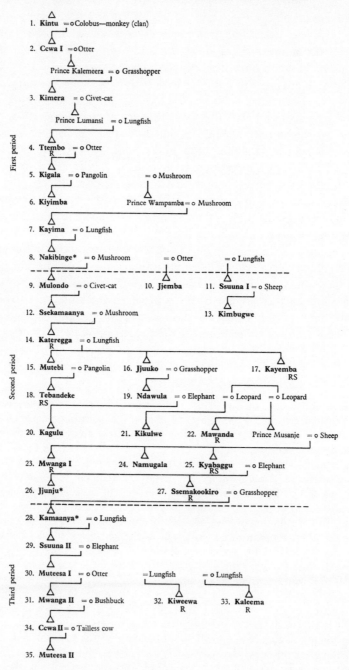

APPENDIX III.
RULES OF HEREDITARY SUCCESSION

This list is intended for reference only; the rules are not all of equal validity, and should be assessed in the light of the comments made in the text.

PRESCRIPTIVE RULES

Rule 1 (p. 97). Only a prince, that is any male descendant in a male line from any Kabaka, was eligible to succeed to the throne.

Rule 2 (p. 97). Among princes, only the Princes of the Drum were eligible. These were defined as men who were the sons, or son's sons, of any Kabaka.

Rule 3 (p. 98). The first-born son of the Kabaka had the name/title of *Kiweewa*, and was barred from the succession.

Rule 4 (p. 98). Princes of any generation above the reigning Kabaka (i.e. classificatory 'fathers', etc.) were ineligible.

Rule 5 (p. 98). A grandson of the late king could be chosen only if all his sons were dead or otherwise not available to succeed.

PREFERENTIAL RULES

Rule 6 (p. 101). By the principle of *kusikirana*, if the succession remained in the same generation, a first cousin was the preferred successor.

Rule 7 (p. 104). A brother was preferred to a son.

Rule 8 (p. 107). After one fraternal succession, subsequent succession by a third brother was disfavoured.

Rule 9 (p. 108). An elder 'brother' was, other things being equal, preferred to a younger.

Rule 10 (p. 108). By the principle of *kusikirana*, a brother's son was preferred to an own son.

Rule 11 (p. 108). When the succession dropped to a junior generation after passing through a set of brothers, a son of the senior of the brothers was preferred.

Rule 12 (p. 110). The king's full brother, if any, was the preferred successor.

Kintu, Kabaka; Prince Wampamba, non-ruling member of the royal house ; R, Kabaka by rebellion; RS, Kabaka by rebellion by sorcery; *, Kabaka by apparent accession war; O Otter, Mother of a Kabaka or prince with her clan (to which he was attached).

Note. This king-list is essentially identical with that given by Roscoe (1911: 231). I have checked it against information given by Kaggwa and Nsimbi; the only correction required concerned the clan of the mother of Kaleema (K33). I have added Muteesa II and his mother; the fact that the mothers of Kikulwe (K21) and Mawanda (K22) were sisters; and the details concerning rebellions, etc.

I have not attempted to give all the royal wives or their sons; much of this information is given by Roscoe (1911: 175–80).

NOTES

[1] If Roscoe (1911 : 200) is right in saying that the capital extended for 5 or 6 miles by 4, its population would have been much in excess of 10,000 persons.

[2] The Baganda had no beasts of burden, and did not use the wheel.

[3] I put the titles of chiefs and other officers in italics, to distinguish them from personal names; but because I use them so frequently, I have not done this with the titles 'Kabaka' and 'Katikkiro'.

[4] Every successor, however humble, was linked with a kinswoman, the *lubuga*, in the ceremonies of personal succession.

[5] By Mr I. N. Kakungulu of Mbale, the son of the last *Kimbugwe*.

[6] Kaggwa (1905: 319) writes: 'When the Kabaka was tired of his Katikkiro and wanted to dismiss him and replace him with another man, he would first stop confidential matters from passing through his hands, and they would be issued through the Kimbugwe...until the Kabaka had chosen another Katikkiro.' In the English literature the duties of the *Kimbugwe* are represented as mainly ritual; but this is because our information has been largely funnelled through Kaggwa, who was himself Katikkiro, and who rightly judged that to represent the *Kimbugwe* as a pagan official would persuade the British to agree to the abolition of the post.

[7] The term *bakungu* is ill-defined: most often it is used in a broad sense to refer to all senior chiefs and officials, but sometimes in a narrow sense to distinguish sub-chiefs from *ssaza* chiefs. I cannot say that the sense I have chosen is the most usual; but I find it the most useful.

[8] A Kabaka belonged to his mother's clan. The clan affiliation, if any, of Kintu, the first king, is doubtful; the other thirty kings down to Mwanga II belonged to only ten clans in total, of which two provided but one king apiece. Analysis of the record of appointments to major chiefships indicates that some other clans were also important; but I doubt if there are more than twenty clans to be seriously reckoned with.

[9] This, and all other quotations from Baganda authors, are given in my translation of the Luganda text.

[10] I have here stated the principle; that some clans in fact realized their interest more than others is another matter.

[11] 'Indeed, wondrous great is the kingship—surely it seals up a man's ears' (Kaggwa, 1901: 118, commenting on an evil deed done by Muteesa).

[12] I use this term for simplicity; analysis shows that the Luganda word *kojja* does not *mean* 'mother's brother', but rather something like 'man of the clan which bore me by an affine (of my agnatic clan)'.

[13] Citing, like Nsimbi (1956: 167), the fact that a prince does not pass this totemic allegiance to his son, as he would do if he were fully a member of that clan.

[14] Kamaanya (K28) is especially noted for having favoured his 'mother's brothers' (perhaps because Kaggwa himself was of their line) and Kaggwa (1901: 77 and 80) lists a number of the chiefships they received: even here it is striking how few of them were really senior.

[15] Although very little of the material I have used here is the product of my own fieldwork, its unravelling and interpretation certainly is. I acknowledge my indebtedness to the East African Institute of Social Research, and to the International African Institute, whose generosity made my fieldwork possible. I should add that in my fieldwork I gave little attention to the institutions of the pre-Christian era, and less to the working of the central government; on the matters discussed in this paper there may well be better informants in Buganda than any of those with whom I worked.

[16] I have outlined elsewhere (Southwold 1961: 1–2) my reasons for having more

faith in this history than one often has in oral tradition. Essentially, I find it hard to conceive how an account which can stand such intricate analysis could be a work of fiction. I would certainly concede that the first two kings are most probably largely legendary figures; and there is reason, inside or outside his narrative, for doubting the truth of some of Kaggwa's statements. However, I think it is fair to argue, especially when one remembers that at least the skeleton of the history is assuredly factual, that fictions are likely to be still more pregnant of custom than are facts.

[17] For instance, Kaggwa (1901 : 112) says that Muteesa I was chosen out of one hundred sons of his father, not counting young children. There would have been many more eligible princes if Muteesa's father, Ssuuna II, had not executed fifty-eight of his brothers (Kaggwa, 1901: 93). If the Baganda are right in asserting that earlier kings did not marry such large numbers of wives, there would presumably have been fewer princes.

[18] Kaggwa's account would imply, in my judgment, not less than a year later.

[19] Other than Kigala (K5) who abdicated in his son's favour, and Namugala (K24) who abdicated in his brother's—this of course is a different matter.

[20] In most cases it is impossible to determine whether the king's own mother was alive. When Ssemakookiro (K27) told his son Kamaanya he would succeed, he referred to the fact that his mother had been killed (Kaggwa, 1901 : 77); but in the light of the way Ssemakookiro's own mother had behaved (see p. 114), this may well be taken as the kind of exception which proves the rule.

[21] In a personal communication; her informant was Mr M. K. Kawalya Kaggwa, himself a former Katikkiro, and son of Sir Apolo Kaggwa.

[22] In reality, as Kaggwa well knew, they were of Elephant clan; but at this time this clan was in disfavour, and its members represented themselves as belonging to the Civet-cat clan.

[23] The election of Ssuuna II (K29) is technically an exception; but the clan concerned (Lungfish) is so large as to function rather as a coalition of clans, and the link between Katikkiro and prince was doubtless of minimal political significance. This clan in fact provided seven of the thirty Kabakas from Ccwa I to Mwanga II— and the first two Kabakas of the Christian era. Its large share of the total number of kings may be merely a direct function of its size—it is conceivable that as many as a quarter of all Baganda are members of this clan.

[24] Hence it is hardly likely that sons of the king not 'born in the purple' were excluded. In any event we learn from Kaggwa (1901: 77 and 83) that Kamaanya's (K28) son Nakibinge was born before his father's accession, yet was later killed by him because Kamaanya feared he 'wanted to eat the kingdom'.

[25] Roscoe's statement is imprecise, as he writes 'a king', not 'the late king'. His words could thus be interpreted as meaning that Princes of the Drum whose father never reigned were eligible only in the absence of any prince whose father had been king. This is refuted by the reigns of the three sons of Prince Musanje, the brother of Mawanda (K22). Of these, Mwanga I (K23) was a rebel, and Kyabaggu (K25) a rebel by sorcery; but Namugala (K24) was apparently peacefully elected. We know that Mawanda left sons, since two of them are described as fighting for the throne in Kyabaggu's reign, after having been invited to do so by Kyabaggu (Kaggwa, 1901 : 62). It may be inferred from this that they had not previously laid claim to the throne, although, on this interpretation of Roscoe's words, they would have had a title superior to that of their cousins. (Kiyimba, (K6) is another case of a grandson of a king succeeding in preference to a son of a king (his own father, Prince Wampamba). But— at least if we may suppose that his father's brothers were dead—this case does not bear on the point, as Wampamba is stated to have been passed over on account of having contracted an incestuous marriage.)

[26] This was essentially the choice of a personal successor to the name and

personality of the deceased, even though it is evident that he was going to receive the chiefship too; in general chiefships were permissively but not prescriptively heritable.

[27] The priests were typically *bataka*, between whom and the Kabaka I have already remarked (p. 85) that there was continuing opposition.

[28] Divided succession, as found in Busoga (Fallers 1956: 86) is fairly common in Buganda also; but this is the only instance in the record of royal successions. The facts of this case are probably sound, since, to this day, when a king succeeds, a prince of the line of Jjuma is chosen to succeed to the religious office of his ancestor.

[29] In the history of the dynasty of Turkish sultans (Alderson 1956: 10–11) we also find an initial period of filial successions, changing to a pattern of fraternal succession; and here too the change occurs when a sultan dies leaving only young sons. In view of the particular circumstances in each case, I hesitate to base conclusions on the coincidence, without knowledge of further parallel cases.

[30] I think their insistence derives from the belief that if the successor is publicly known in advance, murder will ensue.

[31] Kayima (K7) succeeded his father's brother Kiyimba, who apparently had no sons (Kaggwa, 1905: 31). As Mwanga I (K23) was a rebel, his case alone can hardly be taken as indicating a preference.

[32] After the arrangements that had been made to separate the mediumship from the kingship, Jjuma Kateebe would hardly have been allowed to reunite them by becoming King. Kaggwa (1905: 44) shows Jjuma as Tebandeke's only son; as Tebandeke had five wives and one hundred concubines, it requires an effort to believe this.

[33] Ccwa I was succeeded by his grandson Kimera, as his son was already dead; very likely his brothers were also dead by this time. But since in reality Kimera was almost certainly an invader from Bunyoro, and no descendant of Ccwa at all, it is not worth pursuing the subject.

[34] It was normal to execute any man who shed royal blood, even in the cause of a successful rebel. But if this had been all there was to it, Kaggwa would not have related in detail how the whole regiment responsible was hunted down for execution.

[35] The bite of the *mbwa* fly (*Simulium damnosum*) is very painful and transmits onchocerciasis; it used to infest the Mabira forest, and rendered it almost uninhabitable. Although Kaggwa (1901: 67) indicates Jjunju's homicidal intent, subjection to the *mbwa* flies was not the most certain or rapid means of killing a man.

[36] His predecessor was killed by his mother's brother; while this was not done in the interest of Namugala, it would probably not have been done at all if the kingdom could not have been transferred to another sister's son.

[37] One word, *mirembe*, means both 'a reign' of a king, and also 'peace'.

SUCCESSION TO THE CHIEFSHIP IN NORTHERN UNYAMWEZI

By R. G. ABRAHAMS

INTRODUCTION

The Nyamwezi[1] are a Bantu-speaking people whose country, Unyamwezi, nowadays consists of the Tabora and Nzega Districts and the eastern half of the Kahama District of west-central Tanzania.[2] They numbered 363,258 in the official census of 1957, and as such they are the second largest tribe in Tanzania, being smaller only than their very closely related northern neighbours the Sukuma. Most Nyamwezi live in Unyamwezi, which has an area of about 34,000 square miles, and they are for the most part both the politically dominant and the numerically preponderant tribe there. Members of many other tribes live in the area as subjects of the Nyamwezi chiefs. Sukuma, Sumbwa and Tusi form the largest of these 'foreign' elements in the population.

Most of the inhabitants of Unyamwezi are farmers, though some Tusi do not practise agriculture. Various staple crops are grown including maize, sorghum, bullrush millet and cassava. The year falls into two main seasons, a rainy season from around October until April and a dry season. The average rainfall is slightly under 35 inches per year, but rain is unpredictable from year to year and is often very poorly distributed. Much of the land is of poor quality. Various cash crops have been tried with little success, and for more than a century the people have sought wealth as porters, traders and labourers outside Unyamwezi. Cattle, though numerous, are mainly to be found in the Nzega district where there has been much Sukuma immigration. Sheep, goats and chickens are much more evenly distributed.

Unyamwezi is a multi-chiefdom area which has apparently never been politically united. It is divided among several distinct ruling dynasties, and most of these control a number of contemporary chiefdoms. The total number of chiefdoms has varied greatly from one period to another. In 1959 there were thirty-one, ranging in area from about 60 to 10,000 square miles, and in population from a few hundred to a little over 70,000 persons. Each chiefdom has its own ruling family and a chief who bears the title of *ntemi*.[3]

Towards the end of the German colonial period (1890–1916), and during the subsequent period of British rule, a more or less uniform pattern of patrilineal succession to the chiefship was followed throughout Unyamwezi. During the pre-colonial period, however, patrilineal succession to the chiefship was the rule in some parts of the country, and matrilineal succession to the office was the rule in other parts. In addition, traditional histories assert that some chiefdoms had changed over from a matrilineal system to a patrilineal one before the period of pre-colonial European contact (1857 and 1858–1890).

I shall not attempt to cover all these variations in this essay. Rather, I shall confine myself to an examination of past and present institutions and practices surrounding succession to the chiefship in some chiefdoms of the Kamba dynasty of northern Unyamwezi and what is today officially the south-west corner of Sukumaland. The Kamba chiefdoms practised matrilineal succession to the chiefship right through into German times, before adopting patrilineal succession to the office.

THE PRE-COLONIAL KAMBA CHIEFDOMS

There were eleven Kamba chiefdoms in 1959, but it is clear that this has not always been the case. Traditional historical accounts collected in different parts of the Kamba region agree that there was originally a single Kamba chiefdom, and that the present chiefdoms have resulted from a series of divisions of that former unit, tempered by occasional re-amalgamations. The accounts collected differ in some details but these do not appear to be significant in the present context.

According to a version collected in the present-day Ukamba chiefdom, Chief Nkumbi was the last single chief of the whole Kamba area.[4] His sister, Nyabakamba, gave birth to a son, and Nkumbi gave this child the southern and the eastern districts of his chiefdom. He is said to have done this partly out of gladness at the birth and partly because lion skins which came to him from these southern and eastern areas were rotten by the time they reached him. When this sister's son grew up, he himself divided out the country given to him by Nkumbi. He gave the chiefdoms of Nindo, Lohumbo, Mwangoye and Mwakarunde to four of his sister's sons and retained the present-day Kahama and Ukamba chiefdoms for himself. One of his successors later gave Kahama chiefdom to a grandchild.

These divisions occurred, according to genealogical data, some seven or eight generations before my oldest living informants, which would seem to place them some time in the eighteenth century. All the above chiefdoms were in existence when the Germans first took over the area, and the six southern and eastern units still exist today. The chiefdom which Nkumbi retained for himself was called Nsalala and was divided up in German times.[5]

There were, then, seven Kamba chiefdoms in the nineteenth century. Some picture of their internal organization before the coming of the Germans can be gleaned from a variety of data. Information can be abstracted from accounts

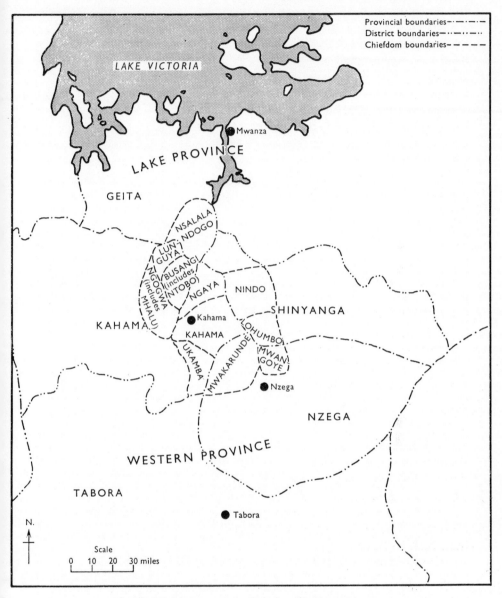

Fig. 9. Sketch map of the Kamba chiefdoms in 1959.

of the traditional history of ruling families, and this can be supplemented by more direct statements about particular aspects of past organization collected in interviews. There is also some material in the works of previous writers from Speke onwards. Finally, some inferences can be drawn from certain present institutions, which are found in similar form over a wide area and which seem unlikely to have spread simply during colonial times.

The interpretation of this material, however, poses certain problems. The latter half of the nineteenth century was, according to both European and indigenous sources, a period of political manoeuvring and conflict in the Kamba chiefdoms. On the other hand, it is clear from most accounts of this conflict that it was taking place within an institutional framework in which a major element was a rule of matrilineal succession to the chiefship, coupled with a rule of patrilineal succession to the headmanship of territorial divisions of the chiefdom. Moreover, when the nature of this framework is elaborated by informants, there emerges a picture of a system which in many ways appears to be geared, albeit unsuccessfully, to the prevention of the sort of strife which typifies this period. It is difficult to say for certain just how real this picture of the institutional framework is, although the detail into which informants enter on occasion, and the similarity to material collected in neighbouring areas are among the factors in its favour.[6] A second question is whether there was ever a period of Kamba history in which actual behaviour closely coincided with the rules which this framework embodies. If such a period existed, it must definitely be placed before the coming of the first Europeans (1858), and possibly before the coming of the Arabs to the area (c. 1820–30). Political conflict in the latter half of the nineteenth century, however, seems to have been connected with developments engendered from outside the area, and particularly the development of large-scale trading. To this extent, I believe it probable that early Kamba political organization fitted the ideal more closely.

The main elements of the institutional framework appear to have been as follows. At the head of the chiefdom was a chief, *ntemi*, whose office was succeeded to matrilineally. Succession was not confined to a single matrilineal line. Female matrilineal kin of chiefs, including classificatory mothers and their daughters, were called *batemi kazi*, and a child of any of these women was apparently eligible to rule. The chiefs themselves were always men.

The chief was ritual guardian of his chiefdom. There was felt to be an intimate connexion between his person and the well-being of the chiefdom Good rains, bountiful crops and victory in war were all considered to depend upon him, and a series of ceremonies in which he played a leading part existed to ensure these benefits. Some say that in time of drought the chief was beaten till he cried, so that his tears might cause the rain to fall. One chief is said to have abdicated when he saw his rule was not blessed with good rains. The person of the chief was carefully guarded and he seems not to have travelled beyond the borders of his chiefdom. If he was ill and seemed unlikely to recover, he is said to have been strangled by the ritual elders of the chiefdom in collusion with his great wife.

The chief had few administrative duties beyond the settling of disputes in his own immediate vicinity. The main administrators, and also the leading warriors, were the greater headmen who controlled the major territorial subdivisions of the chiefdom. The large majority of greater headmen were patrilineal descendants of chiefs. The others were descendants of the rulers of formerly independent units which now lay within Kamba territory. Those headmen who were sons of chiefs were called *banangwa*, and the sons of these were known as *bizukulu* which is the ordinary word for grandchild. The sons of *bizukulu* were again *banangwa* and so on. Under the greater headmen there were lesser headmen, and some of these were also patrilineal descendants of chiefs. Other lesser headmen were those men, and their descendants, who had been the first to clear bush in a particular area. Matrilineal descendants of chiefs did not, it seems, hold headmanships.

Annual meetings between the chief and greater headmen are said to have taken place. At these meetings the affairs of the chiefdom were discussed, laws were made, and edicts issued for the coming year. At the same time headmen brought the chief a portion of the tribute which they had collected from their subjects. Similarly they brought a portion of the fines they had exacted and a part of any booty they had gained in warfare. Chiefly generosity was highly valued, however, and the chief was not expected simply to reserve his wealth for his own use.

The existence of ritual officers in the chiefdom has already been mentioned. The main body of these were known as 'men of the chief's court' (*banyikulu*). These men were always slaves or their descendants. They formed the chief's bodyguard, helped him in his ceremonial and other duties, and looked after the sacred objects and regalia of chiefship. It was they who strangled a sick chief, and they also played a major role in burying him and in installing his successor. In addition to the *banyikulu*, each chiefdom had a ritual officer known as the *ngabe*. His office was held by a patrilineal kin group of non-royal descent, and his most important duty was to supervise the process of succession to the chiefship. Apart from these permanently established ritual officials, there was the office of *kitunga* which was held only when a new chief was to be installed. The *kitunga* tied on the regalia of the chief and his main wives in preparation for the installation and he was banished from the chiefdom after the ceremony.

When a chief died, his successor was chosen in a divination which was conducted by the ritual elders and the greater headmen of the chiefdom. The interregnum was supposed to be a closely guarded secret, and the death of the chief was only spoken of in euphemistic terms by those who knew of it. The chosen successor was ideally unaware of the death of his predecessor until he himself was seized and taken to the initiation chamber. A story which is often told in this context emphasizes this point strongly. It relates how Nsabi, a chief of Nsalala who reigned in the mid-nineteenth century, was originally living outside Nsalala in the neighbouring non-Kamba chiefdom of Mbogwe where his mother had been married. At the time of his succession, ritual elders went at night to seize him, and he did not know what was happening until the rituals of installation had begun.

Such, then, were apparently the main features of the institutional framework of the pre-colonial Kamba chiefdoms. Considered as a system *in abstracto*, it displays a neat division of labour and appears to be designed to ensure the peaceful and unimpeded continuity of chiefly office. By virtue of his annual meetings with his headmen, the chief can be considered as the central point of the administrative and economic life of his chiefdom. He was also the ritual figure-head and guardian of the country, and its well-being was embodied in his person. Most of the day-to-day administration of the chiefdom, and the more practical aspects of warfare, were in the hands of greater headmen and their territorial subordinates. Ailing chiefs were killed, and their successors were chosen secretly by ritual elders and the greater headmen, who were themselves ineligible to succeed. The need for a successor was not known to eligible candidates, and these did not hold territorial office in the chiefdom.

Let us now turn to consider actual behaviour in the latter half of the nineteenth century. Speke, who was the first European to visit this part of Unyamwezi, passed through Nsalala in the course of his famous visit to Lake Victoria in 1858. He tells us that the country was in a state of war involving various 'sultans' who were fighting over their father's estate, but he makes no mention of an overall chief of the country (1864: 285, 288 and *passim*). These 'sultans' seem to have been greater headmen. I have not been able to identify the particular dispute in question, but traditional accounts collected in the field make numerous references to the sorry state of chiefship in this period of the nineteenth century, and relate how various greater headmen, including the ruler of Ngogwa whom Speke met, quarrelled and fought with one another on a number of occasions. Sometimes they fought when one tried to extend his territories at the expense of another, and they are also said to have fought about which of the various eligible sister's sons should hold the chiefship. It is further related how, in the course of expanding his domain, one greater headman even drove the chief away from his own headquarters and forced him to seek sanctuary in another part of the chiefdom. As far as I can ascertain, such internecine disputes in Nsalala reached an unprecedented frequency and intensity during the reign of chief Nsabi, mentioned above, and it is interesting that a young boy, Gagi, was eventually installed as his successor.[7]

Writing at the end of the nineteenth century, Desoignies confirms the weakness of the Nsalala chief's position, although he probably overestimates the power of earlier chiefs (1903: 277). 'Kingly office has become only a name' he writes. 'A certain number of headmen (*Häuptlinge*) have made themselves independent of the chief (*König*) or *ntemi*, and they have become much more powerful than him. Those great headmen have a number of vassals under them, who obey them blindly and have therefore left the chief without support. He no longer possesses any authority at all.' He goes on to say that each of these headmen rules his own district quite independently (*willkürlich*) and that the only time when all the headmen come together is when a new chief has to be chosen. This is, of course, in contrast to the annual meetings, noted earlier, at which the headmen were supposed to bring their tribute to the chief and arrange with him a common policy for governing the chiefdom in the coming year.

A comparable situation seems to have obtained in the Kahama chiefdom. The following account describes the events there in the period preceding German occupation of the country.[8]

When Ntemi Shilinde died, Ntemi Zelele, his brother through his mother, ruled... This Ntemi Zelele was driven out by Mwanangwa Nkandi...When Zelele was deposed, Nkandi installed Ntemi Nkola who was his father's elder brother...This Ntemi Nkola was similarly driven out by Mwanangwa Nkandi who took Nkola's sister's son Kuhenga and installed him as chief. Ntemi Kuhenga only ruled the western part of Kahama. In eastern Kahama there arose a warrior headman called Magulu who took Machibya, one of those eligible to be chief, and installed him. Now the one country had two chiefs...A great war arose. Mwanangwa Nkandi fought to have his chief and so did Mwanangwa Magulu...Neither side was able to defeat the other...Then in western Kahama Nkandi became ill and in accordance with our traditional custom the diviners were consulted. They revealed that Ntemi Kuhenga was the witch. Ntemi Kuhenga was seized by Kishimba, the son of Nkandi, and was tortured with rope because of his witchcraft. The rope killed him. After recovering, Mwanangwa Nkandi installed another chief, Ntemi Kadundu, and he likewise became chief of western Kahama. Nor did the war between the headmen finish...There arose a war against another chiefdom...Kishimba the son of Nkandi was killed (in this war)...and Ntemi Kadundu was deposed as a witch. It was said that his medicine caused the son of Nkandi to be slain by his enemies. Then Nkandi sought another man in accordance with the custom of the land of installing as chiefs the children of women, the sister's sons of the country. Thus Kalima ruled and became chief of western Kahama...(Eventually) Mwanangwa Nkandi and Mwanangwa Magulu came to an agreement, and this was at the time when the Germans entered the country. These two headmen resolved to remove these two chiefs, and Ntemi Machibya and Ntemi Kalima were both deprived of their regalia. The two headmen decided to instal a single chief and they went to seek out Sawasawa that he might become chief. Ntemi Sawasawa became chief of all Kahama.

It appears then that greater headmen in the Nsalala and Kahama chiefdoms felt it worth their while in the latter half of the nineteenth century to try by violence to extend their territorial influence and control succession to the chiefship. I do not have sufficient data to say at present just how typical this situation was for all the other Kamba chiefdoms. A similar situation is said to have existed in some of them, but in others, and particularly the most southern units, the chiefs themselves seem to have obtained rather greater power than that enjoyed by their Nsalala and Kahama counterparts. A second point which is not clear from the information at my disposal is exactly what the greater headmen sought to gain from their activities, apart from power in a very general sense. Further inquiries are clearly needed on these points. Some tentative suggestions on this second question may, however, be made here.

The Kamba chiefdoms never felt the full impact of the entry of the Arabs into Unyamwezi.[9] Nevertheless, Arab caravans did pass through the area, and Speke mentions an attempt to enlist Arab help, and a plan to make further use of it, in the Nsalala dispute he encountered (1864: 288, 354). It is also clear that a considerable amount of indigenous trading was taking place at this time. Speke records that Kulwa, the greater headman of Ngogwa, had trading interests in Karagwe to the west and in 'the northern kingdoms' and he also met a number of native caravans on his way to Lake Victoria (1864: 268, 271, 273, 350, 356). Large scale Nyamwezi and Sumbwa expeditions to the coast were made at this time.[10] The overall result seems to have been that new forms of storable wealth, especially cloth and later guns, became available in considerable quantities in the region. Warfare, raiding, trading and the taxation of caravans offered greater rewards than ever before, and I suggest that it was competition for the fruits of such activities which led to fighting between greater headmen and to their desire to control the chiefship. The chief, at least in theory, was the recipient of tribute and other forms of wealth from all parts of his chiefdom, and it would seem to have been to the advantage of headmen to be able to control, and perhaps in some cases to further, his activities in this respect.

THE PERIOD OF GERMAN ADMINISTRATION

The above discussion brings us to the period of German rule. The German colony of East Africa was established under the Anglo-German Agreement of 1890, and in Unyamwezi as elsewhere the Germans were faced with two basic problems. They had to pacify the country and they needed to set up a satisfactory system of administration.

Unyamwezi was pacified by 1893. The only serious opposition to the Germans was in the Tabora area where Isike, the chief of Unyanyembe, fought and lost an eight months' war against them. The Kamba chiefdoms appear to have presented no problems in this respect.

Contrary to their general policy in East Africa, the Germans adopted a form of indirect rule in Unyamwezi. A similar policy was adopted among the Sukuma and the Haya.[11] Many indigenous chiefs were recognized by the

Administration, and the main mark of such recognition was the giving out of large account books in which the chiefs had to keep a record of the fines and taxes they exacted. Some ruling families still possess these books.

In many cases, however, such books were also given to people who were not legitimately independent rulers in the indigenous organization. In the Uyui chiefdom in Tabora District, for example, the Germans gave a book to the chief, but they also gave one to the ruler of a subdivision of the chiefdom and recognized him as an independent chief. The number of Nyamwezi chiefdoms was considerably increased by such actions. In the Kamba area, Nsalala was divided over a period of years into eight new chiefdoms. These were Busangi, Bunakoba, Lunguya, Mhalu, Ngaya, Ngogwa, Nsalala Ndogo and Ntobo. Busangi, the chief's headquarters, was left under the control of the chief himself. The other units were held by former greater headmen of the chiefdom. Each of the eight chiefs was given a book, and it was only later, in some cases not until the early years of British rule, that all of them obtained traditional regalia. In Kahama chiefdom, Nkandi was made chief of the western half of the country, only the eastern portion being left in Sawasawa's hands.

In addition to these changes, the Germans introduced patrilineal succession to the chiefship as the general rule in the Kamba area. The notion of the sons of chiefs succeeding to the chiefship, as opposed to holding headmanships within a chiefdom, is said to have at first caused consternation to many subjects living in the Kamba chiefdoms. For they feared that the country would be struck by drought. Chiefs' sons themselves, however, appear to have welcomed the change.

The change to patrilineal succession to the chiefship brought the Kamba chiefdoms in line with other parts of Unyamwezi. Although a patrilineal system was perhaps more easily intelligible to the Germans, its adoption in the Kamba area seems also to have been consistent with their attitude to chiefship. For the Germans, the main functions of chiefs were the maintenance of law and order in their chiefdoms and the efficient collection of taxes. Sons of chiefs, in their capacity as headmen, were often more experienced in such matters than were sister's sons. Similar arguments apply, moreover, to the German recognition of such rulers as the Nsalala greater headmen, in so much as they had been the main administrators in the former chiefdom.

Under the Germans, then, there was a further increase in the number of Kamba chiefdoms, and patrilineal succession to the chiefship was adopted. The chiefship became established as the most important administrative office in the chiefdom, though it may be mentioned here that the office has never fully lost its ritual connotations. It should be added that chiefs were now largely the agents of the Central Government, and their holding office was dependent on the good will of that Government. It is significant here that it was more important for a chief to hold a book than to possess traditional regalia. If the chiefs carried out their duties satisfactorily, they were supported by the Germans. If they failed to do so, they were subject to dismissal, and a number of chiefs were in fact deposed for such failure.

THE PERIOD OF BRITISH ADMINISTRATION

By the time the Germans were driven out of Unyamwezi in 1916, succession to the chiefship followed patrilineal lines in all parts of the country. This pattern was maintained under the British. Succession has with few exceptions been confined within a narrow group of agnates, and in most cases the successors have been sons of former chiefs.

The British formally took over the administration of Unyamwezi in 1919, and like the Germans they have used indigenous rulers as administrative agents in the area. This was at first done on an *ad hoc* basis. By 1929, however, a number of Ordinances had been passed implementing the well-known policy of Indirect Rule throughout Tanganyika. Through these and later Ordinances, Nyamwezi chiefs and their chiefdoms have obtained a legally recognized position in the administration of the region. A system of popular election of chiefs from a number of eligible candidates has also been introduced.

In order to improve administrative efficiency, the British have made various efforts to reduce the number of Nyamwezi chiefdoms. They have also tried to ensure that suitable persons, from their point of view, should hold the chiefship. They prefer that chiefly successors should be literate and have experience of clerical or administrative work. It is worth mentioning in this respect that Tabora School was originally founded in 1925 as a school for sons of chiefs. Many chief's sons have also been given work as court clerks or as minor officials in various governmental departments. What is of particular interest in the present context, however, is that the British have occasionally been led to the manipulation of periods of interregnum in the Nyamwezi area in the pursuit of their aims of reducing the number of chiefdoms and obtaining suitable successors to the chiefship. Two examples taken from the Kamba region may serve to illustrate this point.

As has been mentioned earlier, the greater headmanship of Mhalu in the old chiefdom of Nsalala became an independent unit during German times. In the early years of British administration the ruler of Mhalu died leaving three young sons. The ritual officers of the chiefdom wished to instal Mashimba, the eldest of these sons, as chief. The British, however, decided that the boy was too young to rule, and they put the chiefdom under the 'temporary' control of the neighbouring chief of Ngogwa chiefdom which had also been a greater headmanship. When Mashimba grew older, another attempt was made from within Mhalu to instal him as chief. This time it was decided by Government that the burdens of chiefship were too heavy for an

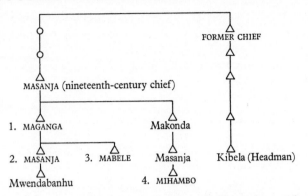

Fig. 10. Genealogy of a Kamba chiefship. Numbers show order of chiefs after the change to patrilineal succession.

untrained youth and that he should therefore first obtain some suitable experience. To this end he was given work as a court clerk in the nearby chiefdom of Kahama.

In 1935 Mashimba died in a car accident. Up till this point, Government had always said Mhalu would again become an independent chiefdom. From the death of Mashimba onwards, however, they took the standpoint that Mhalu was a part of Ngogwa and would remain so. Attempts to alter this state of affairs by the younger sons of the late chief have gone on steadily since their elder brother's death, but without success. Finally in 1959 a compromise was reached and one of them was made the headman of a section of his father's former chiefdom. The area is part of Ngogwa for once and all.

The second example is a more recent one from another Kamba chiefdom. Figure 10 is useful here.

In the late 1940s Chief Mabele was deposed by the Administration and a successor was sought. Public opinion in the chiefdom was apparently at first divided between two main candidates. The first of these was Mwendabanhu, a young son of Mabele's elder brother and predecessor in office. The second was Kibela, a rather old headman who was only distantly related to the ruling line of chiefs. After a time, popular support became concentrated upon the young Mwendabanhu. The District Commissioner, however, is said to have been keen to have someone who had worked in a Government Department, and he had heard from Mabele that Mihambo was an employee of such a department and was also eligible to rule. According to my information, he overruled the popular choice by telling people that Mwendabanhu was too young, and he asked them who was eligible and at the same time had experience of work for a Government Department. Eventually Mihambo was mentioned, and the District Commissioner is said to have asked why they had not mentioned him before. He was told that they had thought that

Mihambo would not be willing to leave his Government work. The District Commissioner is then alleged to have told the people that Mihambo was in fact willing to become chief and, having convinced them of this, to have set about convincing Mihambo to give up his work and take the office. Shortly afterwards, Mihambo was installed as chief.

THE INSTALLATION CEREMONIES

So far in this paper, I have concentrated on the description of developments and changes which have taken place in the system of succession to the chiefship in the Kamba chiefdoms. It would be mistaken, however, to conclude from this that the history of chiefly succession in the area was in all respects a history of change. I mentioned earlier that certain present institutions are found in similar form over a wide area and seem unlikely to have spread simply during colonial times. For our present purposes, the most important of these comparatively stable institutions are the actual installation ceremonies of chiefs.[12] The following account of the installation of a Kamba chief in 1941 will illustrate the form of these ceremonies.

On the evening prior to his public installation, the chief was seized by two of the ritual elders of the chiefdom and was taken inside the initiation house (*itindikilo*). The ritual elders enveloped him in a lion skin when seizing him, and beat him with sticks. He spent the night inside the initiation house along with his two main wives (*nyihanga* and *nyihojo*). Also present were the ritual elders and some diviners, and with them was a small black dog with a patch of light hair above each eye. Such a dog is called a 'four-eyed dog' (*iwa lya miso anne*).[13]

While in the initiation house, the chief and his two wives were given various instructions by the ritual elders. They were told never to eat zebra, giraffe, guinea fowl, spurfowl, the greater ant-eater, and wild pig nor were they to allow these creatures within the royal residence. Most of them are spotted or striped and are symbolically associated with leprosy by the people. The chief and his wives were also told not to have sexual intercourse in the open nor to eat at night or inside their huts. They should eat outside so that others might eat with them. They were forbidden to have anything to do with sorcery, and they were told to be very careful where they spat or urinated. They were warned not to see the *kitunga* after the ceremonies, though in this case he was not banished from the chiefdom. The *kitunga*, it will be recalled, tied on the regalia of the chief and his wives for the installation. The two wives were instructed to keep secret anything they saw or heard in the royal household.

During the night the diviners were busy preparing medicines for the installation, and in the early morning the ritual elders prepared new straps for the regalia of the chief and his wives. Those of the chief and of the senior wife were of lion skin. Those of the junior wife were of cow skin. When this work was completed, the chief and his wives were seated upon the royal stools and, having had their heads shaved, they were invested with their various regalia by the *kitunga*.

At about 4 p.m. they were taken out for the public part of the ceremonies which is called *wanila*. A space for this had already been prepared and the royal drums had been set up there. Since the death of the previous chief, the striking of these drums had been forbidden. The procession from the initiation house was led by one of the ritual elders, since at this time the chiefdom had no *ngabe*. The chief wore his regalia and carried a variety of royal objects including a bow, a spear, a shield and a lynx skin. The main wife carried a wooden spoon. The stools, a tray with millet on it, some gourds and a basket-work cup were carried by the ritual elders. The substitute *ngabe* carried a metal-shafted spear to which was attached a bell, and as he walked he sang repetitively *Kamunhenga, ng'wize wilolelwe* which means 'Come out and be seen, *kamunhenga*', this being the name of a pretty, little bird.[14] The royal drums were now being beaten and a large crowd followed the procession. Women in the crowd threw millet on the chief and his wives.

On arrival at the prepared space, the chief and his wives were seated on the stools. The drums were silenced and the acting *ngabe* took a new gourd and split it over the heads of the chief and his wives. As he did so he warned the chief that if he did not act carefully, his chiefdom would be split as the gourd had been. The chief, he said, had no father or mother; all, even these, were his children. He should not hesitate to share his food with any of his subjects. He should be just in court, neither favouring the rich nor mal-treating the poor. The prosperity of the land was in his hands and he must follow the customs of his predecessors. He should be ever mindful of his subjects and respect them.

The speaker then turned to the subjects who were assembled there and told them to help and respect their chief. He then announced a new name for the chief. During the course of these speeches, a mixture of millet and water had been prepared in the basket-work cup and the speaker now spat it upon the chief and his wives in blessing. This is a form of blessing which recurs throughout Nyamwezi ritual. Then a neighbouring chief who had been invited to the installation made a similar speech to the crowd, and gave a further name to the chief.

When the speeches and the naming were completed, the subjects came forward to greet their new chief and give him gifts. The royal drums were beaten once again, and the chief and his wives retired to their house to rest while their subjects danced outside. Later on, the three of them returned to watch the celebrations.

The final event of the installation ceremonies was the kindling of fire by rubbing sticks together. Before the subjects came to the installation all fire had been extinguished in the chiefdom. Now on their return to their homes the new fire was taken with them. In this way the commencement of a new reign was symbolized throughout the chiefdom.

Such then are the actual ceremonies of installation. Their comparative stability through time appears to have been due to a variety of factors. One of these is that control of the ceremonies has been kept in the hands of the ritual officials of the chiefdom. It may be pointed out that these men are in many ways the centre of conservatism in a chiefdom. They tend to be men of little or no education in the Western sense, and Government exerts no economic influence upon them since they receive no official payment for their work. Moreover, the very nature of their duties as guardians of the royal relics and as experts in traditional ritual encourages their interest in the past.

In addition, it seems clear that the installation ceremonies traditionally served functions which are still meaningful today. One of these, as has been seen by Beattie (1959: 108–9) and Cory (1951: 5) is the need for ceremonial to mark off as chief a person who was, until his accession, merely one of a number of eligible candidates for chiefly office. Secondly, the ceremonies serve to point out in their admonitions to both chief and subjects the existence of an interdependence between them which, although its content has been modified, has apparently always been a major feature of chief-subject relationships.

CONCLUSION

In this paper I have tried to survey some of the changes and continuities in chiefly succession in the Nyamwezi Kamba chiefdoms during the last hundred or so years. These changes and continuities are, I believe, important indices of certain developments which have taken place in the form of the chiefship itself. I have suggested that the struggles of the Kamba headmen to control succession to the chiefship in the latter half of the nineteenth century were connected with changes in the economic potentialities of the office. Further, there appear to be clear links between the new functions of the chiefship in a colonial setting and the modifications in succession practices introduced by the German and British Administrations. I have also argued that a major reason why the installation ceremonies have remained comparatively stable amid all this change is that they are still meaningful today and represent realities which are common to both modern and traditional chiefship. I will merely add here that the interstitial position of Nyamwezi and other African chiefs between forces for continuity and change is neatly encapsulated in the need for a chiefly successor, chosen largely for his literacy and experience in modern government, to pass through a traditional installation ceremony controlled by the most conservative elements in the chiefdom.

That all this should be the case is not, of course, surprising. Processes through time, whether they be ones of change, growth or continuity, are not simple, uniform phenomena involving smooth movement along an undifferentiated path. Rather, it appears that certain points in their progress are more critical and influential than others. In the progress of an office through time, the succession of a new incumbent is such a critical and influential point. As such, one may expect that the alteration or maintenance of the system of succession will be intimately connected with the form the office takes through time.

NOTES

[1] I carried out fieldwork in Unyamwezi between October 1957 and February 1960 as a Junior Research Fellow of the East African Institute of Social Research. The present tense in this essay should be taken as referring to the period of fieldwork. In the second case discussed on pp. 137–8 the names of the actors have been changed.

[2] This definition of Unyamwezi is the most convenient for the discussion of modern political organization but, as will be seen, it is a little too rigid for discussion of the past.

[3] Throughout this essay, I use the term 'chief' to refer to the ruler of an independent chiefdom. I refer to his subordinate territorial office-holders as 'headmen'.

[4] This version of Kamba history was written about 1927 in Swahili by the then chief of Ukamba. It was in the possession of the present chief.

[5] Some features of present-day inter-chiefdom behaviour lend support to these stories. Thus, Busangi chiefdom, which is the direct continuation of Nsalala chiefdom, is still in some ways considered as the ritual centre of the Kamba area. Replacements of lost or damaged regalia should be obtained from there, and in 1959 ritual officers of Nindo chiefdom went there to ask for such a replacement.

[6] Cory (1951) gives a comparable picture for some non-Kamba matrilineal chiefdoms of Sukumaland.

[7] The missionary Hannington met the young Gagi in 1883 (Dawson 1888: 237).

[8] This is taken from the Ukamba version of Kamba history noted above and it appears to be generally accurate.

[9] The Arabs were most influential in the south and central areas of Unyamwezi. For a picture of their impact there see *inter alia* Stanley (1872), Cameron (1877), Whiteley including Smith (1959), Bennett (1963) and Smith (1963).

[10] Cf. Burton (1860: I, 341–2 and *passim*), Krapf (1860: 420–1), and the writers noted in note 9. According to material quoted by Gray (1957: 245–6), Nyamwezi profits from this caravan trade increased considerably towards the middle of the nineteenth century.

[11] Cf. Eberlie, R. F. 'German Achievement in East Africa,' *Tanganyika Notes and Records*, 55, 1960, 191 and *passim*).

[12] A comparison of my material with the account in Cory (1951: 13–28) reveals the strong similarity between the Kamba ceremonies and those said to have existed in the chiefdoms of the Siha dynasty in Shinyanga District. See, too, the account in Bösch (1930: 494–500). In a comparison of past and present installation ceremonies in the Mwanza District of Sukumaland, Tanner (1957: 207) also points out the considerable degree of continuity to be found there.

[13] According to Bösch (1930: 498), such a dog represents the hunting ancestry of Nyamwezi ruling families. I myself did not encounter this idea in the field.

[14] Cf. Cory (1951: 24).

CIRCULATING SUCCESSION AMONG THE GONJA

By JACK GOODY

INTRODUCTION

The history of monarchy is stained with the blood of close kin. In southern Africa, the great Zulu chief, Shaka, was assassinated by his brother Dingane. In the Near East the Turkish sultans, fearing their brothers as rivals, killed them upon taking office. Nor are these dynastic conflicts found only in African kingdoms and among oriental invaders from the Asian steppes. They are equally characteristic of European history. Such was the story of monarchy among the Franks. And, yet nearer home, the tales of the princes in the Tower, of Richard and John, bear witness to the constant struggles among close kin for the highest office in the realm.

Gonja political theory presents us with a type of succession directly opposed to that with which we are familiar in the monarchical régimes of Europe, or indeed in most of eastern and southern Africa. Important offices are handed down not between close kinfolk, but between distant members of the dynasty representing different segments of the ruling estate. Consequently the whole of the dynasty, which is a large one at that, is directly concerned in filling the main offices of state.

Political practice does not of course always accord with the theory. I know of no way to measure the gap between the two, the degree of correspondence between the 'ideal' and the 'actual'. But in Gonja the ideology of circulating succession certainly exercises a powerful influence on the process of selecting the holders of office. In this paper I want to sketch the way in which succession works, to analyse the variables involved in this and other circulating systems and to spell out some of the correlates and consequences for the social system.[1]

Immediately to the north of Ashanti, beyond where the Black Volta river cuts eastwards across the state of Ghana, lies the kingdom of Gonja.

Compared to the country to the south, it is a land with poor soil and few resources. This poverty is reflected in the low density of the population; even in 1960 there were only some 85,000 people in an area of about 200 miles across and up to 100 miles from north to south, that is, less than 6 persons a square mile. These inhabitants live in small compact villages of up to three hundred people, separated from the next settlement by anything from 10 to 15 miles. In addition there are some larger townships, which were formerly important centres involved in the trade of kola and gold that led from Ashanti in the south to the Hausa states in the north-east, to the Mande kingdoms in the north-west and to the Mossi empire in the north.

It was down these trade routes from the Mande area that the ruling dynasty of the Gonja kingdom claim to have come. These invaders, mounted on horse-back, conquered the area between the Black Volta and the Togo hills where dwelt a number of small tribes speaking a variety of Guang and Voltaic languages and possibly under the loose hegemony of the Dagomba-Mamprusi group of states. Assisting the Gonja in their wars by mystical means were a number of Moslems of Mande origin. And also drawn along in the to and fro of war were other groups of commoners and slaves who were to settle in the conquered lands alongside the earlier autochthones.

The Gonja probably first settled in the Banda-Techiman area to the north-west of what later became Ashanti some time in the sixteenth century. From here they moved north to establish the state of Gonja, although this was at first more to the south than at present. They were forced north by attacks from the Akan peoples and in 1744 an Ashanti expedition crossed eastern Gonja and reached Dagomba. From then until the British entered Kumasi in 1874, eastern Gonja at any rate was tributary to the Ashanti. But the traffic was not all one way. An uneasy reciprocity existed in that the Ashanti needed the Gonja markets as an outlet for their produce, although the relationship was often interrupted by raids or by wars.

THE SOCIAL ESTATES

This sketchy outline of Gonja history indicates the major groups in the society. These were:

(i)   the ruling estate;
(ii) the 'Gonja' Moslems;
(iii) the commoners;
(iv) the slaves;
(v)   the strangers.

All the ruling element of Gonja claim to be affiliated through males to the conqueror of the country, Sumailia Ndewura Jakpa. In his wars of conquest, Jakpa enlisted the services of a Moslem priest by whose supernatural powers he was enabled to defeat his enemies and seize the whole land of Gonja. Most of the important Imams (*Limami*) of the country, the Moslem priests attached to the main divisions, are descendants of this man, Fatu Morukpe, also known as Mohammed Labayiru, The White One. At major ceremonies, which are largely Moslem in character, chiefs and Moslems (*Karamo*) each have distinct tasks, but their joint participation is necessary for a successful outcome. The ruling estate is fully aware that the well-being of their kingdom depends partly upon its ritual practitioners, whilst the Moslems fully recognize the political role played by the chiefs. A chief, however, could not be a wholehearted Moslem; [2] and the Moslems declare they want no part in chiefship.

The Moslem estate consists of those groups traditionally associated with the ruling dynasty who fill the post of divisional Imam; the wider Moslem community includes most of those living in the strangers' quarters of the trading towns, as well as some slaves (in the past), and converts from other estates.

The commoner estate (*Nyamasi*) consists of both the autochthones and of groups who came as followers, as refugees and recently as farmers in search of new land. The newer immigrants, mainly LoDagaa in the west and Konkomba in the east, hold no special roles in the social system; the refugee groups are often owners of medicine shrines (*agbirwura*); the autochthones have the priesthood of the Earth (the *kasaweliwura* of the Gonja, *tendaana* of the Dagomba, or *heoheng* of the Vagala); and all groups may provide leaders in war (*mbongwura*).

Chief and *tendaana* are not the complementary roles they are among the Tallensi. Indeed it will be apparent from my analysis of the role of the Earth priest among the LoDagaa (Goody 1956, 1957) that his importance in acephalous systems is heavily bound up with social control and must inevitably suffer a thorough transformation in a centralized state. In Gonja, the Earth priest plays a comparatively minor part. More significant are the other plebeian roles of war-leader and diviner; certain types of divination are carried out only by the autochthones, others by the Moslems. The plebs are usually considered to have more powerful 'medicines' than the other estates. In fact all are well supplied.

Many commoners and Moslems have come from other parts, settled among the Gonja and become identified with them. But in the main trading towns, Salaga in the east and Bole in the west, there are a number of stranger groups who, though they are mostly permanent residents, remain peripheral to the political system. On the other hand, members of these groups were the main props of the long-distance trade on which the national economy largely depended. Since Gonja trade was latterly mainly along the north-eastern route, these groups are largely Hausa speaking; in Salaga, this is the first language of many of the inhabitants.[3]

Lastly, there was the slave population, which was particularly important in the farm villages around the big market town of Salaga. Slaves were part of the annual tribute the Gonja paid to the Ashanti, and they were obtained by raiding acephalous groups to the north and east. But they also played a significant part in the productive system in many parts of the country.

In the remainder of this paper I shall be concerned only with the patricians themselves. The ruling estate refers to itself collectively as *Ngbanya* (alt.

Ngbanbi, Ngbanyabi). In its widest application, the name includes all members of the nation; and the word Gonja (which I use to denote the state and its inhabitants as a whole) is merely the Hausa form which has been adopted by most outsiders.[4] However, applied internally, the name *Ngbanya* (or Gbanya) differentiates the rulers from the ruled and isolates that group in which chiefship (*kowura*) is vested from the remainder of the population. Indeed the members of this group also speak of themselves collectively as *Mbiwurbi*, Sons of Chiefs, Princes. Although not every individual among them is the offspring of a chief in the sense of the holder of a specific title, all are descendants of the conqueror Jakpa and all are eligible for the highest office in the land, that of *Yagbum Wura*; in eastern Gonja they are known as *ewura-jipo*, 'those who become chiefs'. For among the *Ngbanya*, as in the Napoleonic Army, Soviet Russia and the United States of America, universal access to supreme office is part of the accepted myth of the group, each member of which has the carrot of paramountcy dangled before his eyes. Among the Gonja, the relevant group is only a section of the total population; on the other hand, attainment of paramountcy is a somewhat more practical proposition.

CHIEFLY TITLES

I have said that only the ruling estate has access to chiefship and the Gonja themselves speak of chiefship in this way. But the statement raises problems of definition which concern the study of most other political systems. For in fact the Gonja apply the word *wura*, chief or leader, to ritual officiants, such as Earth priests, *kasaweliwura*, to compound heads, *langwura*, and to the paramount chief himself, the *YagbumWura*. The patrician estate has access not to leadership in all its various forms, but to a special series of titles at the head of which stands the paramountcy itself.

Not all of these titles are offices in the sense of carrying specific duties or having authority over a particular set of human beings.[5] Some chiefships bear the name of deserted villages, and today a number of these titles lie vacant, waiting for a candidate who meets the approval of the divisional chief and his own dynastic segment. Formerly, no doubt, such vacancies were rarer, but the continuation of titles bearing the names of dead villages gives the chiefs of divisions and of lesser segments some room for manoeuvre. But whether titles in the dynastic series are attached to specific offices or diffuse roles, the holders are equally eligible for higher office.

There are three types of chiefly title among the Gonja. There are the titles allocated to plebs in their own right, which I call chiefships of the third rank. Although these incorporate the suffix *wura*, members of the ruling estate will sometimes differentiate them from chiefships proper and speak of the incumbents as 'councillors' (*begbangpo*). These chiefs are representatives of the plebs, often with specific ritual and courtly roles, and become especially important at the funerals and enrobements of chiefs of the first rank.

Secondly, there are a number of chiefships available to the offspring of women of the ruling estate, regardless of the paternal filiation of the children. Some of these second-ranking title-holders are plebs, others are members of the ruling estate living in their maternal rather than their paternal divisions. Like third-ranking chiefs, such men play an important part at critical junctures in the political system, at interregna and in dynastic disputes; knowing that a 'sister's son chief' cannot succeed to his office, a divisional ruler can freely employ such a man as a personal adviser.[6] Because they constitute no threat to the divisional ruler, chiefs of the second and third rank often have precedence over those of the first rank.

Finally, there is the category of full-ranking chiefships which are in principle reserved for those descended in the male line from the conquering hero, Jakpa. Only these chiefs, who partake of chiefship proper, are eligible for promotion to senior offices, the highest of which is the paramountcy itself. To understand this system of promotion, we must look at the relationship between chiefship on the divisional and national levels.

THE DIVISION AND THE PARAMOUNTCY

The kingdom of Gonja is divided into a number of divisions or primary political segments (Fig. 11). In most cases these divisions emerge as territorially compact segments, with more or less specific boundaries, although in fact there is a continuing conflict between rule over land and rule over people. The rulers are locally resident chiefs, each of whom claims descent from a different son or grandson of the founder of the state, and divisions themselves fall into two categories, which from a functional point of view correspond in a way to the difference between chiefships of the first (patrifilial) and second (matrifilial) rank. The first category includes the paramountcy itself (for the capital of Nyanga and its nearby villages formed a kind of division) as well as the five chiefships now eligible for promotion to the paramountcy.[7] These are the 'gates' to Yagbum (the title of the paramount). The second category comprises all the other divisions, the chiefs of which have reached an 'executive menopause' and cannot succeed to the paramountcy. So the assertion that all members of the ruling estate are eligible for the paramountcy requires correcting, for it only holds for the members of that estate who belong to the eligible divisions. But the Gonja themselves speak of the paramountcy as open to all, and in fact there seems to have been some movement between the two categories of eligible and terminal division from time to time.

The present YagbumWura is said to be the first paramount from Daboya; and while this appointment was made under the colonial régime, there are

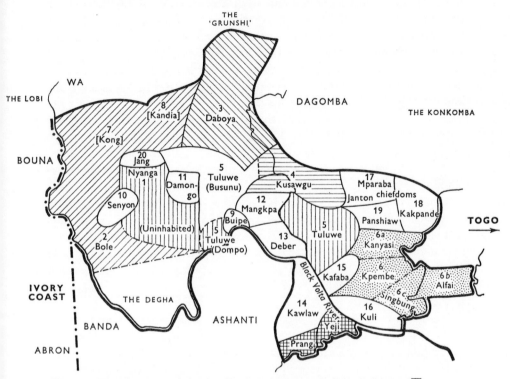

Fig. 11. The divisions of Gonja. Shaded areas are eligible divisions; ⊞, areas included in Gonja District for administrative purposes (1956).

reasons for thinking that the national myth, which regards the heads of all divisions (excepting Kafaba) as descendants of Jakpa, always allowed for some flexibility. It is a long time since Kpembe has provided a paramount, a fact that reflects its independence of Western Gonja (and possibly the degree of Ashanti influence), but all recognize the right of this division to succeed.

The capitals of these terminal divisions are sanctuaries for fugitives from other areas as well as from the justice of the paramount himself. Some of these chiefs perform advisory and ceremonial functions on behalf of the kingdom, especially during the transition from one reign to the next. Indeed, the one regular time when they and other divisional chiefs are likely to gather at the capital is to choose a new ruler. In this respect their role is analogous to that of second and third ranking chiefships within a division. Indeed, both are known as councillors (*begbangpo*), a term that implies the incapacity to succeed to higher offices, though the paramount also has his own local councillors.

In the legendary charter of the state, which has been recorded in a number of documents, both in Hausa and in Arabic, all the divisional chiefs are regarded as descendants of Jakpa, whether or not they succeed to the kingship. That some are eligible while others are not is explained by accounts of how, in the dead-end divisions, an earlier ruler is said to have refused the offer of the paramountcy when his turn came, preferring to remain in his own town rather than uproot himself and his family to go and live in the nation's small capital of Nyanga, remote from his own home. Chiefs of this kind are often heard to deprecate the value of the paramountcy, emphasizing their own autonomy, the strength of their position as councillors, and the advantage of staying in the country one knows.

The most important of these dead-end or terminal divisions is that of Gbuipe (Angl. Buipe). It is this chief who arranges the installation of the new Yagbum Wura, and after this has taken place, the two men are not permitted to see each other again. Nevertheless, the chief of Buipe keeps in regular touch with national events, for it is the Moslems resident in his town who provide the nation's Imam. This position makes it possible for him to intervene on a variety of issues; and it was his advice that recently enabled one division to reject the chiefly candidate who had the paramount's approval and select another in his stead.

This role as the most important councillor in the realm is buttressed by strong sanctions. In earlier times, Buipe was the main kola market on the route which ran from Kumasi north through the centre of modern Ghana. [8] But supernatural agencies as well as commercial interests were involved. For Jakpa, wounded in battle, is said to have been buried there while being carried to his capital. The burial place is now a shrine, whose guardians, in typically Gonja style, are Moslems and commoners, rather than members of the ruling estate. At the same time, the Mohammedans say, Buipe is a Moslem town; unlike other divisions there is no war leader, nor yet an Earth priest, though one resides in a nearby village. And war is said to be banished from its precincts.[9]

It is some time now since Buipe lost its connexion with the kola trade, which moved to the east. But the central route was important in the itineraries of early European travellers to Ashanti and again in pre-European times after 1874, when Kintampo replaced Salaga as the main kola market.

In theory, the paramountcy circulates among the five eligible chiefships. Whoever is head of the next division in line quits his own town, relinquishes his former title and settles in the nation's capital with his wives, sisters, children, foster-children and other of his close kin. There he takes over a set of chiefs, known as councillors or as courtiers (*mpotassibi*, 'those who sit around'), who act as his personal advisers; these title-holders are the heads of non-royal villages situated in the vicinity of the capital and under the immediate jurisdiction of the paramount. Most of these chiefs claim not to be autochthones but to have accompanied the invading Gbanya as fighting men or in some other subordinate capacity.

In most cases the villages belonging to a division form compact blocks of territory. The chief's authority over this area is expressed in his control of hunting rights. Within its borders the chief has a claim on one leg of any large animal killed, just as he does on part of any domestic animal killed. Strangers wishing to hunt in his territory should first obtain permission and present him with both a front and hind leg of their victims. This manner of acknowledging subordinate status extends also to the national level, for when an elephant is killed one leg should go to the divisional chief and a tusk to the YagbumWura.

In some instances, however, a few of the division's villages are separated from the main part of the principality. The Gonja themselves regard chiefship as pertaining to people as well as to land. The arrangement whereby an isolated village is 'owned' by a distant ruler may be seen as inconvenient but not as illogical. 'Ownership' in this context has nothing to do with the control of land as a productive resource. It is quite inappropriate to regard the tribute given to the chiefs as a rent paid for the use of land. In the first place, since the population is so sparse, rights in the productive capacity of land not actually in use are almost non-existent. People farm where they wish. Secondly, if any rights in the productive capacity of land can be said to exist beyond the user level, they are the largely ritual rights vested in the Earth priest (the Owner of the Earth) and these (as I have suggested) are not of great moment. In other words, generalized rights to land are associated with autochthones rather than rulers, with the plebs rather than the patricians. It is possible to regard tribute to chiefs as protection money but not as rent for the land; in fact, these presentations bear a closer resemblance to the offerings which stateless peoples of the region make to the Owners of the Earth in order to acquire ritual protection against supernatural forces, except that such offerings are made to the Earth rather than to its priest. This is very clear in the division of Kpembe, where an annual tribute from certain villages is rendered at the Damba festival and consists of token amounts of ingredients for soup and firewood to cook them. These augment the supplies with which the women of the ruling estate prepare the feast and serve both to acknowledge the suzerainty of the Gbanya and to bring the commoners into the most important ceremonies of the state.

The material revenues of the chiefs came not from the land, nor indeed from the commoners at all, but rather from taxes on trade, from slaving, and to a lesser extent from production by servile labour.

I have already spoken of the relative independence of the divisions when discussing the reasons people gave for the existence of dead-end chiefdoms. This autonomy is also explicit in the political history of Gonja, though further discussion of this point falls outside the scope of the present essay. After the original conquest, the organization of the state became more decentralized. Distances were great and the population sparse. There was no regular communication by king's messenger. The national army consisted of the temporary co-operation of divisional forces—those that were made available. Consequently the paramount had no monopoly of physical force. War between the divisions was not altogether unknown, and when it broke out the monarch had no adequate force of his own with which to restore peace. All judicial proceedings were conducted locally in the first instance, although there was the possibility of appeal by oath to the paramount in a manner similar to that of Ashanti. But since the paramount had at his disposal little control of physical force, the sanction was ritual; here, as in Ashanti, the oath implicated the dead.

The centrifugal tendencies inherent in so great a degree of regional autonomy are only too apparent. But countering these were the centripetal attractions offered by the circulation of the paramountcy through the major territorial segments, which meant that the greater part of the ruling estate were directly concerned to maintain the existence of the state as a whole. Consequently, despite the chequered history of the over-kingdom of Gonja, there was not the constant tendency to fission (as distinct from decentralization) that occurs in next-of-kin succession as found, for example, among the Azande, the Alur, and some of the south-eastern Bantu.

TITLES WITHIN THE DIVISION

In each division are found the three types of title-holder mentioned earlier. There are titles of the first rank from which men are promoted to the divisional chiefship and, in the eligible divisions, to the paramountcy itself. There are titles of the second rank, reserved for 'sister's sons'; these are personal and do not lead further. And there are the third ranking titles reserved for non-Gbanya, usually plebs, but in a few special cases for persons belonging to a subgroup of the Moslem estate. Sometimes these titles form part of a small-scale promotional series; in Kpembe, before a man becomes Imam, he has to fill the two junior offices of Nso'oWura and Nyami; here the offices do not circulate between local segments of the Moslem estate (which is small), but such rotation does occur elsewhere in Gonja. Finally, there is a fourth category of women's titles.

A member of the ruling estate can only hold a chiefship of the first rank in the division in which his father had a similar right. In other words, only members of the locally domiciled segments of the ruling estate are eligible. Just as the paramountcy has five primary dynastic segments which supply the monarch, so each divisional chiefship is selected in turn from two or three secondary segments.

In the Deber and Tuluwe divisions, these secondary segments are located in separate villages, in the same way that the primary units of the dynasty are each situated in one division; here I speak of scattered segments. Unlike the paramountcy, however, the reigning chief makes his segment's own village the divisional capital. More usually, the secondary segments are located in the capital, as at Bole, where they may form distinct wards of the town; these I call compact segments. The third possibility, found at Kpembe, is a combination of the two, where each segment is represented both in an outlying village and at a central capital; here I speak of dispersed segments. In each instance, according to Gonja political theory, the divisional chiefship should rotate in fixed order among the secondary segments, whether or not the chiefship is terminal.

Each dynastic segment in a division includes a number of title-holders; it is the senior chief of the next segment in line who should assume office at the death of the present incumbent. This seniority is usually indicated by appointment to a 'gate' chiefship, an office which may lead to higher things.

In a few of the smaller divisions there is no pre-selection through appointment to gate chiefships. Senior title-holders of the first rank are eligible for direct promotion to the divisional chiefship if the segment to which they belong is next-in-line, although in any particular instance some chiefs will be better placed than others; this system obtained at Busunu and Mangkpa. In all the other divisions, however, specific chiefships were recognized as leading to higher office. In some cases (as in Buipe) there are several free-floating gate chiefships to which all lesser chiefs can aspire and which designate the senior chiefs in each segment; the senior chief of the next segment in line is the proper successor, whichever of these titles he holds. In a number of other instances, where there are only two dynastic segments (as in Tuluwe and Daboya), there is a single gate chiefship, so that the heir apparent is always known by a special title.

The advantages of this prince-of-Wales system are discussed in the Introduction (p. 14). Here I would add that a less explicit indication of the successor is said to have been made at the installation of the paramount himself. After his enrobement by the senior representatives of the Moslems and of the plebs, the assembled members of the ruling estate set him on a horse to take him from the sacred grove where the ceremony has been performed back to the capital of Nyanga. At this point the chief of the division next-in-line seized the bridle of the horse and led him forward, thus making a public demonstration of his division's claim to provide the next king.

Kpembe (the largest and most easterly division) is organized on different lines from the rest of the kingdom; in several ways it mirrors more closely the structure of the state itself and was indeed the most independent of the divisions. Each secondary segment has a certain number of village chiefships,

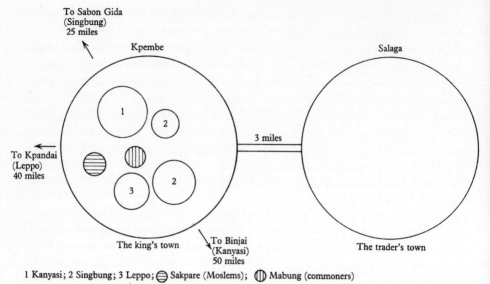

1 Kanyasi; 2 Singbung; 3 Leppo; ⊜ Sakpare (Moslems); ⦀ Mabung (commoners)

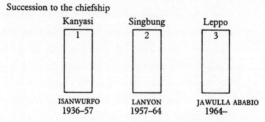

Fig. 12. The dynastic segments of Kpembe.

which form a more or less compact territorial segment. Hence promotion depends upon the occurrence of a vacancy within the titles vested in a particular dynastic segment, not in the division as a whole. The gate chiefships are the senior positions in the three secondary segments, each of which has a specific title.

In all these cases there are subsidiary rungs in the promotional ladder between first appointment as a junior title-holder and elevation to the senior chiefship of a division. Sometimes the only intervening step is the gate chiefship. But in the larger divisions, such as Bole, a man's first posting is to a relatively small and distant village, from which he gradually advances in the shoes of dead and promoted men to the bigger townships, in a manner not unlike the progress of officials in the British Colonial Service and similar bureaucracies where spatial and hierarchical movements are interrelated.[10] Except for the chiefships of terminal divisions, and for those a patrician might occupy as a sister's son in another division rather than as a resident member of his own segment, each title held by a member of the ruling estate is part of a promotional system that extends throughout the kingdom.

Not every title held by a member of the ruling estate necessarily carried the headship of a particular village, and to put this in context I want briefly to consider the duties associated with various kinds of title. Those of the third rank usually have specific duties of a ritual kind, but in some cases they also imply the headship of local groups, such as a ward or village. Title-holders of the second rank quite often hold village headships. From this standpoint they are identical with chiefships of the first rank, which imply but do not always confer the headship of a village. Although most of the titles seem to be derived from village names, the villages themselves may have ceased to exist because the inhabitants have died out, joined other villages or started a new one; for unlike villages among some mobile agriculturalists, a change of location (which is in any case but a rare happening) may involve a change of name.

The holders of these titles without villages usually reside in the divisional capital, forming part of the personnel attached to the chief's court; they greet him formally every Monday and Friday and hold themselves in readiness on those days to take part in any discussion, either in the chief's meeting hut or in their own, and they perform all the manifold duties of chiefs at customary ceremonies, both at the regular festivals (some of which follow the seasons and others the Moslem calendar) and at life-cycle rituals, especially funerals.

The titles which carry village headships are considered to be more rewarding (or 'sweeter') than those without. It is true that the latter are closer to the divisional chief and do not involve residence in distant villages. But it is those chiefs who reside in villages mainly composed of plebs who get more material rewards; at yearly festivals, a portion of each wild animal killed, a tithe of the fish caught in certain streams, and communal labour for their farms, although this last benefice has now been transformed into a fixed monthly payment from the funds of the District Council.[11]

The situation in a Gonja division is typically that of a conquest state. A group with the traditions of an invading horde is scattered over the country-side as the rulers of a subordinate people. The bulk of the ruling estate is concentrated in divisional capitals, from which chiefs are sent out to rule the predominantly plebeian villages. I say predominantly plebeian, because the villages may contain elements of the ruling estate who originally came there through an earlier chief. For instance, a man is appointed to a town, marries a local girl, begets a son there, and dies. The son may remain, either because he is being fostered by his maternal kin, or because his mother continues to live there, or simply because it is the only home he has ever known. In time he and his descendants will constitute a local element of the politically dominant group in an otherwise commoner village.

The cultural distinctiveness of patricians and plebs varies from division to division. In Central Gonja the rulers and the ruled spoke one language, and the domestic organization of the two estates was broadly similar. But in other parts the Gbanya chief of an outlying village may be divided by both language and culture from the people among whom he lives and over whom he rules. This cultural heterogeneity is most marked in the east and in the west, especially in those areas into which new immigrants are coming, the Konkomba from the north-east and the 'Lobi' in the west.[12]

Apart from these recent immigrants, the plebs have close links with the patricians. Intermarriage is frequent, and as a result of the transfer of children between kin (kinship fostering), the links with maternal relatives are particularly strong, even though political status is determined by paternal filiation. Indeed I have been present when the paramount chief and the son of one of his paternal half-brothers (who was at that time acting as my research assistant) conversed with one another in a language of one of the commoner groups; this language, Tampluma, was literally their mother tongue and they seemed to find it easier for speaking about domestic matters. This was no isolated instance; the same happened on a number of occasions, with other senior chiefs, and I am assured in my own mind that this practice was not merely a way of imparting information so that bystanders like myself could not understand what was being said. Rather, I interpret the incident as a striking example of the difference between ruler-subject relationships in the political and in the domestic domains; the position and influence of commoner women as wives and mothers of the ruling estate emphasize that political subordination is quite consistent with domestic equality.

Not only do the members of the ruling estate marry commoner girls, many of them declare a preference for such wives, as against women of their own estate. For Gbanya women, they declare, are too proud to make good wives, and their links with their natal homes are strong; only there can they succeed to women's titles (b'wuriche), only there do they fully occupy the role of 'Gbanya women' (Ngbanyiche) as distinct from 'Gbanya wives' (or 'chiefs' wives'). Because of these stronger ties, they are often deemed to make less permanent and consequently less satisfactory wives. In fact the divorce rate seems much the same for plebs as for patricians; in each case, both the jural and conjugal instability of marriage is high (Goody, E. 1962).

There remains one point concerned with the distribution of titles within a division which requires some clarification. It has been said that a member of the ruling estate can only become a chief of the first rank in the division in which his dynastic segment is permanently resident. Why then should he accept a chiefship in another division, not through paternal but maternal filiation, when his mother is also a member of the ruling estate?

The residential system of the Gonja is marked by an extensive practice of kinship fostering, whereby offspring are sent to be brought up by close kinsfolk of the parents. As inter-village marriage is frequent, children are often found in villages other than the one in which their father was born, and sometimes in another division altogether. Of the children resident with maternal or other kin, some may return to their father's home, but others will stay. In addition, older men may go and live with their maternal kin for a number of differing reasons. The residential flexibility of childhood extends to adults as well. For a member of the ruling estate, the father's home always exercises a strong centripetal pull; only there can a man attain high political office. Nevertheless, at any one time, there will always be a percentage of individuals, even among the ruling estate, who are living with their maternal kin; for one thing, they stand to gain a larger share of the property of their mother's brothers. And it is these men with mothers from the local segment of the ruling estate who are eligible for the sister's son chiefships.

The dynastic segments are not merely local aggregates of those members of the ruling estate who happen to be residing in a particular division at a particular time. Membership is determined by paternal filiation and a man is only eligible for chiefship of the first rank in the division to which his father belonged by right of birth. Eligibility for chiefship is a combination of blood royal and residential qualifications.

APPOINTMENT TO CHIEFSHIP

Any member of the ruling estate may be appointed to a chiefship of first rank in the division in which his segment is located. Titles are expected to go to the next most senior untitled person in a dynastic segment, but this is by no means always the case. Membership of a local segment is the only unvarying criterion of eligibility. There is of course an explicit ideal personality pattern a chief should have, but how far approximation to this ideal plays any part in the choice is difficult to say. What is certainly more important is that the candidate should have sufficient funds to make the traditional gifts to the divisional chief, to the non-royal electors and to the local members of the ruling estate. Anyone who can command such funds, either from his own pocket or by borrowing from kith, kin or friends, and who is at the same time a senior member of his own dynastic segment, is in a favourable position to secure election. But chiefship depends on motivation and support more than money, for the sums required are low; the Gonja sharply contrast their system with that of the Dagomba, who, they say, buy chiefships.

After a man has shown by gifts that he wishes to be considered for a particular office, the selection is theoretically in the hands of the enrobers, who usually consist of the senior representatives of the other two estates. In fact the choice is made not by the enrobers, although they may act in an advisory capacity, but by the divisional ruler, in concord with other chiefs, on the basis of gifts received, of loyalty anticipated, and of past relationships. Under such a system, a divisional chief will clearly be under some pressure to appoint members of his own dynastic segment when offices fall vacant. But there are contrary pressures. For the members of other secondary segments will not willingly see the claims of their own senior members overlooked; their segment would be downgraded and everyone's chances of chiefship diminished. Consequently they assist their candidates to make the necessary gifts and make their support clear by other more subtle pressures. Chiefs in a position to command or influence appointments realize that the exclusion of one segment might lead to non-co-operation and finally armed rebellion, which would weaken the position of the ruling estate in relation to the commoners inside and hostile powers outside. This is precisely what happened in the Kanyasi wars of Eastern Gonja, where, in 1892, the attempt to set aside the claims of one party to the divisional chiefship led to a prolonged war. Rebellion is the final safeguard of a neglected segment, and this the ruling estate is anxious to avoid. Moreover, most chiefs appreciate the advantage of having junior offices more or less equally distributed throughout the various parts of the community, as such dispersion is a valuable instrument of control.

It might be supposed that there would be considerable disagreement within a dynastic segment over which members should fill available titles. For the segment has no comprehensive internal genealogy by which seniority is reckoned, and any attempt to use merit alone as the basic criterion for promotion could lead to considerable friction between sibling groups, and possibly within them too. I have not observed any great degree of conflict of this kind at any level. Within the large secondary dynastic segments an equitable sharing of chiefships among constituent houses is seen as necessary to maintain the unity of the segment. This explicitly entered into the deliberations over succession to a Kpembe chiefship in 1964. The holder of the segment's senior chiefship first proposed a candidate from his own house. Strenuous objections came from the other houses of the dynastic segment and the chief was forced to choose a distant rather than a close agnate. His capitulation was explained as due to the danger of losing the support of part of his segment if they were denied access to the senior chiefships. On this level, the threat of withdrawal of active support is a more realistic sanction than armed rebellion. A secondary segment must appear united to achieve recognition in divisional councils. A chief who everyone knew represented only his own family would count for little. It is probable that in the past similar considerations acted against a monopoly of divisional chiefship by a single secondary dynastic segment or part of a segment.

But even in divisions where secondary dynastic segments are small, there is relatively little overtly hostile competition for chiefships. First, chiefship of the first rank is not in itself a scarce good. While those carrying village headships are of course limited, it is always possible to appoint a man to the chiefship of a 'dead' village. Providing these are chiefships of the first rank, the incumbents are equally eligible for promotion to higher office. Secondly, a man would rarely attempt to become a chief until his elder brother had been offered the chance; there is little competition within the group of paternal siblings.[13] Thirdly, a chief has to stay in his village, and the young men of Gonja are addicted to travel; others are living with maternal kin, some hunting in a distant village, others trading or working for wages. Nowadays others have been to school and are working as teachers and administrators. The younger men do not want chiefship; they recognize its drawbacks and they recognize that age, experience and some wealth are prerequisites of the successful chief. Motivation therefore limits the number of possible candidates at any one time.

The appointive element is necessarily lessened in the selection of the divisional head, as compared with a junior chief, since the paramount, the only person who could act in this capacity, was formerly too distant; the office had to be filled early in the series of funeral ceremonies. In the case of dispute, recourse was sometimes had to ineligible electors (in Kpembe, the Kilibu-Wura, the NjaiWura, the KorassiWura and the KafabaWura) who tried to find the least unacceptable solution.

VARIABLES IN CIRCULATING SUCCESSION

Circulating succession is a system whereby offices pass between two or more units of organization. It necessarily entails a promotional system, but the reverse is not true. In certain of the Mossi states the paramountcy is obtained only by promotion through a series of gate chiefships but there are apparently no dynastic segments involved (for Dagomba, see Rattray 1932: 574; Manoukian 1951). So too in Barotseland and in Buganda chiefs moved from village to village but there was no explicit movement of chiefship between different kin groups. It is the latter I refer to as circulating succession. It may involve the spatial movement of a chiefship as well as of a chief, as when the dynastic segments are located in distant towns, which become the nation's capital in turn; the state of Gyaman (or Bondoukou) in the Ivory Coast had twin capitals of this kind (Tauxier 1921).[14]

The units of organization involved may be dynastic segments, political parties or even national states.[15] Here I want to consider three ways in which the first of these, polydynastic systems, vary amongst themselves, since this is a necessary preliminary to discussing gains and costs.

First, the transfer of office between groups may vary between open competition and strict rotation, although the extremes are unlikely to occur in actual situations. Unrestrained competition between dynastic segments would lead to the domination of one by the other, the subsequent elimination of the subordinate segment, and the collapse of the polydynastic system. Strict rotation, while it may be the desiderated aim, is always liable to be set aside because of the temptations that kingship offers to an ambitious prince. Nevertheless, polydynastic systems do vary according to the regularity of the swing between the segments, both in ideology and in practice. Although the variations lie along a continuum, I find it useful to speak of irregular circulation as oscillating succession and regular circulation as rotational succession.

An example of an oscillating polydynastic system is found among the Eastern Anuak of the Sudan. These people form a loosely knit kingdom, in which the senior office, a kingship with largely ritual functions, circulates rapidly among the sons of the former kings who seize the emblems of royalty by force, or by threat of force (Evans-Pritchard 1940, 1947). The noble clan is divided into two branches and the king-list shows a tendency, it certainly cannot be put more strongly than that, for the office to alternate between the two branches.

The example of the Anuak points to the relationship between circulating succession and 'corporate' dynasties on which I have remarked in the Introduction. In the absence of a highly determinate method of designating the heir, all members of the sibling group are seen as alternative candidates for the throne, both by themselves and by the nation at large. Temporary factions or permanent segments of the community easily accrete around the rival princes and succession may then be determined by a civil war that annihilates or expels the losers. But the defeat of princes does not necessarily lead to the destruction of their followers; among both Zulu and Barotse, for example, 'the commoner who followed his prince or chief in rebellion was not guilty of treason' (Gluckman 1963: 22).

A more determinate type of circulating system is found among the Shilluk, a neighbouring group of the Anuak. Despite Seligman's denial that there was 'no basis for the belief...that there were two, or even three or four, branches of the royal house from which the kings were elected in turn', Evans-Pritchard maintains that the royal clan was in fact so divided, that there has been in recent times 'an alternation on the throne of branches of the royal house' (1948: 30–1) and that this alternation is related to the division of Shillukland into two territorial segments, the north and the south. [15] In the more recent period, the system worked relatively smoothly, for the reigning monarch took under his wing a scion of the rival line (i.e. a tanist), thus nominating him as his successor. The new king does likewise, and each thus tries to insure not only against rebellion by the rival segment but also against the future exclusion of his own line. The recent history of the Shilluk dynasty, with its relatively strict rotation, stands in contrast to the less determinate system of the Anuak, with its greater degree of disruption.

The second variable has to do with the relationships between dynastic segments. Under the term 'polydynastic system' I have included those in which a single dynasty of kinsfolk is divided into two or more subsections, as well as those in which the eligible groups consist of unrelated dynasties. Gonja, like Wa and Nupe, has a single but subdivided dynasty which traces descent from a common ancestor, while the Hausa and the Bariba possess a number of distinct descent groups between which the chiefship circulates. Structurally, the difference is not great; in both cases a balance is preserved between the different dynastic groups. But where the segments are of diverse origin, this function may be of considerably greater importance. In the Hausa emirate of Zaria, for example, the dynastic segments consist of three kin groups, each of which was involved in the Fulani seizure of power at the beginning of the nineteenth century (Smith 1955, 1956, 1960). The initial passage of the paramountcy between these groups ensured that the rewards of office were equally distributed among those taking part in the conquest. The subsequent history of the emirate showed a tendency to irregular oscillation rather than strict rotation, and since the end of the last century one segment has dominated the others. Nevertheless, at the ruler's death, the kingship has always passed to a different segment with the result that, although eligibility is restricted to the sons of former rulers who have held territorial office, close kin never succeed one another on the throne (1960: 110).

Among the Bariba of the Nigeria–Dahomey border, there is rather more emphasis on rotation. Here the ruling estate consists of six dynastic segments, three of Bariba (Gur speaking) descent and three of Boko or Busa (Mande speaking) origin (Lombard 1957). Rotation is essential to secure an approximately equal participation of these culturally diverse groups in a common chiefship. Here as elsewhere circulating succession is a system for distributing power.

A third major way in which polydynastic systems differ among themselves relates to the method of selecting or eliminating candidates for high office.[16] Among the Bariba of North Dahomey, there are a number of dynastic subdivisions, but only sons and grandsons of previous chiefs can act as candidates. This elimination of potential claimants creates a separation of the ruling estate into royals and nobles, eligible and ineligible members.

Restricted eligibility seems also to occur among the Shilluk. The fact that chiefship is vested in a segment of a descent group while the remainder are ineligible for the senior offices must clearly lead to an imbalance, one obvious outcome of which is the severance of descent ties, and more especially of those genealogical ties which form the framework of lineage organization. Another example of this process is given in Lienhardt's recent account of headmanship among the neighbouring Anuak (1958), where some of the difficulties of reconciling hereditary authority with lineage organization are clearly brought out.[17]

Among the Gonja, any member of the ruling estate who belongs to one of the divisions eligible for chiefship is himself eligible, though he should not of course directly follow a member of the same segment either in the paramountcy or in a divisional chiefship. As in the Ashanti divisions (as distinct from the paramountcy), the chiefly dynasties are large-scale dynasties. A new chief in Ashanti is selected from within the lineage by joint consultation between its members and the divisional council. In Gonja, the paramount is in principle selected in rotation from the chiefs of the constituent divisions, who have themselves achieved their positions by promotion within the secondary segments. Below them are a number of other chiefs of the first rank, any of whom may step into their shoes providing they are of the right segment at the right time; ultimately all members of eligible dynastic segments can become candidates for these chiefships. By extending the rotational system to secondary segments, and by avoiding 'elimination', all members of the eligible divisions are included in a promotional ladder at the top of which stands the paramountcy itself. While some practical advantage accrues to sons of former chiefs, every Gbanya sees himself as having the field marshal's baton in his knapsack.

The implications of rotational succession, its costs and gains as compared with other systems of transferring office, are examined in the following section.

THE PROFIT AND THE LOSS OF CIRCULATING SUCCESSION

(i) *Political*

Circulating systems are essentially ways of distributing power; next-of-kin systems are ways of concentrating it. In terms of the relationship between incumbent and successor, office-holder and heir, the former is a type of distant succession, the second a close one.

In this section I want to consider the costs and gains of circulating succession from two angles, the structure of the political system and the relationships within the dynasty.

From the first standpoint, circulating succession distributes office among the constituent, power-holding segments of the political system. In Gonja, as well as in the other cases we have been considering, these segments are groups of kin with local affiliations, but they may well be colleges, political parties or nation states. The United Nations selects leaders such as the President of the Security Council by rotation among its members. The office of Vice-Chancellor in the University of Cambridge passes in a less regular manner between the heads of the constituent colleges. In these cases, the circulation of office reflects the relative strength of the segments as against the central organization.

But circulating systems may also ensure that power is diffused among a wide section of the population, thus increasing the direct support an office receives.

In monarchies, the circulation of the kingship augments dynastic numbers by extending the range of eligibility and by increasing its 'corporate' character. Of course, even in next-of-kin systems a large dynasty can be maintained by other means; for instance, where the excluded members regard the king as representative of the kin group as a whole; this semi-corporate attitude to the crown maximizes the willingness of the dynasty to provide support and is often linked (as among the Basuto and the Mossi) to their active participation in the government as holders of important offices. But when the dynasty is divided into segments for the purpose of succession, a large number of persons are involved in a more direct way, even given the limited eligibility of many rotational systems, such as those found in Ireland and Nigeria. There is not the same tendency to fission that is revealed in the history of the Mossi and the South-East Bantu. For the representative character of the chiefship becomes stronger when the office rotates between opposed segments of equal status, the loyalty of whose members is reinforced by alternating periods in the wilderness.

The reasons for distributing power by circulating succession are many. In societies that approach the acephalous end of the political continuum, it may solve some of the problems of combining office with a 'segmentary' system of social groups that are relatively equal in status. The difficulties of allocating authoritative roles (outside the group of descendants of a living man) have been perceptively analysed for the Tiv of Nigeria (L. Bohannan and P. Bohannan 1953), and the same difficulties emerge in connexion with any exclusive role in such societies. Among the Nuer, the mediatory position of Leopard Skin Chief is vested in an 'outsider', in someone who is not a member of the locally dominant lineage. In other societies such as the Tallensi and the Yakö, the problem is handled by making offices pass successively through all the major segments concerned.

In state systems, chiefship circulates not among the whole community but between segments of the ruling estate. Although it is possible to envisage a monarchical state in which the major offices passed between segments that embraced the whole population, in every case I know of, access to the highest office is limited to the members of a single group (usually a descent group, or plurality of such), set apart (in this way at least) from the bulk of the population. The exception is the nation state, where there are no overt restrictions on eligibility to political office, aside from membership of the party. In monarchical systems, rotation spreads access to high office within a kin-based dynasty, or dynastic association, which for this purpose must be divided into exclusive segments. In other words, the dynasty has a unilineal character about it. One of the obvious features of the early dynasties of Scotland (the Cenel of Fergus Mor) and Ireland (the Cenel of O'Neil) that distinguished them from the Norman royal family was their greater inclusiveness and the fact that they constituted one segmented descent unit in a society consisting of a number of similar units.[18] I would stress this point by recalling that where monarchical rotation is found together with a basically bilateral kinship system (as among the Gonja, the Hausa or the Nupe), the ruling estate is nevertheless divided into dynastic segments that have a distinctly unilineal character. For members of the ruling estate had not only to be defined by agnatic filiation, they had also to be allocated, in some more or less defined way, to specific segments of that estate.

The function of rotational succession in weakly centralized organizations like the United Nations is clear enough; it tends to occur for the same reasons as in 'acephalous' systems of a different kind, such as the Tallensi. But in West Africa circulating succession is found in some of the most complex and organized states in the continent. Among the Nupe and the Hausa it serves partly as a means of distributing power amid the various elements that shared in the conquest of the kingdom. But rotation has its present as well as its past functions. For it means that the ruling groups who fill many of the major territorial offices of state have a direct stake in the kingship. Among the Southern Bantu, princes are often used to rule the territorial segments, but filial succession denies them access to the paramountcy itself; this they can attain only by setting up their own kingdom through an act of rebellion or secession.

The Gonja system of rotation is more extensive than the Nupe and the Hausa in two respects. First, in Zaria and Nupe, fief-holders have to live in the capital; the dynastic segments are centrally located and come directly under the supervision of the paramount. This system of 'compact dynastic segments' gives the ruler a greater control over other members of the ruling estate. But it does so at the expense of the relationships with the subject peoples, with whom there is less local identification (Nadel 1942: 118). The Gonja system of rotational succession between locally resident units ('scattered segments') achieves closer contact with subject peoples while counteracting to some extent the centrifugal tendencies of a purely local chiefship, a divisional set-up where the chiefs have interests of a wholly local kind. For the rulers of all the major territorial units, being eligible for supreme office, have a stake in seeing that the kingdom to which they might eventually succeed is not damaged by attack from without nor by secession from within. The problem of secession is particularly acute in political systems such as the Gonja where segments of the ruling group are locally resident.

Secondly, by taking the promotional principle down to the grass-roots level, the whole of the ruling estate is directly involved in the perpetuation of the state as a unit; there is no elimination or limitation of eligibility within the dynasty. The most junior member of the ruling estate may one day become paramount. One divisional chief might find it opportune to attempt independence, but if he achieved his aim he would deprive all other members of the local dynastic segment of the possibility of succeeding to a yet higher office, now and for evermore. Consequently he may find among his closest supporters reaction against any suggestion of secession. While the same argument does not apply to the terminal divisions, it will be recalled that these are not only numerically smaller, but their status as ineligible is not altogether immutable.

The fact that the highest office had in some ways less 'power' than the divisional chiefships did not mean it was necessarily less attractive as a goal. The importance of the paramountcy lay partly in the strength of the Gbanya myth, in itself a potent factor in the maintenance of the unity of the state (Goody 1966a). The myth specifies the paramountcy as the supreme office, and it is therefore established as a desired object apart from any consideration of 'power'. A not dissimilar situation can be seen in the recurrent struggles between Fellows of Oxbridge Colleges to appoint a Master of their corporation, as readers of Charles Snow will be well aware. To outsiders, the significance of holding such an office, limited in power and scope, may seem of little importance, particularly for those engaged in academic work. But membership of a College involves a man in a powerful process of secondary socialization, instilling values which, though different from those of the academic profession as such, become accepted by the participants as fully worthy of ardent pursuit. Once a man steps on the bottom rung of such a promotional system, he tends to strive for the top, regardless of the pragmatic utility of getting there; for he acquires a personal commitment to the system itself.

From the administrative angle, then, rotation gives a large number of persons a direct interest in maintaining the unity of the state, which is particularly liable to fission when it includes many different ethnic groups and covers such a large and sparsely populated area as Gonja. But the maintenance of a large dynasty was not simply an administrative convenience; it was also a military necessity. As in the case of most other kingdoms of the West African savannah, this conquest state was established by virtue of the military superiority of the incoming conquerors. This superiority lay mainly in their use of cavalry. Cavalry requires the investment not only of time in acquiring the necessary skills, it also needs a considerable accumulation of wealth (or exchange ability) to supply the horses themselves, especially when, as in Gonja, these have to be bought rather than bred. Nor is this an investment that can readily be made by the monarchy itself. Both skills and horses were supplied by the ruling estate. There was no standing army; indeed under these conditions a military technology based upon the horse is very difficult to centralize. What rotation did was to give the nobility, those who provided the armed might of the nation, the promise of power. And the importance of this promise was dramatically illustrated in the civil wars that took place in Eastern

Gonja towards the end of the nineteenth century, when the Kanyasi segment of Kpembe rebelled against its continued exclusion from the divisional chiefship.[19]

The greatest threat to rotation comes from the section in office. Where titles are not permanently allocated to individual segments, the divisional chief may attempt to fill vacancies with members of his own. What is there to stop the segment in power acting in this way, or indeed replacing one dead ruler by another from the same house?

The checks upon such action are embodied in the system itself. The successor who has been cheated of office automatically gets backing from his own segment; he does not have to search around, as he would in a system of close succession, for disgruntled or ambitious men to support him. The segmental structure has built-in factions. The important counter-balancing factor is the threat or actuality of civil war, and the effectiveness of this sanction is directly related to the nature of the military technology. The Gonja forces largely depended upon armed cavalry provided by the ruling estate. Consequently, if the segment in power attempted to consolidate its position, it was faced with the possibility of rebellion by a force of roughly equal size and military potential. Indeed, where the number of dynastic segments exceeded two, the military force at the call of the have-nots exceeded that of the haves.

But the circulating system of succession does not work only because there is a threat of force, even where military power has a segmentary distribution. A further check is the fact that rotation is a quite explicit feature of the political ideology. Of course, there are instances of the order having been broken. Nevertheless, succession by rotation is, in the last analysis, the legitimate system from the actor's point of view. The Gonja say that a son can never succeed his father, only a 'younger brother' (*supo*) can; that is to say, office should pass horizontally to another dynastic segment. This statement represents more than a generalized feeling that offices ought to move from segment to segment. Rotational (as distinct from oscillating) succession is part of the accepted order of things political.

(ii) *Interpersonal*

I began this paper by commenting on the internecine strife to which systems of hereditary succession give rise among close kin. Behind such struggles lies the fact that in most parts of the world it is between near relatives that the incumbent-successor situation falls. So that even where open conflict does not occur, a hostile component is still present in the relationship, for a man has much to gain from the death of his close kin. Psychological theory suggests that the suppression of this hostility may in itself cause additional wear and tear upon these nuclear bonds. Of course, the individual behaviour of incumbent and successor, conscious or unconscious, may vary considerably within any system. But however firm their relationship, the actors are likely to be thrown into conflict as the result of their relative positions in the order of succession. Even if there is no legal provision for the dismissal of a ruler, the heir apparent is bound to provide a possible focus for the discontent of subjects, particularly those who hold important positions in the state. Rivalry is forced upon the members of the sibling group, and the relationship of brothers (or other close kin) is strongly coloured by the fact that they offer alternative choices for the paramountcy, irrespective of their personal inclination; coloured too by the fact that the consequences of the rivalry are so critical, since the replacement of one monarch by another almost inevitably leads to the death or banishment of his predecessor. No two suns can shine in the one firmament.

Even the death of the previous incumbent does not altogether remove him as a focus of alternative aspirations, unrealistic as these may be. For as Gouldner shows in a bureaucratic context, there is a strong tendency for a Rebecca myth to form about the previous office-holder, which heightens his supposed qualities at the expense of the man who has taken his place. The relations between incumbent and successor may thus contain a hostile component even after the death or departure of one of the parties.

Like other systems of succession, rotational chiefship of the Gonja type has its hidden tensions and its open conflicts. The point I wish to make is that, here, conflicts over office do not generally fall between those who have to co-operate closely in a domestic context, but between persons who are socially distant one from another. As compared with a next-of-kin system, close relatives are somewhat freed from the burden of succession tensions. In Gonja, a man's near kin are no great threat to his position, for his legitimate successor comes from another dynastic segment. Unlike next-of-kin systems, a member of the ruling estate has little or nothing to gain when his close kinsman ceases to be his political superior. Indeed, quite the reverse, for he is more likely to benefit if his kinsman remains in office than if the title passes to the dynastic segment next in line.

The difference in terms of interpersonal ties is clearly seen in the fact I have already noted, that when the paramount succeeds, a number of his close kinsmen accompany him to the capital as supporters. Of the present Yagbum-Wura's brothers, some are chiefs in their own local division of Daboya; the others have come to live near him, even though this move means they cannot be elected to chiefships in their own division. His sisters too have followed him; they have less reason than most Gonja women to stay with their husbands and less reason than their brothers for continuing to reside in their natal division. For holding a woman's title in their own locality is of minor importance compared with the kudos they get from being attached to the national court.

What is true on a national level also applies within the divisions. A man's close kin are his political supporters rather than his rivals; and in consequence a ruler's siblings and children of both sexes tend to cluster round the court. There is no banishing of heirs; rather heirs are automatically distanced by the system of succession.

The reduction of tension between close relatives (as compared with next-of-kin systems) is evident in both aspects of the incumbent-successor situation, in the relations between incumbent and successor as well as in the relations between the potential successors themselves. But whereas it is rarely that two rulers follow one another from the same segment, it does happen that two claimants present themselves from one dynastic sub-division. At the death of KpembeWura Isanwurfo in 1957, the senior chief of the next segment in line was already an old man, who appeared unlikely to last for long. Some members of his own segment proposed that a chief junior to him should be put forward as their candidate, for in this way they would have a longer spell of close association with the reigning chief. The previous ruler had been in office over twenty years and his house was firmly established in the changing political scene; junior members had been sent to school, so that they were now well placed in the various branches of modern administration. The members of the next segment in line now wished to secure the same advantages for their own people. But the other two 'gates', appreciating the fact that the older the chief the quicker the turnover, strongly supported the candidature of the old man on the grounds of law and custom. And in due course he it was that prevailed both with the local electors and with the paramount himself, who now plays a more important role than formerly in the selection of divisional chiefs.

Where internal rivalries of this kind occur, the alternative candidates tend to be distantly related within the dynastic segment. There is a constant tendency for struggles for promotion to be thrown outside close relationships and on to socially distant ones. As I have remarked, brothers rarely compete with one another for appointment as chiefs. Nor do fathers and sons; indeed in eastern Gonja a man cannot hold a senior chiefship during the lifetime of his parents. The inclusive eligibility of the Gonja system, in contrast to the son-grandson limitations in the polydynastic systems of Northern Nigeria or of the Anuak and Shilluk, means that even when the office returns to the segment, the new ruler is unlikely to be a close relative of its previous representative. In segments with limited eligibility, a brother might intrigue against the ruler in the hope that he would gain from a quick turnover; that the sooner the office became empty, the earlier would it return. But in Gonja, with its large dynastic units and inclusive eligibility, the chiefship would rarely come back to the same sibling group or even to an immediate descendant of its previous representative. Support of a brother or father in office usually payed better dividends than intrigue against him.

Polydynastic systems with limited eligibility (e.g. those of Northern Nigeria) do increase the social distance between an office-holder and his successor, but in effect they operate a delayed next-of-kin rule; while this does not externalize succession conflicts from nuclear relationships to the same extent as in Gonja, there is a ban on close kin following one another.[20] The Gonja system does indicate a potential successor, in some cases more precisely than in others (and not always does he succeed). But he comes from another segment.

The externalization of political conflict from close kin is a negative aspect of rotational succession. It corresponds in some ways to the function that certain 'double descent' systems play in the domestic domain, where the splitting of the holder-heir situation between uterine and agnatic kin gives some relief to the parental tensions (Goody 1962). In a rotational system, conflict is shifted on to relationships which are relatively free of strain. In this way political conflicts are largely confined to the political domain and do not impinge upon the domestic sphere.

In suggesting that rotational succession at once relieves nuclear relationships and strengthens the unifying forces in a locally autonomous state, I am not implying that it is a tension-free system. The history of Ireland gives plenty of evidence to the contrary. Conflicts of considerable intensity occur in Gonja, but characteristically they fall between socially distant persons or segments. A typical instance of this occurred in the subdivision of Busunu, regarded as an offshoot of the eligible division of Tuluwe but in practice operating as a terminal division. The ruling estate consisted of two effective secondary segments, both resident in the capital. In 1957, the chief, a very old man, was attached to one of these. The senior chief of the other secondary segment was the MoroWura, who considered himself to be the legitimate successor. Tension had reached such a point that the MoroWura no longer accompanied the other title-holders every Monday and Friday to pay their respects to the chief of Busunu; most of the day he remained quietly in his own room, receiving visitors and biding his time.

The tension between incumbent and successor appears not only in open behaviour of this kind, but also in covert ways. One of these is gossip, and the claimants to office are often only too anxious to display the chief's dirty linen, if not in public, at least in the open privacy of their own compounds. But the tension manifests itself mystically as well as in words. A chief is always supposed to have strong 'medicine' to protect himself from the attacks of witches and sorcerers; indeed he is thought to have eaten witchcraft medicine, and thereby made himself a witch (a defender witch, in Wilson's phrase), so that he might better protect himself and his people. It was said to have been the power of his medicine that prevented the divisional chief of Bole from being killed by a senior sub-chief, who was himself killed by the medicine as a result of his attack. Characteristically, this attacker was seen as the head of the next segment in line. The circulating system does nothing to prevent such conflict between incumbent and successor; it merely throws it outside the nuclear relationships.

It is not only incumbent-successor conflicts which are intersegmental. Although conflict situations between different claimants to the same office do occasionally occur within one dynastic division, they more regularly arise between members of different segments.

For although rotation tends to inhibit such disputes by providing a specific successor, the rewards to be got by jumping the queue sometimes override obedience to the accepted rules. Variation in the order of rotation is a means whereby the segments are kept roughly equivalent in strength; smaller units may have to merge into larger ones if the members are to get their fair share of high office. There must be some flexibility in the system to allow for such adjustment and in Gonja this is well understood.

There is one further aspect of polydynastic systems I want to mention, although only briefly since it touches upon certain aspects of the role of conflict which cannot be dealt with here. All systems of authority generate some hostility between the ruler and the ruled which receives expression in such forms as the Swazi *incwala*, the office party, the exaggeration of inter-generational differences, rituals of rebellion of innumerable kinds. In monarchical states, the desire to change the existing scheme turns not so much on the offices as the office-holders, on rebellion rather than revolution (Gluckman 1954; Evans-Pritchard 1948). But in this context all transfers of power, even legitimate succession through death or retirement, may have cathartic or chiliastic implications; the new lord ·comes to cleanse the kingdom and sweep away old injustices. Such a prospect carries more con-viction where the new ruler comes from a different line. The analogy with modern states is close. In multi-party systems, the conflicts are overt and distant, the promise of change direct. In one-party régimes, the hostilities are covert and close, the expressions of open conflict being mainly directed to the outside world; the prospect of change is much reduced when succession means the transfer of power to a close associate in the same clique. The problem of intra-party succession arises of course in all nation states, but since one-party systems have a more centralized organization and have generally abandoned electoral in favour of acclamatory procedures, the problems arising from the transfer of leadership are more critical for the social system. It is not altogether a paradox to point out that in one-party states, stable government is bought at the price of unstable succession.

That these comparisons between party and dynastic systems have some relevance is apparent from the contemporary scene. It is customary for leaders to justify the one party system by reference to the corporateness of traditional society. In the words of Kojo Botsio of Ghana, 'the previous arrangement was incompatible with our traditions because the concept of an organized opposition was unknown in Ghana's traditional ruling houses'.[21] On the other hand, it has been argued that 'the struggle between rival royal houses for the succession to a Stool provided an excellent training ground for the operation of a modern two-party system' (reported in Austin 1964: 33–4). While few multi-party systems work by deliberate rotation, though nineteenth-century Portugal may provide an example (Duffy 1962: 27), all presume some degree of oscillation; not only does the principle offer some appeal to electors ('it's time for a change') but the continued failure of one party to win power leads to adjustments of membership and programme.

However, the analogy between dynasties and parties overlooks the full implications of the difference between ascribed and voluntary membership of social groups as well as the limited nature of the usual changes (structural rather than organizational) involved in dynastic succession. But from other angles its relevance is brought out in an account by C. W. Welman, himself a lawyer-administrator, of the southern Ghanaian state of Peki:

The system which we find in Peki of succession to the Stool by selection from each of several families or branches of a family is not uncommon among the States of the Gold Coast. It appears to be one of those stabilizing devices which political experience has found necessary in this part of the world, where the fickleness of peoples and the untrustworthiness of princes are perhaps even more pronounced than elsewhere. It has the effect of securing the interest of a large number of the most influential people in the State in the maintenance of the existing order, by which a particular Stool is the premier Stool among the many associated Stools that make up the political organism. It operates against the risk of one small group becoming so powerful and consequently so unpopular as to precipitate a revolution of the political arrangement. It secures in a way what the party system secures in England, carefulness on the part of the section in power that no occasion shall be given for its displacement and watchfulness on the part of the sections not in power for abuses which might lead to the deposition of the reigning Chief and hasten their own accession. (1925: 43–4.)

The situations in Gonja and Peki are not altogether parallel. For in Peki chiefs may be dethroned, whereas in Gonja the only possibility of replacement was by rebellion or the threat of rebellion; otherwise a chief rules until his death. However Welman states with admirable clarity the political significance of circulating succession in Gonja.

But the rotational system of the Gonja has other important repercussions on the interpersonal relationships of members of the ruling estate. As a type of 'distant succession', it throws the weight of such hostilities outside the nuclear relationships. Unlike the next-of-kin systems of Western Europe, the Middle East and most other parts of the world, the shedding of the blood of close kin was rarely, if ever, a passport to high office.

JACK GOODY

APPENDIX I. OFFICE, ROLE AND TITLE

The term office requires some elucidation for the purpose of this analysis. Although concepts such as role and status have received considerable attention from comparative sociologists (especially Nadel 1957), terms such as office, officer, chief, chiefship, title, title-holder, although in constant usage, have been left virtually undefined.

The most extended discussion of the concept of 'office' is Weber's *Theory of Social and Economic Organization*, where it is inseparably linked to his typology of legitimate authority, rational, traditional and charismatic. The pure type of rational or legal authority is found in systems which employ a bureaucratic administrative staff. One of the mutually dependent set of ideas upon which bureaucratic arrangements are built is that

the typical person in authority occupies an 'office'. In the action associated with his status, including the commands he issues to others, he is subject to an impersonal order to which his actions are oriented. This is true not only for persons exercising legal authority who are in the usual sense 'officials', but, for instance, for the elected president of a state. (1947: 302.)

In an editorial footnote Parsons defines Weber's use of office (*Amt*) as 'the institutionally defined status of a person' (305). This usage seems wider than Weber's. It is true that Weber speaks of 'officials' in non-bureaucratic systems. But he is not happy about this and always tends to equate 'officialdom' with 'bureaucracy' (305). And while he states that bureaucracy 'first developed in patrimonial states with a body of officials recruited from extra-patrimonial sources', slaves, eunuchs and senechals, nevertheless 'these "officials" have originally been personal followers of their chief' and certain central features of a bureaucratic administrative staff, such as appointment and promotion on the basis of free contract, are absent (315).

Weber's use of 'office' is a highly specialized one, limited in the pure type to bureaucratic systems, and excluding most of the roles an anthropologist would include, e.g. chief, priest or Grand Vizier. Parson's interpretation, while closer to comparative usage, appears to be rather too wide, for, unless 'institution' is very narrowly defined, the concept surely comprises the totality of roles and becomes redundant.

A more restricted meaning is given to 'office' by Lasswell and Kaplan, who define it as a position of authority, where authority = formal power, and power = participation in the making of decisions (1952: 75, 133, 198). Thus the term is at least restricted to superordinate roles, although it would apparently cover that of father as well as king. I suggest that this inclusiveness overlooks an important difference between these two roles.

Indeed the difference is overlooked even in the most comprehensive attempt at a comparative analysis of roles, in the 'role chart' which Nadel puts forward in his book, *The Theory of Social Structure* (1957). Here the basic dichotomy is between 'achievement' and 'recruitment' roles, the latter category being similar to, though not identical with, 'ascriptive' roles, as defined by Linton and Parsons. In other words, the primary differentiation is concerned with how a role is entered into. Nadel's taxonomy is admittedly 'tentative' and the author refers to the possibility of alternative classifications. But no distinction is made between those roles which are at some stage occupied by all the members of a social group and those which are necessarily the prerogative of a few, e.g. between 'father' and 'king'. When I speak of 'office', I refer only to the latter type, to a superordinate role, entry to which is restricted, selective, i.e. to a scarce resource. Only in a limited sense is 'office-holder' the semantic equivalent of the Gonja *wura*, for the latter could refer to any leadership position such as household head (*langwura*), which is not restricted in the way I mean here. But the Gonja would make this distinction by context rather than by morpheme.

In the Gonja situation it is useful to draw attention to a further distinction between 'title' and 'office', although again the actors use the one word. A title, of course, refers to the name rather than to the network of rights and duties. The Concise Oxford Dictionary defines a title as being, among other things, 'personal appellation, hereditary or not, denoting or implying office (e.g. king, queen, judge, mayor, etc.) or nobility (e.g. duke, etc.) or distinction of merit (e.g. baronet, knight) or degree qualification (e.g. D.D., M.A.) or used in addressing or referring to person (e.g. Lord, Lady, Sir, Mrs, etc.)'. This wide definition logically includes the appellations of all role and quasi-role categories, all kinship terms of reference or address. I use the term in a more specific sense. In the first place, titles are designations for restricted role categories; which means they are scarce resources. Secondly, they are individualized role names, like the duke of Plazatoro, rather than plural role categories like doctor; which means they can be ranked in ordinal series. Thirdly, they are generalized terms of reference or address; which means that the role extends its influence over the social personality of the title-holder, producing what Nadel speaks of (in a different context) as a halo-effect (1957).

A title is conferred upon a member of the ruling estate by a ceremony very similar to that by which he was named seven days after birth. Chiefship, too, involves being shut in a room for a week; from then on a man's former name is set aside and anyone addressing him except by his title is liable to be fined. The acquisition of chiefship among the Gonja, like the acquisition of a husband in Western society, is thought of as 'changing one's name'; in both cases change of name implies change of status.

But this change is a matter of degree. The acquisition of a title may not necessarily mean that an individual takes on a role with any specific set of rights and duties, such as are usually considered the attributes of office. In the British political system the kind of distinction I am referring to is between appointment as minister of the Crown and the acquisition of an earldom either by appointment or by heredity. The latter is an award, which as far as duties are concerned places the individual in a general category of advisers through membership of the House of Lords. From this standpoint, titles and offices are not complementary.

The same is true in Gonja. Appointment to a chiefship, that is, to a specific chiefly title, may mean that the chief becomes an office-holder, in the sense that his title carries with it, not merely the general rights and duties of a person of chiefly status, but the specific rights and duties of a particular chiefly office. On the other hand the title (especially one that takes its name from an abandoned village) may simply give its holder a 'titular position', placing him in a general category of persons of rank.

It must be stressed that the true Gonja refer to all holders of titles as *biwura*, chiefs, whatever the duties involved, and what we are dealing with here is essentially a continuum between hierarchical positions with specific duties and those with diffuse obligations. Offices may be specific with regard to:

(*a*) people (i.e. village chiefs, who govern directly), or

(*b*) duties (e.g. electors, advisers of the divisional ruler, those who have special tasks in the major ceremonies).

This distinction between the line and staff organization tends to correspond to that between first ranking and other chiefships, and to a lesser extent between chiefs who reside in the capital and those who live in the villages. But it should be added that not all of the former are courtiers or advisers. Many chiefs of the first rank reside in the capital; some of these are absentee rulers of commoner villages, while others are holders of titles carrying only duties of a diffuse kind.

APPENDIX II. THE DISTRIBUTION OF CIRCULATING SUCCESSION

The development of polydynastic succession is most notable in West Africa, where it is a political mechanism of first importance. But it has a wider distribution than this and I summarize the results of a somewhat sporadic reading below, in the hope that it will provide the starting-point for further comparative work.

West Africa

(a) Ghana

In the Mampon division of Ashanti, there are three dynastic units located in the capital and there is a saying in the rest of Ashanti that 'The Mampon people say, "We do not cultivate twice in the same spot"' (Rattray 1929: 235, n. 1). In another Akan-speaking kingdom, the Gyaman of Bondoukou in the Ivory Coast, also known as the Abron, two dynastic segments resided in separate capitals (Ward 1948: 135; Tauxier 1921: 89 ff.). A similar situation exists in another Akan-speaking kingdom of the Ivory Coast, the Anyi of Ndenye, where again the ruler is drawn from the representatives of two immigrant dynasties, who established themselves in the area in the middle of the eighteenth century after being driven westwards by the Ashanti; each dynastic segment is again located at a different village, the Techiman dynasty descended (matrilineally) from Ano at Abengourou and the Nzima dynasty descended from Efui-Ba at Amélékia (Tauxier 1932: 19; his information on Sikasso suggests a similar system might have operated there). A similar system is found in the Nafana kingdom of Banda.

Further south in Ghana, polydynastic succession is found in the state of Peki (Welman 1925) as well as among the Ewe (Crowther 1927) and the Sefwi (Holts-baum 1925). It occurs also among the Ga of Accra, where, under the Akwamu domination of the eighteenth century, the governorship rotated between two segments of Akwamu 'royals', one local, one not (Wilks 1959); there is also some rotation in the military office of *Mantse* (Manoukian 1950: 82).

In most of Ashanti and the Akan kingdoms, a single dynastic unit prevails, but immediately to the north, the Guang speaking kingdom of Gonja take the principle right down to the divisional level. Further to the north, some of the great Mossi group of states have polydynastic systems, Nanumba (2 groups, Amherst 1931: 17; Anon: 10), Wa (3 groups, Goody 1954: 15; Rattray 1932: 452), Buna in the Ivory

Coast (3 or 4 groups, Labouret in Tauxier 1921: 550) and the two other chiefdoms associated with Wa, namely Dorimon and Wechau. While the states of Dagomba and Mamprusi have 'gate' chiefships, and rules to prevent (or at least inhibit) a king being followed by son or brother, there is no system of dynastic segments, since collateral branches are eliminated from the eligibles. But in Mamprusi Rattray noted a kind of distant succession for 'it was always the son of the *Na* most remote who should succeed' (Rattray 1932: 552). Note that it is the outlying off-shoots of Mamprusi and Dagomba, namely Wa and Nanumba, who practise poly-dynastic succession. Have they retained an older system, or developed a new one? My choice would be the first alternative.

(b) Dahomey

Polydynastic succession is most prominent in the northern part of the country and Lombard has contrasted the rotational system of the 'feudal' state of Bariba (Borgu) with the vertical succession in the centralized kingdom of Dahomey (1957). Lombard shows a circulation between six groups (466). Three of these groups are of Bariba (Gur speaking) and three of Busa (Mande speaking) origin. The Mande-speaking inhabitants of the important Niger town of Bussa (Ilorin province, Nigeria) were associated in the same political system. According to Lombard, Bussa was founded by 'Kisra' in the seventh century and it was from here that the state of Nikki (now the Bariba capital) originated in the thirteenth or fourteenth century. It is also said that the Yoruba kingdom centred on Old Oyo was founded by immigrants from Bussa, a tradition which is reflected in contemporary political relations (468). Other members of the same royal family are said to have gone to Illo, near the Niger, and Tenkodogo in Upper Volta (Mossi), and Yendi in Ghana (Dagomba).

Other circulating systems are reported from Djougou or Zugu in Northern Dahomey (Cornevin 1962: 193). In Middle Dahomey, the Yoruba kingship of Ketou went in rotation first among nine, then five dynastic segments (149). And in Southern Dahomey, the kingship of Porto Novo was transmitted on a circulating basis from its foundation in 1688 until 1908 (87); this port formed the main access to the European trade for the Yoruba kingdom of Old Oyo (Ajayi and Smith 1964: 4).

(c) Nigeria

Polydynastic systems are found in both the Fulani and Habe Hausa states of Northern Nigeria (for the 3-group Zaria system, see Smith 1955, 1956, 1960), in Nupe (3 groups, Nadel 1942), among the Igala (4 groups) from whom the pre-Fulani dynasty of Nupe traced a connexion (Armstrong 1955: 87), among the Igbira (4 groups, Brown 1955: 64) and among various Idoma speaking groups, Boju (3 non-exogamous patrilineal groups, Armstrong 1955: 107), Agala (2 groups, 112), Orokam (3 groups, 118), Igumale (123), Ijigbam (2 groups, 124), Iyala (2–4 groups, 129–30), Etulo (3 groups, 135), Afu (2–3 groups, 139), Akweya (3 groups, 148), and in Ife (4 groups) and other Yoruba kingdoms (Forde 1951: 36; Morton Williams 1955: 175; Lloyd 1962).

(d) Mali and neighbours

But circulating succession links Gonja not only with the Hausa north-east but also with the Mande north-west, the other main area of commercial importance to the Akan hinterland.

Among the Malinke and the Bambara most of the evidence for rotational succession comes from the village level.

'Rotational succession is universal at the village level and general at the *Kafo* (canton, chiefdom) level too, at least in the upper Niger and down the Milo, Baule and Bogore valleys. Only in some small hamlets which lack ritual autonomy is rotation absent. But in the main villages, which usually have from 1,000 to 3,000 inhabitants, there is a tendency for the headship to rotate among three sub-lineages (though two and four are also found). These lineages are usually seen as descended from two sons of the founding ancestor of the village, with the offspring of one son having split into two further segments' (Yves Person, personal communication).

In the centralized states of the Mande area, rotation is less common, e.g. Ségou and Kaarta, although Monteil's genealogies give some suggestion of rotation (1924: 102, 118). Person suggests that the rotation found among the principal chiefdoms of the Senufo (Kong, Korhogo, Sinematioli) is due to the influence of the Mande speaking peoples; no rotation is found at the village level. Rotation is also found in the town of Mousadougou in the Konyor country on the border between the Ivory Coast and Liberia; these are Malinke people, living on the northern borders of the forest.

Stenning refers to a more limited kind of rotation in the Fulani state of Fouta Jalon where 'dissensions between the war leader's party (Soriya) and the followers of the holy men (Alfaya) led, in 1840, to a cumbersome compromise by which administrative offices alternated every two years' (1959: 14). However, rotation appears to be more widespread than this remark suggests, and operates at the village as well as the state level (Cantrelle and Dupire 1964: 537).

Western Sahara

Murdock mentions the existence of tribal 'sultans' with only nominal authority among the Kanouri-speaking Kawar and Teda of the Central Sahara who are selected in rotation from two or more noble lineages (1959: 130; I can find no reference to such a system in Chapelle's account of the Teda of the Tibesti region).

Eastern Sudan

Shilluk (between two groups, Evans-Pritchard 1948); Eastern Anuak (Evans-Pritchard 1940, 1947).

East African Coast

Dynasty of Pate, 1203–1820, where, since 1494, no son has directly succeeded his father, and where there are strong indications of oscillation between dynastic segments (G. S. P. Freeman-Grenville, MS.).

South-Eastern Africa

Nyakyusa (Wilson, M. 1951).

Asia

Gullick (1958) analyses such systems in Malaya; there is mention of a similar institution in the island of Socotra (Botting 1958) and it seems also to have occurred in the state of Sumer and Akkad (Smith, S. 1958: 126). See also Dumont (1957) on Southern India.

Pacific

In Fakaofo in the Union Group (Hocart 1915: 638), the king was elected from 3 families. In Rotuma (Bell 1932: 189, 202–3), the prime spiritual chief or *sou* was elected in turn from 'the 5 principal family groups' for a period of 6 months.

Europe

In Europe circulating succession was long a feature of Irish kingship; it was used when the Irish established the Dal Riadic kingdom of Argyle and it later became the rule when the kingdom of Scotland was unified under Kenneth MacAlpine. In both kingdoms it disappeared under the pressure of Anglo-Norman custom and might. The feudal organization of medieval England required a more specific statement of military obligation than circulation allows. It is one of the penalties of such systems that the rough balance of opposing segments of the dynasty can be readily upset by outside powers who lend their support to one segment, sometimes as the result of an appeal for help by that party. It was by deliberate intervention that the colonizing power of England destroyed the Irish kingship at the end of the sixteenth century; it was by calling on their help that in the eleventh century Malcolm shattered the rotational system of the Scottish kingdom and introduced next-of-kin succession from south of the border.

NOTES

[1] This paper is based on scattered historical sources and on fieldwork carried out by my wife and me in 1956–57 and 1964–5. The only published papers on Gonja social organization are Esther N. Goody, 1962, 'Conjugal Separation and Divorce among the Gonja of Northern Ghana', *Marriage in Tribal Societies*, ed. M. Fortes (Cambridge Papers in Social Anthropology, No. 3); Jack Goody, 1966, 'The Over-Kingdom of Gonja', *West African Kingdoms*, ed. P. Kaberry (London).

[2] The situation has changed in recent years, but although a chief may recite the Moslem prayers, neither he nor any other member of the ruling estate will attend the Friday mosque. For Gonja chiefs have their own ritual practices which are unacceptable to Islam, and they are rulers over Moslems and non-Moslems alike.

[3] In fact the Hausa speakers are mainly of Bornu origin, having learnt Hausa during their sojourn in that country.

[4] To the Ashanti, they are the *Ntafo*, to Mossi speakers, the *Zabagsi*.

[5] For a discussion of specific and general offices, see Appendix I.

[6] Such *eche pibi* chiefships are less common in Eastern Gonja than in other parts.

[7] The capital was moved to Damongo in 1944 as its central location was deemed more suitable for administrative purposes. The eligible divisions have certainly varied from time to time; before the advent of Samori and the Europeans, there were six.

[8] Through Kintampo, Buipe, Busunu, Daboya and the former capital of Dagomba at Diari (Old Yendi).

[9] I should add that this statement hardly accords with the evidence of Buipe's activities in the mid-eighteenth and early nineteenth centuries (see the Gonja Chronicle, in Goody 1954; Dupuis 1824: 241, 248).

[10] I have been told that the British Administration put pressure on chiefs to live on the job, so that I cannot be sure of the extent to which chiefs traditionally lived in their villages, rather than the divisional capitals where their segments were located. On the interrelationship between spatial and hierarchical movement in industrial societies see Watson on 'Spiralism' (1964: 145 ff.).

[11] I am unsure how far this difference obtained in the past.

[12] Where land is sufficient, these groups shift not only their farms (which the Gonja do) but also their houses (elaborate constructions that they are); since shifting agriculture has a double significance, I speak of this as mobile farming.

[13] A striking instance of this occurred after I had written the above passage. When the late chief of Buipe died, the SilimaWura was the next-in-line; he had an elder brother resident in Daboya and offered him the chance of returning to fill the vacancy, which he did.

[14] It is worth mentioning that the existence of this institution may help to account for the difficulty historians and archaeologists experience in trying to locate the capitals of some medieval empires in West Africa.

[15] As was the case in Ireland, with the northern and southern O'Neils.

[16] The internal structure of dynastic units varies of course in other ways, e.g. as to whether or not they have a specifiable genealogical structure as well as in the extent of incorporation (and hence 'social mobility'), degree of control over major offices, numerical strength and number of units in the circulating system. But a consideration of these factors is beyond the scope of the present essay.

[17] In this connexion, see also Barth on the Kurds (1953: 43) and Smith on the Hausa (1960: 241).

[18] The nature of medieval Scottish and Irish clans is a tricky subject; the only point I want to make here is that they certainly differed from the Anglo-Saxon and Norman kin-groups of England.

[19] I cannot do more here than refer to the series of complex events that began even before the end of the Ashanti domination. But an account of them has been written by a member of the Kanyasi family, J. A. Braimah, which will shortly be published under the title of 'The Two Isanwurfos' (see also Goody 1966b).

[20] The same in general holds for the Dagomba-Mamprusi system of Northern Ghana, where sons of the paramount are appointed to chiefships which lead to the paramountcy itself. But recent appointees do not automatically displace the offspring of earlier paramounts; they take their place in the queue, which is one reason why father-son succession is virtually unknown (Rattray 1932: 552).

[21] Quoted by Dennis Austin, *Politics in Ghana 1946–60* (1964: 33), who presents a detailed discussion of the growth of the one-party state in Ghana.

BIBLIOGRAPHY

AJAYI, J. F. A. and SMITH, R. S. (1964), *Yoruba Warfare in the 19th Century*, Cambridge.

ALDERSON, A. D. (1956), *The Structure of the Ottoman Dynasty*, Oxford.

AMHERST, H. W. (1931), 'Report on the Constitution, Organisation and Customs of the Nanumba People', unpublished.

ANDERSON, A. O. (1928), 'Tanistry in United Scotland', *Scot. Hist. Rev.* 25 (1927–8), 382–4.

ANON. (n.d.), 'The History of Nanum' (Local History Committee), MS.

ANSON, W. R. (1935), *The Law and Custom of the Constitution*, vol. II, *The Crown, Part I* (4th ed.), Oxford.

ARMSTRONG, R. G. (1955), 'The Igala and the Idoma-speaking Peoples', *Peoples of the Niger-Benue Confluence* (Ethnographic Survey of Africa), London.

ASHTON, H. (1952), *The Basuto*, London.

ASHE, R. P. (1894), *Chronicles of Uganda*, London.

AUSTIN, D. (1964), *Politics in Ghana, 1946–1960*, London.

BARKER, E. (1910), 'Electors', article in *Encyl. Britt.* (11th ed.).

BARTH, F. (1953), *Principles of Social Organization in Southern Kurdistan*, Oslo.

BAXTER, P. T. W. and BUTT, A. (1953), *The Azande, and Related Peoples of the Anglo-Egyptian Sudan and Belgian Congo*, London.

BEATTIE, J. H. M. (1959), 'Checks on the Abuse of Political Power in some African States', *Sociologus*, 9, 97–115.

BELL, F. L. S. (1932), 'A Functional Interpretation of Inheritance and Succession in Central Polynesia', *Oceania*, 3, 167–206.

BENDIX, R. (1960), *Max Weber: An Intellectual Portrait*, New York.

BENNETT, N. R. (1963), *Studies in East African History*, Boston, Massachusetts.

BLACK, D. (1958), *The Theory of Committees and Elections*, Cambridge.

BLOCH, M. (1961), *Feudal Society*, London.

BOHANNAN, L. and BOHANNAN, P. (1953), *The Tiv of Central Nigeria* (Ethnographic Survey of Africa), London.

BÖSCH, Rev. P. Fr. (1930), *Les Banyamwezi, Peuple de l'Afrique Orientale*, Münster; Anthropos Bibliothek.

BOTTING, D. (1958), *Island of the Dragon's Blood*, London.

BRADBURY, R. E. (1964), 'The historical uses of comparative ethnography with special reference to Benin and the Yoruba', *The Historian in Tropical Africa* (ed. J. Vansina *et al.*), London.

BROWN, P. (1955), 'The Igbira', *Peoples of the Niger-Benue Confluence* (Ethnographic Survey of Africa), London.

BURN, A. R. (1952), *The Government of the Roman Empire from Augustus to the Antonines*, London.

BURTON, R. F. (1860), *The Lake Regions of Central Africa* (2 vols.), London.

BUSIA, K. A. (1951), *The Position of the Chief in the Modern Political System of Ashanti*, London.

CAMERON, V. L. (1887), *Across Africa* (2 vols.), London.

CANTRELLE, P. and DUPIRE, M. (1964), 'L'Endogamie des Peuls du Fouta-Djallon', *Population*, 19, 529–58.

CHAPELLE, J. (1957), *Nomades noirs du Sahara*, Paris.

CHILVER, E. M. (1960), 'Feudalism in the Interlacustrine Kingdoms', *East African Chiefs* (ed. A. I. Richards), London.

BIBLIOGRAPHY

COLSON, E. (1958), 'The Role of Bureaucratic Norms in African Political Structure', *Systems of Political Control and Bureaucracy in Human Societies*, ed. V. F. Ray (*Proc. Am. Eth. Soc.*), Seattle.

CORY, H. (1951), *The Ntemi*, London.

CORNEVIN, R. (1962), *Histoire du Dahomey*, Paris.

CROWTHER, F. G. (1927), The Epwe Speaking People, *Gold Coast Rev.*, 3.

DAWSON, E. G. (1887), *James Hannington: A History of his Life and Work*, London.

DELOBSON, D. (1933), *L'Empire du Mogho-Naba*, Paris.

DESOIGNIES, P. (1903), 'Die Msalala', in S. R. Steinmetz, *Rechtsverhältnisse von eingeborenen Völkern in Afrika und Ozeanien*, Berlin.

DUFFY, J. (1962), *Portugal in Africa*, London.

DUMONT, L. (1957), *Une sous-castes de l'Inde du Sud*, The Hague.

DUNCAN-JOHNSTONE, A. (1932), *Enquiry into the Constitution and Organisation of the Dagbon Kingdom*, Accra.

DUPUIS, J. (1824), *Journal of a Residence in Ashantee*, London.

ELLENBERGER, D. D. & MACGREGOR, J. C. (1912), *The History of the Basuto*, London.

ENSSLIN, W. (1939), 'The End of the Principate', *The Cambridge Ancient History*, 12, Cambridge.

EVANS-PRITCHARD, E. E. (1940), *The Political System of the Anuak of the Anglo-Egyptian Sudan* (L. S. E. Monographs on Social Anthropology, No. 4), London.

―― *The Divine Kingship of the Shilluk of the Nilotic Sudan* (the Frazer Lecture, 1948), Cambridge.

―― (1947), 'Further Observations on the Political System of the Anuak', *Sudan Notes and Records*, 28.

FALLERS, L. (1956), *Bantu Bureaucracy*, Cambridge.

FESTINGER, L., RIECKEN, H. W. and SCHACHTER, S. (1956), *When Prophecy Fails*, Minneapolis.

FIELD, M. J. (1948), *Akim-Kotoku*, London.

FORDE, D. (1951), *The Yoruba-Speaking Peoples of South-Western Nigeria* (Ethnographic Survey of Africa), London.

FORTES, M. (1962), 'Ritual and Office in Tribal Society', in D. Forde *et al.*, *Essays on the Ritual of Social Relations*, Manchester.

FORTES, M. and EVANS-PRITCHARD, E. E. (1940), *African Political Systems*, London.

FRANKFORT, H. (1948), *Kingship and the Gods*, Chicago.

GLUCKMAN, M. (1940), 'The Kingdom of the Zulu of South Africa', *African Political Systems* (ed. Fortes and Evans-Pritchard), London.

―― (1954a), *Rituals of Rebellion in South-East Africa* (The Frazer Lecture, 1952), Manchester.

―― (1954b), 'Succession and Civil War among the Bemba—an Exercise in Anthropological Theory', *Human Problems in British Central Africa*, 16.

―― (1963), *Order and Rebellion in Tribal Society*, London.

GOODY, E. N. (1962), 'Conjugal Separation and Divorce among the Gonja of Northern Ghana', *Marriage in Tribal Societies* (ed. M. Fortes) (Cambridge Papers in Social Anthropology, No. 3).

GOODY, J. R. (1954), *The Ethnography of the Northern Territories of the Gold Coast, West of the White Volta*, London (Colonial Office, mimeo.).

―― (1956), *The Social Organization of the LoWiili*, (Colonial Research Studies, No. 19), London.

―― (1957), 'Fields of Social Control among the LoDagaba', *J. R. Anthrop. Inst.*, 87.

―― (1958), 'The Fission of Domestic Groups among the LoDagaba', *The Developmental Cycle in Domestic Groups* (ed. Goody), Cambridge.

―― (1959), 'The Mother's Brother and the Sister's Son in West Africa', *J. R. Anthrop. Inst.*, 89, 1.

—— (1962), *Death, Property and the Ancestors*, Stanford.

—— (1966a), 'The Over-Kingdom of Gonja', *West African Kingdoms* (ed. P. Kaberry), London.

—— (1966b), 'Salaga in 1876', *Ghana Notes and Queries*, Accra.

GOULDNER, A. (1954), *Patterns of Industrial Bureaucracy*, Glencoe, Ill.

GRAY, Sir J. (1957), 'Trading Expeditions from the Coast to Lakes Tanganyika and Victoria before 1857', *Tanganyika Notes and Records*, 46, 226–46.

GRISCOM, A. (ed.) (1929), *The Historia Regum Britanniae of Geoffrey of Monmouth*, London.

GULLICK, J. M. (1958), *Indigenous Political Systems of Western Malaya* (L.S.E. Monographs on Social Anthropology, No. 17), London.

HERSKOVITS, M. J. (1938), *Dahomey, an Ancient West African Kingdom*, New York.

HOCART, A. M. (1915), 'Chieftainship and the Sister's Son in the Pacific', *Am. Anthrop.*, 17, 631–46.

HOGAN, J. (1932), 'The Irish Law of Kingship, with special reference to Ailech and Cenel Oeghain', *Proc. R. Irish Academy*, 40 (1931–2), 186–254.

HOLLAND, A. W. (1911), 'Germany', article in *Encycl. Brit.* (11 ed.).

HOLTSBAUM, F. P. (1925), 'Sefwi and its People', *Gold Coast Rev.*, 1.

HOMANS, G. C. (1957), 'The Frisians in East Anglia', *The Economic History Review*, 10, 189–206.

JONES, G. I. (1951), *Basutoland Medicine Murder*, London.

KAGGWA, Sir A. (1901), *Basekabaka be Buganda* ('The Kings of Buganda'), edition of 1953, Kampala and London.

—— (1905), *Mpisa za Baganda* ('The Customs of the Baganda'), edition of 1952, Kampala and London.

—— (1908), *Bika bya Baganda* ('The Clans of the Baganda'), edition of 1949, Kampala.

KEITH, A. B. (1936), *The King and the Imperial Crown*, London.

KRAPF, J. L. (1860), *Travels, Researches and Missionary Labours in East Africa*, London.

KUPER, H. (1947), *An African Aristocracy*, London.

LAGDEN, G. (1909), *The Basutos* (2 vols.), London.

LASSWELL, H. D. and KAPLAN, A. (1952), *Power and Society*, London.

LEVENSON, B. (1961), 'Bureaucratic Succession', *Complex Organisations: a Sociological Reader* (ed. A. Etzioni), New York.

LE VEUX, PÈRE (1917), *Vocabulaire Luganda—Français*, Algiers.

LIENHARDT, R. G. (1957–8), 'Anuak Village Headmen', parts I and II, *Africa*, 27 and 28.

LLOYD, P. C. (1960), 'Sacred Kingship and Government among the Yoruba', *Africa*, 30, 221–37.

—— (1962), *Yoruba Land Law*, London.

LOMBARD, J. (1957), 'Un système politique traditional de type féodal: Les Bariba du Nord-Dahomey. Aperçu sur l'organisation social et le pouvoir central', *Bull. I.F.A.N.*, 19, 464–506.

MAC NEILL, E. (1921), *Celtic Ireland*, Dublin.

MAIR, L. P. (1934), *An African People in the Twentieth Century*, London.

—— (1962), *Primitive Government*, London.

MANOUKIAN, M. (1950), *Akan and Ga-Adangme Peoples of the Gold Coast*, London.

—— (1951), *Tribes of the Northern Territories of the Gold Coast*, London.

MAQUET, J. J. (1961), *The Premise of Inequality in Ruanda*, London.

MILLS, C. W. (1959), *The Power Elite* (1st ed. 1956), New York.

MONTAGNE, R. (1930), *Les Berberes et le Makhzen dans le sud du Maroc*, Paris.

MONTEIL, C. (1924), *Les Bambara du Ségou et du Kaarta*, Paris.

BIBLIOGRAPHY

MORTON-WILLIAMS, P. (1955), 'Some Yoruba Kingdoms under Modern Conditions', *J. Afr. Admin.*, 7.

MUKASA, H. (1934), '"Ebifa ku Mulembe gwa Kabaka Mutesa" (followed by English translation by Cook, A. H., as "Some Notes on the Reign of Mutesa")', *Uganda Journal*, 1, 2, 116–23, 124–33.

MULIRA, E. M. K. and others (1952), *A Luganda-English and English-Luganda Dictionary*, London.

MURDOCK, G. P. (1956), 'Political Moieties', *The State of the Social Sciences* (ed. L. D. White), Chicago.

—— (1959), *Africa*, New York.

NADEL, S. F. (1942), *A Black Byzantium*, London.

—— (1957), *The Theory of Social Structure*, London.

NORTHCOTT, H. P. (1899), *Report on the Northern Territories of the Gold Coast*, War Office, London.

NSIMBI, M. B. (1956), *Amannya Amaganda n'Ennono Zaago* (Baganda Names and their Meanings), Kampala.

PANKHURST, R. (1961), *An Introduction to the Economic History of Ethiopia*, London.

PARKINSON, C. N. (1958), *Parkinson's Law or the Pursuit of Progress*, London.

POLLOCK, F. and MAITLAND, F. W. (1898), *The History of English Law* (2nd ed.), Cambridge.

RADCLIFFE-BROWN, A. R. (1952), *Structure and Function in Primitive Society*, London.

RATCLIFF, E. C. (1953), *The Coronation Service of Her Majesty Queen Elizabeth II*, Cambridge.

RATTRAY, R. S. (1927), *Religion and Art in Ashanti*, London.

—— (1929), *Ashanti Law and Constitution*, Oxford.

—— (1932), *The Tribes of the Ashanti Hinterland*, Oxford.

RICHARDS, A. I. (1960), 'Social Mechanisms for the Transfer of Political Rights in Some African Tribes', *J. R. Anthrop. Inst.*, 90, 175–90.

—— (1961), 'African Kings and their Royal Relatives', *J. R. Anthrop. Inst.*, 91, 135–50.

ROSCOE, J. (1911), *The Baganda*, London.

ROUCH, J. (1953), *Contribution à l'histoire des Songhay* (Mém. I.F.A.N., No. 29, ii), Dakar.

SCHAPERA, I. (1955), *Tswana Law and Custom* (2nd ed.), London.

—— (1956), *Government and Politics in Tribal Societies*, London.

SHEDDICK, V. G. J. (1953), *The Southern Sotho* (Ethnographic Survey of Africa), London.

—— (1954), *Land Tenure in Basutoland* (Colonial Research Studies, No. 13), London.

SIMMEL, G. (1950), *The Sociology of Georg Simmel* (trans. K. H. Wolff), Glencoe, Ill.

SKINNER, E. P. (1960), 'Traditional and Modern Patterns of Succession to Political Office among the Mossi of the Voltaic Republic', *J. Human Rel.*, 8, 394–406.

—— (1964), *The Mossi of the Upper Volta*, Stanford.

SMITH, ALISON (1959), Historical Introduction to Whiteley's translation of the autobiography of Tippu Tip.

—— (1963), 'The Southern Interior 1840–84', *History of East Africa* (ed. R. Oliver and G. Mathews), London.

SMITH, M. G. (1955), *The Economy of Hausa Communities of Zaria* (Colonial Research Studies, No. 16), London.

—— (1956), 'Segmentary Lineage Systems', *J. R. Anthrop. Inst.*, 86, 39–80.

—— (1960), *Government in Zazzau*, London.

SMITH, S. (1958), 'The Practice of Kingship in Early Semitic Kingdoms', *Myth. Ritual, and Kingship* (ed. S. H. Hooke), London.

SOUTHALL, A. W. (1956), *Alur Society*, Cambridge.

BIBLIOGRAPHY

SOUTHWOLD, M. (1961), *Bureaucracy and Chiefship in Buganda* (East African Studies, No. 14), Kampala.

SPEKE, J. H. (1884), *What Led to the Discovery of the Source of the Nile*, London.

STANLEY, H. M. (1872), *How I Found Livingstone*, New York.

STENNING, D. J. (1959), *Savannah Nomads*, London.

STEVENSON, J. H. (1927), 'The Law of the Throne-Tanistry and the Introduction of the Law of Primogeniture', *Scot. Hist. Rev.* 25 (1927–8), 1–12.

TAIT, D. (1961), *The Konkomba of Northern Ghana*, London.

TANNER, R. E. S. (1957), 'The Installation of Sukuma Chiefs in Mwanza District, Tanganyika', *African Studies*, 16, 197–209.

TAUXIER, L. (1912), *Le Noir du Soudan*, Paris.

—— (1917), *Le Noir du Yatenga*, Paris.

—— (1921), *Le Noir de Bondoukou*, Paris,

—— (1932), *Religion, mœurs et coutumes des Agnis*, Paris.

URVOY, Y. (1949), *Histoire de l'empire du Bournou* (Mém. I.F.A.N., No. 7), Dakar.

WARD, W. E. F. (1948), *A History of the Gold Coast*, London.

WARNER, W. L. and ABEGGLEN, J. C. (1955), *Big Business Leaders in America*, New York.

WATSON, W. (1964), 'Social Mobility and Social Class in Industrial Communities', *Closed Systems and Open Minds* (ed. M. Gluckman), Edinburgh.

WEBER, M. (1947a), *Theory of Social and Economic Organization* (trans. A. R. Henderson and T. Parsons), London.

—— (1947b), *From Max Weber* (trans. H. H. Gerth and C. W. Mills), London.

WELMAN, C. W. (1925), *The Native States of the Gold Coast. 1. Peki*, London.

WHITELEY, W. H. (ed.) (1959), *Maisha ya Hamed bin Muhammed el Mujerbi yaani Tippu Tip kwa maneno yake mwenyewe* (Autobiography of Tippu Tip), supplement to *Journal of the East African Swahili Committee*, 28, 1958 and 29, 1959.

WILKS, I. (1959), 'Akwamu and Otublohum: an Eighteenth-Century Marriage Arrangement', *Africa*, 29, 391–404.

—— (1966), 'Ashanti Government in the 19th century', *West African Kingdoms* (ed. P. Kaberry), London.

WILSON, C. S. and LUPTON, T. (1959), 'The Social Background and Connections of "Top Decision Makers"', *The Manchester School of Economic and Social Studies*, 27, 30–51.

WILSON, G. (1939), *The Constitution of Ngonde* (the Rhodes-Livingstone Papers, No. 3), Livingstone.

WILSON, M. (1951), *Good Company*, Oxford.

WIRIATH, P. (1910), 'France, History to 1870', article in *Encycl. Britt.* (11th ed.).

WRIGLEY, C. C. (1964), 'The Changing Economic Structure of Baganda', *The King's Men* (ed. L. A. Fallers), London.

OFFICIAL PAPERS

Annual Reports for various Basutoland Districts in Government Archives, Maseru, 1884–1904.

'Claims of the Sons of Jonathan to the Chieftainship of Leribe District'. Resident Commission Court Case No. 158/30 of 9 November 1930.

High Commissioner's Notice, No. 171 of 1939. Schedule of Chiefs, Sub-chiefs and Headmen.

'How Basutoland is governed.' Basutoland Government Publication. Morija, Basutoland, 1944.

Judgment in the Case of Chief Constantine Bereng Griffith *v.* Chieftainess Amelia 'Mantsebo Seeiso Griffith. Mazenod, Basutoland, 1943.

'Laws of Lerotholi.' Basutoland Government Publication. Moriga, Basutoland, 1946.